ALSO BY ROBERT GIRARD . . .

Brethren, Hang Loose

Brethren, Hang Together

RESTRUCTURING THE CHURCH FOR RELATIONSHIPS

Robert C. Girard

ZONDERVAN
PUBLISHING HOUSE
OF THE ZONDERVAN CORPORATION
GRAND RAPIDS, MICHIGAN 49506

BRETHREN, HANG TOGETHER
Copyright © 1979 by The Zondervan Corporation
Grand Rapids, Michigan

Library of Congress Cataloging in Publication Data

Girard, Robert C
    Brethren, hang together.

    Includes bibliographical references.
    1. Church renewal. I. Girard, Audrey I. II. Title.
BV600.2.G493   262'.001   79-9544
ISBN 0-310-39071-0

Unless otherwise noted, Scripture quotations are from *The New International Version of the Bible,* (New York: New York International Bible Society, 1978).

Other translations used, as noted, are: (1) NASB, *New American Standard Bible* (Carol Stream, Ill.: Creation House, Inc., 1971). (2) *The Amplified Bible* (Grand Rapids: Zondervan Publishing House, 1965). (3) Phillips, *The New Testament in Modern English* (J. B. Phillips) (New York: The Macmillan Co., 1965). (4) LB, *The Living Bible, Pharaphrased* (Wheaton: Tyndale House Publishers, 1971). (5) NEB, *The New English Bible* (Oxford University Press, 1970). (6) KJV, *The King James Version of the Holy Bible.*

Printed in the United States of America

To the "O.H." family

Since, then, we know what it is to fear the Lord, we try to persuade men. What we are is plain to God, and I hope it is also plain to your conscience. We are not trying to commend ourselves to you again, but are giving you an opportunity to take pride in us, so that you can answer those who take pride in what is seen rather than in what is in the heart. If we are out of our mind, it is for the sake of God; if we are in our right mind, it is for you. For Christ's love compels us, because we are convinced that one died for all, and therefore all died. And he died for all, that those who live should no longer live for themselves but for him who died for them and was raised again.

2 Corinthians 5:11–15

Contents

Preface

The true nature of the church is *relationship* . . . loving, personal relationship to God and to each other as Christians and as human beings. If healthy, loving, personal relationships are lacking, there is nothing to knit the church together around the Head—in effect, there is no church.

Among the deepest tragedies deriving from the institutionalization* of the church (chiefly since the beginning of the fourth century) has been that Christians have lost touch with this heart of the church's reality and true nature—the primacy of personal relationship. The church itself, because of its institutional focus, has become a major hindrance to the fulfillment of Christ's scheme for effective revelation of Himself in the world. This is extremely difficult (perhaps impossible!) for those commited to the perpetuation of the church as an insitution to see. Much of the American evangelical movement, for instance, is presently engaged in a narcissistic love affair with success, power, and cultural acceptance. On its current crest of prestige and notice it will find it extremely difficult to face the suggestion that it is doing anything wrong. The fact is that evangelicalism has borrowed from the world, means and values and even goals, the very nature of which make it

*Institutionalization, emphasis on organization and establishment in society at the expense of other important factors.

11

virtually impossible to convincingly demonstrate the one distinctive that Jesus said would persuade the world that the church is His.

> By this shall all men know that you are my disciples, that you *love one another.*

The aim of this book is to sharpen the vision of the church by focusing on the *vital relationships* with which it is supplied by its Head, Jesus Christ. This is not a study of psychological principles, though that can be extremely valuable to the church seeking to understand the meaning and practice of relationship building. Nor is this a legalistic look at biblical church relationship structures, designed to give a clear outline of "the only right way to organize the church." My purpose is to show what the vital biblical relationships are and how they can be *loving* relationships.

My hope is that those who read this book will catch a sense of the powerful simplicity of the living church, and will begin to see and believe that God's instrument for glorifying Himself in the world is not a more complicated religious machine which can match wits and works with the world's wonderful systems, but is a very uncomplicated network of human people whose lives are interdependently entwined with each other and the living Jesus Christ.

Earnest attempt has been made here to tell, with honesty, the unfinished story of one church's struggle to be the church. We have sought to reveal weaknesses and imperfections, points of deep pain and sickness, as well as positive progress and spiritual growth. Still, there is a keen sense that words cannot really tell it like it is. We sometimes tremble at the thought that someone may read this and, inspired by a partially told story of renewal, take sling in hand and strike out to confront and conquer some institutional giant . . . one or two stones short!

I expressed this concern to Juanita Ferguson (who typed most of the manuscript, and has lived much of it with us). It reminded her of something her mother once said. After having lived in Peru, she read an article in *National Geographic,* which, with excellent writing and full-color photographs, extolled the beauty of that land, its people, and its culture. Upon completing the article, she commented that the magazine had told the truth—the country was everything they said it was. "But," she added thoughtfully, "it's not the same without the smell!"

To me, this sometimes puzzling plant, called "Our Heritage Church," is a beautiful bud about to open. The half-open petals hint of lovely and delicate colors—love, joy, harmony, bearing one another, human kindness and caring, true goodness and honesty, commitment to each other and to God, sharing, servanthood—about to burst forth into the world in a blaze of His beauty. What some see as a strange aggregation of admitted cripples trying to heal each other in Jesus' name is a single half-opened blossom full of promise—God's promise—and full of hope not yet fully realized, but coming, in God's process of renewal and growth.

Acknowledgments:
This Book and the Body

This book is a practical expression of the interdependent nature of the body of Christ. While the actual writing has been my personal, alternately painful and happy task, the footnotes at the end of each chapter tell how dependent I have been on the input of other Christians.

I have been more than dependent on Audrey Girard—my wife of twenty-six years—who has been more than an editor. She has first lived and died all these things with me, and then painstakingly and skillfully worked through my rough manuscripts to make them more readable, understandable, and palatable. By wisely deleting my most sarcastic and petty tirades, she has helped me to come across with less "neurotic intensity" when discussing things about which I have strong feelings. Many of the most lucid illustrations contained herein are her additions to my needy story line.

Other body members have proven themselves necessary. Juanita Ferguson, our wonderful, unpaid secretary (more than a secretary), typed the lioness' share of the manuscript, with help from Ilene Porter, Carol Graham, Debbie Rogers, Cecilia Stienhoff, and "Ranie." Edward Janos provided the nearly 1,000 copies needed.

Then, there is the little Christian community in Aiea, Hawaii, which received the Girard family as members for ten

Acknowledgments: This Book and the Body

weeks last summer—Dr. Ron and Jeannie Fessenden, Kim and Jennie, Opal O'Neil, her son Neil, Sandy Foote, and Becky Phillips. Clyde and Joanie Hoeldtke (Dynamic Church Ministries) paid the family's air fare from Arizona to Hawaii, to encourage my writing.

The brothers and sisters in our church family in Scottsdale persisted in prayer support and encouragement, lovingly released me to do the work, and, most significantly, with us have lived what is reported here. Their lifeblood and tears are literally mingled with ours in these pages.

The pastoral team (elders) of Our Heritage Church—Pat Porter, Rod Wilke, Howard Graham, and Larry Richards— gave valuable consultation and editing to chapter 10.

Finally, thanks to Zondervan Publishing House, for granting an advance to pay family living expenses while this project has been going on.

Robert C. Girard

1
One Great, Big, Wonderful, Hundredfold Family

O Lord, everybody's home!
Eating, drinking, breathing of the Lord;
O rejoice! the family's all together.
O Lord, everybody's home. . . .[1]

Welcome to the family! Join the singing of the round. Spend five minutes in personal conversation with each other—right in the middle of the morning worship service. Let the song rise out of the din of the conversing human voices. Reach out and take the hand of a brother or a sister, a mother or a child. Sense the warmth of membership in the family. Catch the contagious spirit of the endless song.

I love it. Because I see the church as a family. Without end.

Jesus started it. In Mark 10:29-30 He promised that to become a true follower of His, is to gain, instantaneously, a new hundredfold family! Brothers and sisters and mothers and children galore. Hundreds of them!

I tell you the truth, no one who has left home or brothers or sisters or mother or father or children or fields for me and the gospel will fail to receive a hundred times as much in this present age (homes, brothers, sisters, mothers, children, and fields—and with them, persecutions) and in the age to come, eternal life.

When we follow Jesus we may expect more than to be

part of a following, a crowd, an audience. The people who follow Jesus are promised a *family*! His pledge was not that we would be given a great institution to be proud of, nor a successful business to share in, nor an organization that would thrill us with its effectiveness in getting things done. The church is not anything that Jesus intended if it is not a family.

THE GATHERING OF THE CLAN

Jesus spent three years holding that little aggregation of potential apostles together by the sheer magnetism of His visible presence. During that time He shared all the the important principles for the spiritual family-life experience, the caring community of salt and light and sharing they were to become after He left.

Even after all that they still were a self-seeking, competitive bunch, each pulling in his private direction, watching out for his own skin, and jockeying for power over the others.[2]

Just before He physically ascended to His Father in heaven, He gave them instructions to gather together in Jerusalem to wait to be baptized in the Holy Spirit.[3] They obeyed. And even during the time of waiting and praying they could sense the potential of their oneness.[4]

Then, after ten days of quiet anticipation the Holy Spirit invaded their gathering and their lives.[5] When the upper room doors opened, what had entered earlier that morning as a polite group of friends and acquaintances, came bursting out with arms around each other as a new 120-fold family.[6]

All the principles of family life they had heard Jesus talking about moved out of the theory stage into daily practice. Now they not only knew the principles and gave mental assent to the ideals—they *were* a family. They *acted* like a family. They *cared* like a family.

Fellow followers had become brothers and sisters and

mothers and children . . . not merely theologically, but in reality.

> And the followers of the living Jesus were spending time together earnestly receiving the instructions of the apostles. They also were spending time in "koinonia"—that is, sharing with each other, interacting—celebrating the Lord's Supper and praying together.
>
> Their deep sharing kept them feeling the same sense of wonder they had had from the beginning. Miracles kept happening among them through the apostles.
>
> And in their closeness and love for each other they shared even their material possessions—even to the point of selling what they had in order to have something to share with their brothers and sisters in need.
>
> What oneness they experienced in their daily meetings! Whether they were in the temple or sharing the Lord's Supper together in each other's homes, or sharing meals together, each meeting was marked by gladness, openness, childlike simplicity, and praising God.
>
> The whole city was impressed with their love and care for each other and their devotion to the Lord.
>
> And the forever family grew as the Lord kept adding those who were turning from their old way of life to begin following Him. (Paraphrase of Acts 2:42–47.)

That congregation was no uninvolved "audience." Whenever and wherever they got together it was a family reunion!

In this spirit both Paul and Peter told the readers of their letters not to forget to greet one another with a holy kiss of love.[7]

My wife, Audrey, is from a South Dakota farm family of Danish heritage. There are nine children in this family—six sons and three daughters.

The fiftieth wedding anniversary of Audrey's parents was celebrated with a family reunion. A Christian campground was rented and all but one of the nine children, most of the grandchildren and great grandchildren, along with aunts and uncles and cousins and cousins' children and shirt-tail relatives and in-laws of all shapes and sizes gathered. Seventy-five family members in all.

The first hour after anyone arrived at the reunion site was spent in a spontaneous round of hugging and kissing and weeping for joy and laughing in the sheer delight of being together again. And every time another family member arrived it happened all over again.

No one was embarrassed about being touched, embraced, or kissed. We (yes, even we in-laws) are part of the family. And when we get together it's a celebration!

Peter and Paul and the others saw the gatherings of the church that same way. Every meeting was a get-together with brothers and sisters and mothers and children—a family reunion. Touching and embracing and holy kissing were as normal and natural a part of it as singing and praying and listening to sermons.

Who is to blame that Christians can't be that way with each other today in the church? Saint Augustine? Queen Victoria? Sigmund Freud? Or is it just evidence that the church has come to see itself as a business, an institution, a monument, a weekly sermon-tasting society; and has stopped seeing itself as a close-knit family, a caring community, a sharing fellowship.

GETTING TO KNOW YOU, GETTING TO KNOW ALL ABOUT YOU

By the design of the Head of the clan, the church is to function as a network of loving relationships. And yet . . .

The construction of most church buildings, as well as the way we conduct ourselves together as Christians, declares in strong nonverbal telegrams that we expect the ministry and life of the church to revolve around a few "performers" who will be the church while the rest of us watch. The building in which our church meets, constructed before we began to ask some of the questions we are now asking about the church, was built long and narrow, with a high-peaked roof, and a "chancel" (platform) at one end, from which we expected all activity to take place. It was furnished with rigid oak pews (padded, of course) all facing the front, affording the best possible view of the "performers" and the backs of everyone else's heads!

It all shouts in a nearly audible whisper when you walk in the door: "It's what's up front that counts!"

As I began to see the relational nature of the church, there were times when I wished I could take an ax and chop those hard, unbending branches into two-foot sections. I wanted the freedom to turn them around in circles for five or six people, to discuss the sermon, share the happenings of their lives, and touch each other in prayer and loving personal ministry. Sometimes we did it anyway—stretching around those oak barriers—but the nonverbal message was hard to silence. Eventually, our desire to change the character of our gatherings became so strong that the leadership team of the church (elders) set aside the regular agenda of their Saturday morning meeting to unbolt the pews from the floor and rearrange them in a u-shape facing a side wall. It is disastrous to the architectural perfection of the place, but it provides a "here's-looking-at-you" setting that beautifully facilitates interaction.

The church as a family thrives on getting personal. If you are going to love your brother, you need to know your brother. If you are going to minister to his needs, you have to know what his needs are. If he's going to support and strengthen you, he has to know where you are weak and need support.

Somehow this sharing family-style happened spontaneously with the first Christians in Jerusalem. But we have had such a long tradition of coming together in cold solemnity, that until we get over our impersonal, ingrained religious rigidity, we may require some preplanned new forms designed to place us into face-to-face situations with other Christians. The church will have to make a place for the development of such loving relationships. The structures of most churches will not stimulate it. There will need to be changes . . .

My friend Leon Moniot told about visiting a church after moving to a new community. He and his wife were sure as they sat in the worship service that the man leading it was a guest minister. He seemed to be a stranger to the congregation and they to him. Later in the service, to their surprise, they discovered that he was, in fact, the pastor of the church. As they drove home they reflected on the experience of the morning, and concluded that not only did the pastor seem like a guest but the entire congregation seemed like a guest congregation!

As Leon told the story, I saw that often that is exactly how I had been approaching our church gatherings. We had been treating each other as guests, not as family. Sunday morning service was a time to handle each other as though we were all encased in glass. We carefully "protected" each other from too much touch with reality. Everyone had to leave with a good image of the church. Nothing unpleasant or personal could be shared. Problems had to be soft-pedaled. Even prayer requests were carefully worded so as to "protect" all concerned from anything discomforting or negative. We all had to appear nice and secure and holy. Everything that happened had to be perfectly executed, carefully preplanned, and had to lend itself to an atmosphere of "worship" (whatever that was), "spirituality" (whatever that was) and pleasantness. We had to give the impression that because we believed on Jesus, all our personal and corporate problems were solved and we had it "all together."

Even if we did allow someone besides the "professionals" to speak or share or participate, we always preselected our best—the attractive, articulate, successful and well-thought-of—those sure to make "a good impression" for the gospel and the church. Everyone had to think that at this church we were *all* attractive, articulate, successful, and well-thought-of. We were trying to say, "If you want to be identified with attractive, articulate, successful, and well-thought-of people, you should accept Jesus Christ and join this church."

And who doesn't want that?

But is that an appeal to motives that will actually lead to denying one's self, taking up one's own cross and following Jesus? Is the church, as the New Testament describes it, really built on a commitment to associate with the most attractive, articulate, successful, and well-thought-of group of people one can find?

In the "guest pastor-guest congregation" style of church life, the person who feels that he is not attractive, articulate, successful and well-thought-of is practically forced to build his walls even thicker to protect himself from being found out. He is lost and lonely in the midst of the "superstars."

The gatherings of the church, as well as what happens with its members the other 166 hours in the week, are all meant to be part of a dynamic family life. This is a life together in which the spiritual family comes to grips with the real needs and problems its members are facing in the real world in which they live every day.

In a healthy family, life together involves rejoicing together over the good things that happen and hurting together over the hurts.[8] A healthy family is a context in which you can share the real things that are happening to you, even if what you share reveals some personal inadequacy or weakness. You know you'll be forgiven and will not be drummed out of the family. The family handles problems together. Each one knows that he has the support of the others in the struggles he is having. If you are hurting or hungry or wounded or sick or undecided or doubtful or have a question or have lost some battle in the world, you bring it home and the family shares it with you.

They love you. They take for granted without ever questioning the fact that all the members are part of all the others. And while each is unique and his uniqueness must be protected and nurtured, together they see themselves as all in this together. It's a fact that can't be changed. No matter how miserably I fail or how successful I prove to be, my failure or my success is instinctively shared by my brothers and sisters and parents and children.

Audrey and I have three children. More than once, while coming home from school, one of them has fallen down and gotten hurt. Sometimes the accident happened several blocks from home. Jeans torn and knees bleeding the child would pick himself (or herself) up and walk or ride his bicycle the painful distance home. It hurt badly. But he would never cry until he came through the front door, to where there was a caring family waiting to soothe and salve the wounded body and ego.

The family exists to meet the real, basic needs of its members—spiritual, emotional, social, physical, and material. And some of the most important of these needs are not met by formal, preplanned, well-programmed activities, but in the context of spontaneous interactions with each other in the situations of life as they arise. It is in the context of day-to-day spontaneous interaction that family members learn how to interact meaningfully in society, learn to distinguish right from wrong, are exposed to living models after whom they pattern their lives, discover their roles in the family and in society, and learn to function in the culture and life style of which the family is a part.

In giving us this wonderful, hundredfold family, and declaring us brothers and sisters and mothers and children, and by laying out and exemplifying in His life with the Twelve the principles of caring and sharing as the adopted style of our life together, Jesus shows His intent that the church is to be all those things to the members of the family of God.

The church of the first century caught that ball and ran with it, beautifully. Acts vividly tells it.

The church in this quarter of our century can recapture it!

24

One Great, Big, Wonderful, Hundredfold Family

I know a congregation that seemed as effective and lively as any good church. But some of its members began to hunger deeply for the quality of life together they glimpsed in Acts. At first they became dissatisfied. Then, they became open to fresh truth the Spirit was seeking to show them concerning the church. From there, they began to talk together about their hunger and about the truths they were discovering in God's Word. They began to gather weekly in each other's homes to minister to and support each other in the Christian struggle. As they shared, the Spirit smuggled into their open hearts the conviction that the church must be changed to provide freedom and structure conductive to the development of *koinonia,* sharing—the "family spirit."

The sharing of personal needs, concerns, and insights should be a normal part of every gathering of Christians. We can learn how to listen to each other, to value each other, to esteem even the weaker members. We can learn to give ourselves not only to sound biblical teaching, but also to spontaneous interaction with each other. We can become involved enough with each other to see what God is doing in each other's lives—and this can enable us to live with a sense of wonder at the faithfulness and "working together" of God. We can be in on the miracles God is doing in the family. We can become less afraid to be honest, transparent, and simple in our relationships with each other. We can be real. We can admit to each other that we need each other.

WHY A FAMILY?[9]

The Bible is, in a significant sense, the history of God's family. When our Creator-Father had the world prepared, He crowned His creation by forming Adam, and then Eve, and placing them together on the new earth as the first of the family.

From those first misty days of fledglinghood God has made it clear that His purpose in the world is intended to be

25

fulfilled in a family. Generation after generation of this family is carefully recorded. Even the genealogy of Jesus (Luke 3) tracks His line of human progenitors back to "Adam, *the son of God.*" The father of the clan . . . is God.

In all God's milleniums of dealing with man, He has fulfilled His purpose in man, and the "family focus" continues. The records are kept of fathers and sons. When Noah was saved, he was saved with his family, because God had a plan only a family could fulfill. When He moved to set aside a nation in which to reveal His grand design and through which to communicate His truth, He chose Abraham because he was a man who would "charge his sons and family after him to conform to the way of the LORD and to do what is right and just" (Gen. 18:19 NEB). "And in you," God promised Abraham, "all the families of the earth shall be blessed" (Gen. 12:3) From then on, the Old Testament is the story of Abraham's family.

According to 1 Corinthians 10:11, everything that happened to that family and the families that made up Abraham's extended household, is recorded "as an example . . . for our instruction."

Examination of the structure and life style of the great biblical patriclans uncovers some striking differences between the way we view families in the twentieth Century, and the view the Bible gives of them. Noting the difference may help us to grasp God's purpose for calling the church together as a spiritual family.

In telling the story of the early Bible families, it is not my intent to suggest this as a precise model for life in the Christian nuclear family. It is, however, a forepicture of new covenant family life in which every believer's primary family is the tribe of God, the church (not the institution, which can undermine nuclear family life if given first place, but the network of living relationships in Christ).

The family in the Bible's story is an extended one. It is much more widely inclusive than the tiny westernized household clustered around the marriage relationship. In the Bible (both before and after the law) the idea inherent in the term "family" is of a growing clan including father, mother, sons and their families, daughters, servants and their families, uncles and nephews and their families, maiden aunts, and strangers who have been adopted into the family. All are part of the concept of what the family is, as the term is used in Scripture. It is a whole community of people, of which the "nuclear family" is a part. A nuclear family appears at the foundation of each household, and nuclear families come under the canopy of the household as it grows. In the lives of husband, wife, and "immediate" children, it may always have a place of special significance and purpose. Special instructions are given concerning how it can best function to the glory of God and the fulfillment of its members. But the fullness of the idea of "family" embodies a much more inclusive relational community.

And over it all, spreading the canopy of his influence, protection, direction, supply, and character, and revealing his essential nature through it . . . is the father.

Family life as told by Bible historians focuses on the father. He is the family's head and lord. The father is the one from whom the whole clan derives its name, its character, its uniqueness, its direction, its purpose, its goals, its nourishment, its security. In fact, the whole family exists to express the character, the life, and the spirit of the father.

As you read the ancient story, you discover that the relationship receiving most of the attention in the historical documents of the Bible is the father-son relationship. The central thrust of this primary kinship is the process of the father passing on to the son everything he is and preparing the son to receive everything he has.

The father's hope for immortality lies in his son. The son's chief distinctive lies in the fact that he is the son of his father and will carry on the family traditions and character in the name of his father.

Wives and mothers in this family portrait serve to produce sons for the father, sons to whom he can give his life and nature and, eventually, his authority and power and wealth. This is not intended as a "put down" to women. (Many Bible women occupy places of prominence and great fulfillment both within and beyond their function in the home.) It simply points further to the truth that in the primitive Bible households *everything in the family's life serves to express the life of the father.*

The purpose of the family is the revelation of the father's life.

As adopted sons of God through His Son Jesus Christ our family purpose is the same. As God's "in-Christ" family everything in our life together serves to express the life, the glory of our Father (Eph. 1:12). It has always been the Son's purpose, and now it is the purpose of the entire forever family.

These are some of the concepts Jesus, and later Paul, had in mind when they introduced the truth about our sonship and our adoption into the "hundredfold" family of God. Through our acceptance into the Son, we have entered the extended family of the Father and His favored Son. All that the Father is, all that He has—His character, His life, His essential nature—are the family heritage being passed on to us. We, in relationship with each other as family are, and are becoming, the expression of our Father's life.

GROWTH AND DISCIPLINE IN THE FAMILY

Personal growth and discipline in the family are intensely personal processes. Everything takes place in relationship. The family structure is not a system of rules and protocol. It is a dynamic interaction of related persons, whose first priority is the health of their relationships with each other. Because of who our Father is, and all that He has given to the family, all the problems in the family are relationship problems.

One Great, Big, Wonderful, Hundredfold Family

I was in a denominational meeting not long ago, listening to a discussion among district leaders on the constitutional rules governing movement of pastors from one district to another. It was an in-depth discussion of the minutia of institutional protocol. These were all Christian brothers. And yet it seemed to me that they were trying to work out a foolproof system of transfer that would require the least possible trust between leaders, necessitate the least personal communication, and demand the least amount of humility and servanthood.

One impression stayed with me as I left the meeting: the institutionalization of the church almost invariably strives to make the inefficient and costly process of building and maintaining open, loving personal relationships with each other "unnecessary." We seem committed to setting the church's organizational machinery up in such a way that it will roll on quite nicely without either trust or love. We seem unable to grasp the truth that no amount of assured efficiency and uninterrupted activity can possibly make up for the damage done to the cause of Christ by our lack of relationship to each other. Rather than assuring that the church will still "work" in a relational vaccuum, we would do well to assure that it will fall apart if we do not stay together!

Legislation and enforced systems of protocol are admittedly much more efficient than dealing with problems on the basis of our family relationships with, and love for, each other. Truly, truly, I say to you, efficiency does not happen to be the apex of purpose in the family of God—Jesus only gave that spot to *love*.

Correction and dealing with spiritual lapses is certainly a family function. But the relational priority is to be kept in focus in all corrective or disciplinary action. All the biblical instructions for dealing with spiritual breakdowns in the family call for intensely personal responses. It costs me far less in terms of personal self-giving to preach a sermon, publish a paper, or institute a political action to get the majority to pass a new rule to correct a brother or a "situation," than it costs to go to the brother and appeal to him on the basis of our relationship and the personal affection he already knows I have for him. The tragic fact that I, in my quest for efficiency, may not realize is that my new rule, sermon, or paper may not change the man at all (even though he conforms). A relationship that is alive and kicking has the potential to infinitely change us both.

In Matthew 18:15–17, the teaching concerning confrontation of a sinning brother, we notice that Jesus' concern is not for the purity or efficiency of the church, but for "winning" the brother. In Galatians 6:1–2, the concern of the "spiritual" dealing with the fault of the brother is not to be the perfection of the church, but the restoration of the brother and the bearing of his burden. Even in the drastic situation in 1 Corinthians 5, where everything else has evidently been tried and the incestuous brother is to be separated from the rest of the family, the suggested course of disciplinary action could only be effective if there had been a prior experience of close, continuing personal fellowship between the failing brother and the rest of his spiritual family. In the context of a loving family with relationships in health, such a separation would be the powerful exclamation point at the end of a whole process of loving concern.

Primary concern in all discipling and discipline, correction and confrontation, is not the holiness of the church (Christ has promised to see to that personally),[10] but the "saving"[11] and "winning"[12] of our brother. Our relationships as brothers and our relationship, together, with God are so important that not even the cause of the holiness of the church, nor the efficiency of the church are to be allowed to be treated with greater concern!

Apologies to Mr. Baring-Gould, but I'm not as thrilled as I could be with the idea that "Like a mighty *army,* moves the church of God." It's not that the Christian warfare is not real to me. Believe me, it is. I have the dart scars to prove it. But the depersonalization and human manipulation which characterize the world's military machines is definitely not consistent with our Lord's vision of the church.

When I search the New Testament I find few references to the martial character of the body of Christ—while the references to the family life of the church are found everywhere. It is significant that the most frequent biblical reference to fellow Christians is "brother" or "sister" or "brethren."[13] Older saints refer to the younger as "dear children."[14] And when they gather they greet each other with the kiss of love.

Together, we are just one big, wonderful, hundredfold family.

Notes

[1]From the "Rejoice in the Lord" songbook, Maranatha Music.
[2]Matthew 20:20-24.
[3]Acts 1:5.
[4]Acts 1:15.
[5]Acts 2:4.
[6]Acts 1:15.
[7]Romans 16:16; 1 Peter 5:14.
[8]1 Corinthians 12:25-26.
[9]Some of the ideas in this section were stimulated by a taped lecture, *"God's Authority—A Gift to His Family"* by W. Graham Pulkingham, 1975, The Fishermen, Inc., Houston, Texas.
[10]Ephesians 5:27.
[11]1 Corinthians 5:5.
[12]Matthew 18:15.
[13]The word "brother" referring to fellow believers appears more than seventy times in the New Testament alone. The plural "brethren" is used even more.
[14]1 John 2:1, 12, 18, 28; 3:7, 18; 5:21.

2

Body Consciousness

I like being part of the body!

All of us Christians are in it. Every last member of God's forever family is a member of the body of the Lord Jesus Christ.

I have touched the depths of that great truth. Sometimes, with some people, our hungry spirits unmistakably share the savory richness and gusto Luke caught in the phrase, "All the believers were one in heart and mind" (Acts 4:32).

The members of the leadership team of our congregation come close to this with each other from time to time. This is a small group of men charged with the leadership responsibilities of the church. We have been meeting every Saturday morning, from 7:30 to 10:00, to share a "continental" breakfast, talk, study the Bible, pray, share our lives, minister to each other, and shape the ministry and life of the church.

Often, when in prayer together at the close of an exchange of stimulating ideas and expressions of personal caring, combined with the thrilling potential that we are being led along together by the Spirit, a realization of the genuine oneness and love we have for each other has triggered unashamed declarations of our mutual affection . . .

"Thank God He brought you men into my life!"

"I really need you guys!"

Body Consciousness

"I'm glad you men are going through this with me!"

"You've really taught me something. I'm impressed!"

Would you believe . . . this is a group conducting the *business* of the church? We're savoring the life and the unity of the body there.

Often I forget how important my brothers and sisters in the Lord Jesus are to me. Some of them are easy to prize. Some of them challenge my "body consciousness" to its limits. All of them are precious . . . whether I realize it or not.

And especially, says Paul in 1 Corinthians 12:22–24, the "weaker," the "less honorable," the "unpresentable" parts of the body of Christ are necessary.

I need them. They need me.

There are times when our ministry to each other seems more than anything else like a "ministry of irritation." But even that is precious, because it keeps me from mistakenly thinking that I am a supersaint, full of perfect love for everyone. It gets the hidden potential for resentment out where it can be confessed and cleansed.

Admittedly, some of us Christians are not very smooth, well-educated, poised, polished, disciplined, talented, clever, well-dressed, or hygienic. Sometimes pride makes it difficult to consider ourselves one with some of Jesus' followers. We enjoy being helped, led, ministered to, taught, and sometimes even rebuked, by someone we naturally look up to. But our egos are reluctant to receive ministry or anything else readily from someone we've determined is weaker than we are.

Every brother or sister is a priceless gift, according to the biblical evaluation. There is not one person the Lord puts into my life who can rightly be considered other than genuinely *necessary* to my spiritual well-being and the process of becoming, in which every believer is involved.

See for yourself:

> As it is there are many parts, but one body. The eye cannot say to the hand, "I don't need you! and the head cannot

say to the feet, "I don't need you!" On the contrary, those parts of the body that seem to be weaker are indispensable, and the parts that we think are less honorable we treat with special honor. And the parts that are unpresentable are treated with special modesty, while our presentable parts need no special treatment. God has combined the members of the body and has given greater honor to the parts that lacked it, so that there should be no division in the body, but that its parts should have equal concern for each other (1 Cor. 12:20–25).

If my brother, whether weak or strong, is necessary to me, I should actually anticipate the interaction of my life with his.
The New Testament's evaluation of my brother to me:
  needed
  more important than myself
  highly thought of
  precious
  valuable . . . to me.

THE CARDINAL PRINCIPLE FOR BODY FUNCTION

It's more than just sentimentality.

Other Christians are as important to me, and I to them, as the organs and appendages of a physical body are to each other. Precious? They are indispensable. They are part of my spiritual life-support system.

Paul is the New Testament's principal minister of "body-truth." God began to teach him the body concept from the first blinking moment of his conversion.

The former enemy of the church was on his knees in the Damascus Road dust (Acts 9:1–17). When the Lord introduced Himself to this trembling trouble-maker, it was with the words, "I am Jesus, whom You are persecuting!" As He said this, the risen Jesus was introducing Saul of Tarsus to the principle that *when you touch one of Jesus' followers, you touch Jesus!*

"What do you want Me to do, Lord?" said Paul as he surrendered.

34

But the Lord refused to tell him directly. "Rise, and enter the city, and *it shall be told you* what you must do." It was essential that the one destined to lay the foundation of the gentile church learn early the principle of interdependence, for it is the cardinal principle for function within the body.

God deals with us through one another. With no one is it "just Jesus and me."

So, Paul, the Lord's chosen apostle, must depend on the ministry of an unknown, reluctant, ordinary disciple named Ananias. The Lord's initial instructions would be given, not directly, but through a simple brother.

Paul had still more to learn about the body concept.

In Acts 9:25, 27, Barnabas, a fellow-member with the gift of consolation and encouragement, and with an open heart toward struggling young converts, was Paul's only access into a wary fellowship, skeptical of the one who had practically wrecked the Jerusalem church just a few months before. Baby brother was still learning the truth of interdependence.

We read in Acts 13:1-3 that it was the consensus opinion of a group of brothers with whom he was "ministering to the Lord" in Antioch, that revealed God's plan to Paul about his ministry. There was no direct revelation which might lead to independent action. Again Paul was being taught the vital theology of interdependence. He first had to see himself primarily as a part of the body; then he could be sent out to add to it.

The principle of interdependence becomes a dominant theme with Paul as, in his letters, he spells out the theology of the church. Almost all the biblical references to the church as Christ's body are over his signature. It is no passing reference. It is a strategic aspect of his entire ministry.

THE THEOLOGY OF INTERDEPENDENCE

The following pages are given to a brief commentary on each of the statements in Paul's writings in which he specifically uses the word "body," referring to the church. Even though it necessitates some repetition, all of the body passages are included, in order to show how important this truth is to Paul . . . and to us. This theology of interdependence, of seeing ourselves as believers, as part of a living, indivisible organism, is vital to understanding the purpose of God and where we fit into what He is doing.

Romans 12:3–8. Realistic and accurate evaluation of our personal ministry and value to the church must begin with a clear view of our self as an interdependant member of the body of Christ. We have been given limited faith and a gift, or gifts, according to the grace and allotment of God, which not only equips us for a necessary ministry, but which also leaves us dependent upon all the other members.

1 Corinthians 6:15a. Even our physical bodies are parts of Christ. Since the Ascension and Pentecost, together we believers are actually Christ's physical presence in the world.

1 Corinthians 10:16, 17. The Lord's Supper is not only a remembering of the sacrificial death of Jesus for us; the common bread we share together represents His physical body. As those who eat the "bread of life"[1] (take Jesus into our lives), we celebrate the fact that we are all together in reality His physical body.

1 Corinthians 11:27–29. To truly get the full impact of this passage, it should be remembered that the early church "shared the bread and drank the cup of the Lord" nearly every time they got together. When Paul speaks of the danger involved in eating the bread and drinking the cup of the Lord "in an unworthy manner," he is talking about a danger that he thought of as present *whenever* Christians gather. If there is danger in sharing at the communion table under certain conditions, we are in that same danger at every Christian meeting. "In an unworthy manner," is clearly exposed in verse 29: the problem is failure to "recognize the Lord's body." *Insensitivity* to the body of

Christ. *Insensitivity* to the oneness. *Insensitivity* to the "unity of the Spirit."

Characteristics of unworthy participation in body life include division (v. 18); differences (v. 19); sharing in the body's gatherings to fulfill selfish, fleshly, or individualistic purposes, purposes other than to share the unity of the body, to remember the Lord, and to join in thanksgiving[2] (v. 20); feeding one's own desires first (v. 21); carelessness regarding the people of the church (v. 22); failure to value every member of the body, including those to whom one feels superior (v. 23). All aloofness, pride, self-seeking, separatism, and manipulation of fellow Christians are violations of the body and blood of the Lord, because they are evidences of insensitivity to the body of Christ and its blood-washed members.

Chastisement is upon those who do not rightly discern the Lord's body. Much of present-day Christianity's weakness, sickness, and death are direct judgments brought upon us by our insensitivity to the body of Christ (v. 30).

1 Corinthians 12; 13; 14. The major presentation of the doctrine of the body. Members of the body are identified by their gifts and ministries.

12:3. The uniting confession of the body of Christ: "Jesus is Lord."

12:4–11. The keys to interdependence: diversity of gifts for ministry, diversity of personal ministries, and diversity of effects of those ministries.

12:12–14. There is *one* body, and all who have received the *one* Spirit, have been *placed into*[3] the body by the Spirit. It is not merely the church is *like* a body—that a physical body is somehow a good "illustration" of the church. It goes further than that. A physical body is composed of many members, cells, organs, parts—and yet, inseparably *one* body. That's how Christ is. He does not have many bodies, just one. And all who have His Spirit are physical-and-spiritual members.

37

12:15–27. Apart from the rest of the body, each individual Christian is incomplete and unable to share in the full outworking of the life experience of Christ. They *must* be together. They hurt with each other's sufferings and they rejoice with each other's successes.

12:28–31. Each member is specially equipped for a unique and important ministry in the body. But it's an interdependent ministry. No single piece of this equipment is designated as the one to be given to everyone. In order to benefit from all that God has given the body, I must be ministered to by the other members.

13:1–13. The only thing that makes anything matter, and thus the most important ingredient in the life of the body, is *love.* It is the kind of love that expresses itself in unselfish giving to, bearing with, and respect for, one another. Body members are called upon to lay down their lives, their pride, their self-interest, their "rights," for each other.[4]

14:1–40. The chief goal of function within the body is always "edification"—to build each other up spiritually.

Ephesians 1:23. The church, as Christ's body, is defined here as "the fullness of him who fills everything." The Bible describes no individual in such words, except Jesus Himself. Of Him, Colossians 2:9 says, ". . . in Christ all the fullness of the Deity lives in bodily form." In other words, Jesus is the only One who, alone, gives complete expression of the divine nature.

Yet, here in Ephesians 1:23, the people of God together as the body of Christ are said to be the fullness of Christ. While no single individual expresses fully the personality and nature of Christ, His Body, composed of all who share His Life, is the full and complete disclosure of Himself in the universe. In a very real sense, the body is Christ in the world.

Ephesians 2:11–16; 3:6. The body of Christ is the practical expression of the universal reconciliation provided by Christ through the cross. By shedding His blood to make peace with God for all men, Christ, Himself, replaced the law as the means of establishing peace. The way was opened for gentiles (people without any knowledge of the law; enemies, in fact, of the law) to receive God's promises and to live in close fellowship with God, simply by trusting Jesus Christ. The boundary lines between Jews and Gentiles were erased. And where there had been two men, separated by the demands of the law, now there is "one new man," the body of Christ. Both Jews and Gentiles are a part of it. Enemies wake up to find that they are interdependent members of Christ's body—"family."

Ephesians 4:1–16. Two major emphases are dealt with here: (1) The unity of the body, and (2) the growth of the body.

The unity of the Body (vv. 1–7).

Our calling is to be Christ in the world—*together.* The body is the corporate instrument through which the manifold wisdom of God is made known to the spiritual universe (Eph. 3:10). The maintenance of loving relationships between body members is essential to our faithfulness to that calling.

The body's unity is based on at least seven factors:

(1) *One body.* Anyone who has received Jesus Christ belongs to the one body. Even if we do not see it, the truth is that we are all parts of the same body, and we cannot be separated from it—or from one another—as long as we belong to Christ.

(2) *One Spirit.* If anyone has received the Spirit of Christ, he is a part of Christ, and since I, too, have received the Spirit of Christ, we are one in the same Spirit. We must be diligent to preserve the unity.

(3) *One hope of your calling.* All true followers of Jesus Christ share the common hope of being completely reshaped into His likeness and of being with Him forever. That hope which we share together is meant to bind us together.

(4) *One Lord.* The recognition and acknowledgement

that Jesus is Lord is common to all true believers. The personally acted-upon confession that Jesus is Lord is the basis of our relationship to Christ, our placement into the body, the presence of the Spirit in our lives, and the hope of our salvation and eternal life. If someone is acknowledging Jesus as Lord of his life, and I am also, then we are one.

(5) *One faith.* The faith we share in common as Christians is the faith by which we have all been saved—personal faith that Jesus Christ is the Son of God who died for our sins and lives to give us life. Total intellectual agreement was not the experience of even the church in Century 1.[5] We may struggle with each other over interpretations of Scripture, but we are one from the standpoint of faith for salvation. And we are one when it comes to the object of our faith.

(6) *One baptism.* Whole denominations and separating movements within Christendom are based on interpretations regarding baptism and baptismal methods. One baptism? Our division seems to label Paul's statement as absurd! Watchman Nee suggests that Paul pinpoints the issue for us in 1 Corinthians 1:13–15:

> Is Christ divided? Was Paul crucified for you? Were you baptized into the name of Paul? I am thankful that I did not baptize any of you expect Crispus and Gaius, so no one can say that you were baptized into my name.

The emphasis is on the name into which we are baptized, not the method. All of us who have been baptized into the name of the Lord are one. We have all shared in one baptism.[6]

(7) *One God and Father.* We believe in and worship the personal, supernatural God revealed in the Bible—eternal Creator, loving Father in heaven, who sent His Son to redeem mankind from sin. We belong to His family. We should not be divided.

Ephesians 4:7 adds the important truth that though we are a body, and God deals with the body and is glorified in the most complete sense through people functioning within the context of the body, yet His grace and gifts are given on an "each one" basis. Individually, personally, God gives us His undeserved blessings and favor.

The growth of the body (vv. 11–16).

The keys to body growth are stated summarily in verse 16:

> From [Christ] the whole body, joined and held together by every supporting ligament, grows and builds itself up in love, as each part does its work.

The source of growth and life in the body is the Head, *Christ.*

Two factors keep the body fitted and held together and thus keep it growing and building itself up in love:

(1) *The working of each part.* The individual members of the body each ministering with their gifts (v. 11); (a) to equip one another for service (v. 12a), (b) to help one another to grow (v. 12b), (c) to bring about unity in the body (v. 13a), (d) to help each other to know the Son of God better (v. 13b), (e) to bring the whole fellowship to spiritual maturity (v. 13c), (f) to help bring the body to the point where together we more completely express the personality of Christ (v. 13d), (g) to bring each other to spiritual and doctrinal stability where, instead of being an easy target for deception and error, we are ministering and growing together—all aspects of our lives being brought increasingly under the headship of Christ (vv. 14, 15). This is not a description of a few leaders ministering to the body, but of all the members involved in ministering to each other—whether spontaneously or within structured settings.

(2) *The holding power of every supporting ligament.* The "individual parts" and the "ligaments" are not the same thing. Derek Prince illustrates the difference by pointing to the anatomical construction of the human arm. Between the elbow and the shoulder is one large bone. Below the elbow to the wrist are two smaller bones. The three bones may be in perfect health and strength and yet the arm may actually

be totally useless—*if* the ligament connecting the bones is diseased or deformed. The bones are the individual members of the body. The ligaments are the relationships between the members.

Not only must the members be, individually, in good health, but the relationships between them must be right, or the body cannot do its work or rightly grow. The relationships have as much (or more) to do with the body's growth as the effective functioning of gifted individual members. Whatever growth comes in the body must always be the building up of itself "in love."

Ephesians 5:23 (22–32). Christ, and Christ alone, is the leader of the church. He is its only Savior. He does not leave the leadership, deliverance, sanctification, cleansing, perfecting, nourishing, and cherishing of His body to mere men. He will use Spirit-gifted men in the process, but these tasks are beyond the abilities of men, so the living Lord Jesus sees to them personally. He is pictured as continuously toiling over, and protecting the body. He will present to Himself a glorious church " . . . without stain or wrinkle or any other blemish . . . holy and blameless" (v. 27). The efforts of mere humans to do it for Him only result in frustration and failure. He is the Savior of the body!

Ephesians 5:30. Christ nourishes and cherishes the church as though it were His own flesh and bones—because we are.

Colossians 1:18. Christ is head of the body. He created it. He was the first of its number to rise from the dead. He is to have first place in everything in the church.

Colossians 1:24. Members of the body are often called upon to suffer and sacrifice themselves for the sake of the body and its members. Suffering, even dying, for the body's sake is a normal and necessary function of members.

Colossians 2:19. The body grows from the head. The secret of continuing growth is to stay close to Jesus. Close to Jesus, held together by harmonious, healthy, interdependent relationships ("ligaments") the body will grow—with God's growth.

Colossians 3:15. The ruler, umpire[7], of all body life is "the peace of Christ." Among true believers the shots are called, the boundaries are marked, the paths are pointed out, by peace. Confusion, conflict between members, strained relationships, uncertainty, quarreling, anxiety, are all evidences that something is wrong with the way we are living or thinking or working together. Our relationships are to be marked and guided by peace.

The body is real. Not just a "parable."

The one body is a manifestation of the one Spirit (Eph. 4:4, 1 Cor. 12:13). The Spirit is the hidden reality revealed by the physical reality, the body.[8]

WHERE THERE IS NO VISION . . .

Christians have always found it difficult to clearly "see" the body. Most of church life for us has revolved around denominational structure, local organization, and institution building. When we preach on the church or teach the body passages, we invariably end up applying them no further than as whips to stir up enthusiasm for our own denomination or local church. Often we act as if there were more than one true "Zion," and we were free to take our pick.

Our minds are so fortified with the stubborn walls which such thinking has erected in us through the years, that the Spirit has His hands full trying to break down those world-thinking fortresses and bring our thoughts about the church into the captivity of Christ.[9]

Paul prayed that the Ephesian Christians would be given ". . . the Spirit of wisdom and revelation . . ." (Eph. 1:17), to make them able to see and know the things of Christ He was intending to share with them.

The "revelation" the Spirit is seeking to bring back to the church and its members at this critical moment in history incorporates:

1) a renewed vision of the body of Christ,

2) a sharpened consciousness of its reality and its oneness,

3) a keen awareness of how dependent we Christians are upon each other.

Until we come to "see" God's church, to "see" the body of Christ, to "see" each other as members of each other, we will continue to rationalize our doctrinal, historical, denominational, racial, social, and attitudinal divisions. We will continue to do nothing about them. Until the vision we need breaks in on us *from the Holy Spirit,* we are unable to esteem each other, value and prize each other's ministry and fellowship. Our evaluations of each other often are based on a carnal, rather than a spiritual, criteria. And the body continues to be hindered in the process of building itself up in love. Tragically, the world remains unconvinced about our relationship with Jesus.

Failure to comprehend the body has us blinded to the real spiritual power released in the interaction between believers. When we see the body as a real unity, such interaction is no longer dispensable. It is something the church *must* be experiencing together continually.

The New Testament truth about the body is that God, through the Spirit, has put it together and has put into it all the equipment (gifts) needed to build it up into the Lord. The body in the New Testament has what it needs to build itself up. This is true of every body of believers, in every culture, whatever the size of the group, no matter how limited they are in education and natural talent. Any body of believers, scripturally constituted—alive in Jesus and gathering around Him—can function and grow and express the glory of Jesus together. They simply must be willing to live interdependently with each other. They must be willing to recognize their indivisible basic unity in Christ and be willing to preserve it.

When we "see" the body with its many necessary members, the distance between pulpit and pew begins to shrink and even disappear. The pulpit experiences a centuries-overdue loss of excess weight, and is cut down to size. Everyone in the church becomes important, but no longer is anyone all-important. God seems no longer to be in danger of losing the ball game if some key man is off the field.

Failure to comprehend the body also shows up in every form of disharmony, division, or tension between members of the forever family. Brother with brother. Husband with wife. Parents with children. Pastor with people. Congregation with congregation. Denomination with denomination. Theological camp with theological camp.

BODY CONSCIOUSNESS

There is a body consciousness that accompanies the presence of the Holy Spirit's life. Life is not abstract. It is real. It is possible to be conscious of it. Think about it. When a person wakes up in the morning, how does he know he is alive? Must he pinch himself? Take his pulse? Look in the mirror? No. He knows he is alive simply because he is conscious of life.

There is also a consciousness of spiritual life. I'll never forget how Bill Vipond prayed to receive Christ one night and two weeks later came to me with deep concern because nothing seemed to have happened. As we talked he shared with me how (strangely) in the last two weeks he had been intensely aware of sins in his life that had never seemed wrong before; how, in the last few days, the Bible had come alive to him and he found himself devouring it until late into the night; and how his family relationships had been showing marked improvement just in recent days. I said, "Bill, you've got the life!" He saw it and went home confident.

The life of the body of Christ too is a conscious reality. The solid truth is that those who possess the life of Jesus Christ, the life of the Holy Spirit, possess it in common with all others who have received Christ. And those who recognize the body are conscious of the corporate character of the life they share. The body is a true oneness, a demonstrable life. And having been placed into the body's life stream, it is natural, normal, to develop a growing consciousness of our interdependent relationship with each other.

As the vision of the body grows, so does the sensitivity to what divides it. The Holy Spirit cannot be divided. Neither can the body be divided without causing distress. Whenever disharmony comes between Christians, it is consistent with membership in the one body that a longing arises, an ache develops to remove the obstacles and to get inside the walls and to crash the barriers. The body of Christ is like any physical body. While it has many members, it has only one life. It can live on if it has suffered a wound or amputation or surgery. But it suffers great distress and is left impaired. A spiritual vision of the body, an awareness of its real unity, a body consciousness, will result in a protective experience of pain and distress at the incision of any division.

It was a group of ten women, meeting for Bible study, that first caught the vision of the body at Our Heritage Church. At the start, only two openly confessed Christ as Savior. In a matter of weeks, all ten had received the Lord and were hungrily discovering together what it meant to relate Him to everything in their lives. They saw almost immediately how much they needed each other's support. They began to discover from the New Testament that that was exactly what God had in mind for the church.

The truth became contagious, as these women began to touch, in supportive ways, the lives of many in the local fellowship.

One of these women, Mary, developed a deep sensitivity to anything that would bring tension or strain between body members. And often, it was her prayers and well-timed visits, sometimes even honest rebukes, that moved situations and relationships toward healing. I have seen her weep over wounds in the body, in which she was not directly involved.

46

but which touched the tenderness of her body consciousness. She helped all of us learn that we are a part of each
other and can no longer take the safe, detached attitude,
"It's no skin off my nose." Whatever happens to or between
my fellow-followers of Jesus *is* skin off my nose.

I'll share just two pictures from the album of a whole
developing life style to give a glimpse of how it works . . .

VIGNETTES OF INTERDEPENDENCE

When Margaret Porter was killed in an auto crash, I was in
Saskatchewan, 2000 miles away, on a speaking tour. Her
parents, Pat and Ilene, felt that I should not interrupt my
speaking schedule to return to Arizona for the memorial service; the body would minister to the family. And it did.
Scores of brothers and sisters ministered in a variety of ways
during those days. Sharing the deep hurt, housework,
meals, prayer, encouragement, reminders of the promises,
expressions of love, quiet support and caring. The body in
action. The Porters felt well-cared for, even in the absence
of "the pastor." Pat told me when I returned home, "As we
went through the grieving process, we needed certain kinds
of ministry at certain points. Just when we needed a particular kind of help, God sent someone to us who helped us
in just the right way."

One of our members, a Christian since childhood, is presently going through a period of significant spiritual struggle
and growth. The present growth process began several
months ago at a small spontaneous gathering of friends listening to a taped message on Christian community. Something on tape—not even the main thrust of the message—
was used by the Spirit to expose the man's deep inner dis-
honesty with himself and with God. Here is the story in his
own words:

"In a moment of illumination, the awareness blasted its
way into my consciousness that for many years I had been
looking at the teachings of Jesus, experiencing a growing

hunger to enter into the kind of life style they call for—but invariably had turned away from the most challenging of them. I had been blaming other people in my life for my own failure to respond. This pattern must be broken. I must now accept responsibility for my own decisions and stop sidestepping the responsibility by transferring my own fear and guilt to the people close to me. In that moment of disclosure, the confession spilled forth that the things standing in the way of my freedom to respond were all inner things—fears, anger, guilt, unresolved emotional barriers to relationship and self-giving. We prayed together for my deliverance and freedom. My friends held me in their arms and pledged to go with me through whatever process might be involved."

That was the kickoff to an intensified search for healing and for freedom. The context for this fresh beginning was the body, represented by a handful of supporting friends.

"A few weeks later a 'Yokefellow group' was formed involving some of the members of the church.[10] I decided to join the group. An accompanying personality test provided an in-depth definition of the inner spiritual barriers to growth. The group became both the continued stimulation to press the inner search, and the setting for the mutual confession, affirmation, and acceptance needed to maintain the courage to go on.

"Rod Wilke, one of the original group that had been there that first afternoon, committed himself to meet with me daily—6:30 A.M.—for an hour of sharing and prayer. And there were others, both in and outside the local congregation, who are spiritually related to me, who cared and shared the struggle and loved and affirmed me. There was Al Ransom, whom I called my "weekly confidante-over-breakfast," leader in a sister church, who often had the precise word of explanation needed for some phase of my struggle, and encouraged me to keep going. Often the Holy Spirit seemed to bring people into my life unexpectedly, who would add just the right insight at just the right time (like a friend from 2500 miles away, Stan Jones of Faith at Work, who, in an hour together at Sky Harbor Airport, turned a couple of significant keys to open important doors in the process of healing). It was the body of Christ engaged in body life.

"Continuing body support came from within my own home. My wife, Audrey, has lived with me in a process of spiritual upheaval and growth for far longer than a few months—twenty-six years to be exact. Even though the changes taking place in my life during this time of self-discovery were sometimes extremely threatening to her own sense of security, she provided priceless additional understanding, interaction, and loving reinforcement, close-in.

"I also shared my growing struggle with the congregation as a whole. I found them continuously affirming, supportive, and accepting, even though the intensity with which I pursued this search at times negatively affected my performance as a church leader. I needed help. The body stood by me.

"My fellow members of the church's leadership team have walked through the continuing struggle with me. They stood by me in conspicuous emotional weakness. They listened to the confession of my spiritual hang-ups. At my request, they set me free indefinitely from leadership responsibilities, with full support, so that I could find the ministry and life style the Spirit wants for me, even if that style might not fit the traditional expectations pastors traditionally fulfill!

"In other words, the body surrounded me with caring and support, and dared to set me free to find myself.

"I am now back in active ministry. But it is a ministry with a new shape more suited to my gifts and call. As one member who has felt it, I can tell you that without the loving support of a body of people willing to stick by me even when I am weak, I would not be experiencing the resolution of some very deep, long-standing spiritual problems. Without the body, I would be lost in a sea of unresolved anger and guilt, or forever bound in a prison of stifling conformity.

"I have experienced the power of the principle of inter-dependence on a very personal level. This example may seem "special" because I am admittedly a highly visible character in the life of our church. But it illustrates what I believe is intended by the Head to be the normal experience of the members of the body of Christ—reaching out in need for each other's support, and finding themselves surrounded by a supportive network of caring fellow members, a network corporately capable of miraculous acts of healing and deliverance in the name of Jesus.

"Even beginning to see the body and my place in it, has, in itself, brought new freedom and happiness into my life as a Christian and my work as a minister of Christ.

"I'm not alone any more. The whole responsibility for the work of Christ is not on my shoulders. I can actually visualize the work, the revelation of Christ in the world, get-ting done. I can see Him revealing Himself beautifully through His people, plural. Even when individuals fail, His life is still seen in the body. And it's so big that it cannot be stopped by a seeming collapse in a local area.

"I'm shaking free, within the body, to do the things I'm placed here to do, and to leave the other tasks and minis-tries to the other members, filling their places. I'm not over-burdened by an increasingly exploded evaluation of my own importance.

"I'm drawing life, support, strength, and direction from my fellow members. I depend on them. And in them the living Christ ministers to me and receives ministry from me, in a visible, tangible, feelable way.

"I like being part of a body!"

Notes

[1]John 6:48–58.
[2]Eucharist means thanksgiving.
[3]One of several interpretations of the Greek word meaning, "to baptize."
[4]See also John 15:13.
[5]Romans 14 and 1 Corinthians 8 and 9 were written to deal with differences of opinion, conviction, and "belief" in the church.
[6]*The Normal Christian Church Life* (International Students Press, 1969). p. 62. Another way of looking at this is based on the fact that entrance of every one of us into the one body of Christ was accomplished by a single spiritual baptism in which all true believers are made to share. 1 Corinthians 12:13 tells about this baptism. One baptism, by the Holy Spirit puts us into the one body. And in doing so, makes us one.
[7]Amplified Bible.
[8]Watchman Nee, *What Shall This Man Do?* (Fort Washington, Pa.: Christian Literature Crusade, 1967), pp. 109–112.
[9]2 Corinthians 10:3–6.
[10]Yokefellows, Inc., 19 Park Road, Burlingame, California, 94010.

3

"Pull in Your Oars and Put Up a Sail"

The Bible study group at Glen Schafer's house was engrossed in a study of the third chapter of John's Gospel. In the course of our interaction we came to the eighth verse, in which Jesus explains the work of the Holy Spirit to Nicodemus . . .

The wind blows wherever it pleases. You hear its sound, but you cannot tell where it comes from or where it is going. So it is with everyone born of the Spirit.

Glen was asked what that verse said to him. Without hesitation he answered simply, "Pull in your oars and put up a sail!"

The solid truth is that the wind of the Spirit is blowing wherever born-again believers are gathering. The challenge to this generation of Christians is to stop struggling in the flesh to move "the ship of Zion" along, and instead, to put up something that will catch the wind, and start moving along in His direction and under His power.

The church is dependent on the Holy Spirit for the ability to do and to be all God has called it to.

The success and power of the early church demonstrates one all-important fact that becomes lost amid the gadgetry and gimmickry of the wealthy, over-supplied church of this generation, which cannot imagine itself functioning so simply:

"Pull in Your Oars and Put Up a Sail"

Its living Lord Jesus Christ filling the lives of surrendered people is all the church *really* needs to fulfill its mission in the world.[1]

If that isn't true, the church of the first two centuries could never have made it. It was a movement that had everything stacked against its success.

It was a "federal offense" to be a Christian. There were ten imperial persecutions in the first 250 years aimed at destroying Christianity from the face of the earth.

Those Christians were hated and despised by the rest of society. Slanderous lies were told about them. They were thought to be guilty of all sorts of crimes against humanity. According to one tradition, Nero perpetrated the lie that the Christians had burned Rome.

They were mostly poor. Half the population of the Roman empire was in slavery, and it was among them that Christianity had its fastest spread. For a rich man or government official to embrace Christ often meant confiscation of his goods and dismissal from his office.

They had no church buildings.

There were no educated, professional, paid pastors.

They were virtually without the Scriptures. The New Testament was not written until fifty or sixty years after the movement began. A few copies of the Old Testament were read or quoted from memory on the Lord's Day. But there was no such thing as daily Bible reading or Bible study.

No mass media was available to aid in the gospel's spread. The printing press hadn't been invented. Radio, television, newspapers—nothing like these existed. The Good News was a word-of-mouth project.

Travel was slow.

By all human standards—by all the standards we apply to determine the effective, equipped church—that movement could not succeed. But in Acts 17:6, the worst thing their enemies could say about them was, "These people . . . have turned the world upside down!" (KJV). In 250 years their world, the Roman empire, the greatest empire the world has ever known, had officially bowed its knees to Jesus Christ.

What a church! What an organization! What an administrator they must have had! If we could find someone like that today, we could turn our world upside down!

Their administrator was the Holy Spirit.

He planned, organized, staffed, and empowered the whole movement. The Holy Spirit chose men, filled them, and moved them according to His strategy. Everything they needed was something the Holy Spirit willed, and then did, through men yielded to His control. The movement was utterly dependent on Him.

The gospel literally permeated the empire!

Everywhere something exciting was happening. There was life. God was at work. The things that were happening couldn't be explained any other way.

Even their problems and failures (and they had plenty of them) became opportunities for the Spirit to teach, to revive, and to bring spiritual growth and strength.[2]

And no one could stop it.

THE WIND AND THE WORK

Jesus Christ is alive! No less alive today than He was in Century 1. In fact, it is as true today as it was then, that Jesus Christ lives in every true follower of His. Every person who has genuinely received Jesus Christ has the Spirit of the living Jesus living in him.[3] He is living in His church. Now.

I want to see what will happen if we begin staking everything in the church on the principle stated in Acts 1:8 . . .

You will receive power when the Holy Spirit comes on you; and you will be my witnesses.

This is not a command; this is a promise.

The desire of the Lord is that we be His witnesses. In order to make us His witnesses, He has given us His Spirit. His Spirit, living in us, gives us the ability to be what He wants us to be.

"Pull in Your Oars and Put Up a Sail"

It's a principle stated over and over in the New Testament and applied, not only to being witnesses, but to everything the Lord desires for us to be doing and being.

The principle: All God wants us to do and to be will be produced in us as we enter into, and continue in, a vital, living relationship with the Holy Spirit.

The overflowing spontaneity of the kind of life God wants for the church is promised to us by Jesus:

> "Whoever believes in me, as the Scripture has said, streams of living water will flow from within him." By this he meant the Spirit, whom those who believed in him were later to receive (John 7:38).

Our obedience and performance and production as Christians was never intended to be a dreary, wearisome, duty-bound kind of thing—a reluctant handpump producing a dissatisfying dribble. The Lord has promised a free-flowing, spontaneous river of life, *wanting* to flow, even though we are not always conscious of its output.

In a significant segment from Galatians 2:20, Paul describes the spontaneity and flow of this "river" in another way:

> . . . I no longer live, but Christ lives in me.

It is no mere copy of Christ's life that is our potential as people indwelt by the Spirit. Christ lives His life in us. He clothes Himself in our human flesh, diffuses[4] Himself throughout the totality of what we are, and lives His life in the persons we are. Our lives and His combine.

When it comes to the matters of work, obedience, production of fruit, or of activity, the divine plan is for us to function from this kind of perspective:

> . . . be keener than ever to work . . . with a proper sense of awe and responsibility. *For it is God who is at work within you,* giving you the will and the power to achieve His purpose (Phil. 2:12, 13, Phillips, italics added).

We are workers together, God and His people. If our relationship with Him is living and real, when He works in us, we work it out in our lives. When we work, we know by faith it is because He is at work in us, giving the desire and the ability to do what pleases Him. All our humanness and physical strength are to be involved in the work. Sometimes we work hard. But the desire to do it and the spiritual power in the work is His power flowing like a free river from inside us.

The flesh, alone, can never produce anything that counts. And any effort expended apart from the Spirit's working is wasted effort—what the Bible calls "wood, hay or straw."[5] Frustration. Death. Even if we are trying to be obedient to His commandments. But throwing everything we are into the work in utter dependence, not on human strength, but on His power in us, produces "gold, silver, and costly stones." Work that counts.

What will happen if we stake everything on the principle that all God wants the church to be and to do will be produced in it, if we concentrate on keeping our people in a vital, living relationship with the Holy Spirit? What happens if the local church stops trying to build organizational machinery to carry out tasks we think the Lord has called us to, and instead, simply seeks to stimulate edifying meetings and healthy relationships between Christians that encourage God's people to keep renewed in the fullness of the Spirit?

Will the Spirit do the work through people who are alive to Him? Will people alive to the living Christ and who live their lives in response to his Spirit be involved in doing what God wants to do? Will they pray? Will they love? Will they give? Will they involve themselves in Spirit-directed social action? Will they care about missions? Will they have a zeal for evangelism? Will they study the Bible? Will they, in time, as they grow toward maturity in Christ, become involved in doing whatever is in the mind of the Lord of the church for His people to be doing?

"Pull in Your Oars and Put Up a Sail"

The promise is that they will. I believe that, even though some of these questions have not yet received their full answer among us, and though our answers are not without wide gaps and vast imperfections, our local experience of church life over more than a decade has produced sound evidence that the answer to all the questions is yes. Readers of our story, which is woven into this book, are free to judge for themselves on the basis of the evidence.

And it follows that if believers are *not* responding to what is in the mind of the Lord to be done in the world, the answer still lies in the health of their relationships to the Spirit and to each other. It is to those vital relationships that attention should be directed if the church is failing to fulfill its commissions. The answer cannot be found in management principles, better training, or organization alone (if at all). The final and best answer can be found only in raising the level of sensitivity and responsiveness of the church and its members to the Holy Spirit.

In part, perhaps, it is a matter of getting the horse before the cart.

Perhaps it is not wrong for the church to organize and devise better methodology for reaching the lost with the message of Christ, feeding the hungry, training workers, etc. The issue is that no such organizing and devising can ever be thought to be able to do the work of God as God intends for His work to be done, unless the men and women doing the organizing and planning, as well as those carrying out the plans, are controlled by the Spirit of God and are working in His energy.

The work of God, and any structure that may be necessary to accomplish it, is to grow out of what the Spirit is doing in the lives of God's people.

And when, out of someone's personal life in the Spirit, a plan or ministry emerges which involves other people, others should not be expected to get involved from any other basis than from what the Spirit is doing in *their* lives.

57

How contradictory to be leading from a living relationship with the Spirit, while resorting to the manipulations of the flesh to get others involved.

Many of us have lived our adult lives as "professional ministers," frustrated and overburdened with anxieties and guilt and a sense of failure, simply because we have been taught to see ourselves as responsible to be the church's source of inspiration, leadership, and power. We were told in seminary and even as we grew up in secular society, as well as in every council of church government, that the success or failure of the church hinges on us. The full responsibility for what the church accomplishes or fails to accomplish rests on *our* preaching, *our* planning, *our* programming, *our* calling, *our* ability to inspire enthusiasm, *our* cleverness, *our* strength of character, *our* brilliance as leaders of men.

The whole of our professional lives has been lived in the tight confines of an iron maiden of role expectations. Impaled with guilt and disappointment (mainly in ourselves), we dare not admit the weakness and inadequacy we feel, or the truth that we do not have answers for the church's needs, for fear someone will notice that we are not "God's men of faith and power," as the publicity notices said when we arrived.

There have been times when I felt that I alone, all by myself, was carrying the entire church on my back, and that if it ever reflected the image of Jesus it would be because I, alone, singlehandedly, hammered it into shape with my bare hands!

It is at those times sheer terror sets in! Because I know in my heart it will never happen if it depends on the likes of me to do it. Men can build monuments to human ability that are sometimes impressive, and can even do it in the name of the Lord. But the kind of work God wants can only be done by God Himself.

"Pull in Your Oars and Put Up a Sail"

EVANGELISM AND THE WIND

The New Testament church's application of the principle of dependence on the Holy Spirit in the work, as well as the vital link between the relational health of the church and the ministry of the Spirit through her, are well illustrated in the approach she took to evangelism.

In the church of the first century, evangelism takes place, as a matter of course, when the church is spiritually healthy.

What was the evangelism program of the early church? What was their strategy for fulfilling the Great Commission? For reaching their cities and states and nations and neighbors with the good news about Jesus?

They did a terrific job of it.

Often the story of their progress during the first century is told in terms like those of Acts 9:31 . . .

> The church throughout Judea, Galilee and Samaria . . . was multiplied. (KJV)

Multiplied!

And the same word is used in several other places in the Acts record.

A thousand times we have been challenged with the speed of their spread. We have marveled jealously at how they could do it with so little communications technology.

We have had the Great Commission thrust at us a thousand times to give us an incentive to "get out and win souls." But we are disappointed again and again. For without some plan to "keep the pressure on" and/or some method for "making soul-winning easy," the average church can't even keep a skeleton crew of "witnesses" doing it only once a week. We should know by now that it is going to take more than another new training program to change that.

It is somewhat surprising that in all their dealings with the churches, the apostles in the epistles never once reminded

59

their readers of the Great Commission! Nowhere did the apostle Paul give an extensive rundown on "how to win people to Jesus Christ," or "how to organize your church to fulfill the Great Commission in your city."

Richard Halverson in his book, *How I Changed My Thinking About the Church,* notes that no evangelistic quotas are given, no numerical goals are described for the churches in the New Testament.[6]

This doesn't necessarily mean that the apostles never mentioned the Great Commission. They surely did. I'm sure that every believer understood that the body of Christ and every individual member of it has a responsibility to share the Good News. But it's seldom exhorted about or promoted.

Evangelism seems to be something the early Christian leaders just expected to happen in the lives of believers. Naturally. And it did.

What the early church concentrated on, "promoted," taught, encouraged, pressed for, led to, and exemplified in the New Testament letters, was the development of two vital relationships.

The first concern, a living personal relationship with Jesus Christ, was epitomized by the phrase, "filled with the Spirit."

The second concern, a healthy, harmonious fellowship with fellow believers, was epitomized by the concept, "agape-love."

Halverson:

> . . . the weight of the exhortation and instruction in the epistles has to do with the relationship of believer with believer in the community, in the body of Christ. The implication can be clearly drawn that when these relationships are right, i.e., when the brothers and sisters love one another and when they are abiding in Christ, evangelism and mission will be the normal and healthy result of such relationships.
>
> The last sentence in the second chapter of Acts illustrates this point. There Luke attaches to his description of that New

"Pull in Your Oars and Put Up a Sail"

Testament community, this statement, "And the Lord added to their number day by day those who were being saved." In other words, when all who believed were together and had all things in common—when they were selfless in their attitude toward their possessions—when they worshiped together daily and broke bread in their homes—when they partook of food with glad and generous hearts—when they praised God, they had favor with all the people as a result of which evangelism happened. It was inevitable: "The Lord added to the church day by day those that were being saved" (Acts 2:47).

Other references in Acts bear out this fact. Chapter 6, verse 7, for example, "And the word of God increased and the number of the disciples multiplied greatly in Jerusalem, and a great many of the priests were obedient to the faith." When the word of God increased, evangelism happened, the number of the disciples increased greatly in Jerusalem. The multiplication of disciples was the normal result of the ministry of the Word in the city. In Acts 9:31 Luke records, "So the church throughout all Judea, and Galilee and Samaria had peace and was built up; and walking in the fear of the Lord and in the comfort of the Holy Spirit, it was multiplied." Here again, multiplication is the result of conducive conditions in the community. The church had peace, she was built up, she walked in the fear of the Lord and in the comfort of the Holy Spirit, as a result of which, she was multiplied. So in Acts 16:5, where it is recorded, "So the churches were strengthened in the faith and they increased in numbers daily." The condition was the strengthening of the churches; the effect or result was daily increase in numbers. In these references one is conscious of a spontaneous explosion which resulted when conditions in the body were right for such an explosion or expansion. The emphasis was not on the expansion; the emphasis was upon the conditions which allowed the expansion to take place.[7]

It was not, in Acts, a matter of concentrating on evangelism or the Great Commission or church growth, that produced evangelism, soul-winning and increase of the body's numbers. Instead there is an absolutely vital principle that rises from a study of New Testament church history: When conditions in the body are right, evangelism takes place. When the body's relational network is in tact, the energy and the impetus of the Holy Spirit is there. The wind is blowing, the sails are up, and the thing God wants is happening.

This is not to say that planning and organizing will never be needed to complete the church's evangelistic task. But whatever it takes to do it will flow from a spiritually healthy, supportive, Christ-filled fellowship. That, Halverson points out, is the "Matrix of Mission."

> The church is failing in evangelism and mission today not because she does not know what she ought to do or even how to do it, not because she does not have the tools for such a worldwide propagation of the Gospel of Jesus Christ—but because there is no incentive. And there is no incentive because the conditions in the body which produce that incentive are absent. You cannot legislate evangelism and mission. No amount of organizing and planning, programming, training and exhorting will replace the spontaneous expansion of the church when the Spirit of God reigns in the hearts of believers and they are in fellowship with one another as well as with the Father and with His Son, Jesus Christ.[8]

Jesus Christ is *alive.*

And through the Holy Spirit He is alive in His people. All of them. If that isn't true, they are not His people at all.

I'm tired of trying to do His work in them and their work for them—and then being frustrated because it isn't done right. If Jesus is there (in His people), I want to see it. I want to see Him do the things He has promised to do. So, I do not intend any longer to try to do what He should be doing. Or to try to do what they should be doing. Or try to be to my church what He should be. I'll do my job, according to the gifts and grace and vision and strength His Spirit supplies and within the limitations with which I'm stuck. But I won't try any more (God helping me) to be the life and power of the church. If He is those things—let Him be those things in my church, to the people in my life.

THE SAVIOR OF THE BODY

I struggled with a problem in the church for a whole year. It was a doctrinal issue that I knew had split other churches. I was afraid. I preached to it. Taught on it. Prayed about it. Counseled regarding it. Warned, rebuked, and corrected. Worried, sweated and fretted. But the problem refused to go away. Everywhere I went in the church, I was confronted with it. Everyone was talking about it.

My concern over this stubborn problem that I was afraid would undermine the church, began to take its toll on my ministry, family life, and personal sense of well-being. But nothing I could do was enough to even make a dent in the problem. Many things I did only served to disrupt relationships and build walls between Christians.

After twelve months of increasing fear, frustration, and unrest, I finally realized that the very absence of peace I was experiencing was contrary to everything God says in His Word I have a right to expect as His child. I went into my study at home, cut myself off from the phone, sat on the floor with my Bible, and began complaining and crying to God for help. A couple of hours later I ran into Ephesians 5:23 . . .

. . . Christ is the head of the church, his body, of which he is the Savior.

I shouted for joy and release! For twelve months I had been struggling and fighting and fretting and dying because I was trying to do something I had never been called to do. I had been trying to be "Savior of the body"! I had struggled in vain to "save" the church from this problem, this inroad of error. But savior is not one of my gifts. Pastor, teacher, shepherd perhaps—but Savior and Head are jobs He reserves for Himself. And only He can do them.

I relinquished the whole situation to Him. And I gave up

the idea that the salvation and purity of the body was my responsibility. His people are ultimately His responsibility.

Two beautiful things happened. I was at peace, able to minister with confidence and greater effectiveness. And in a very short time peace came to the church, too. The tension and fear all drained out of the problem. The whole church seemed to take it in stride. In fact, we became stronger because of it.

The Holy Spirit living in every believer can be trusted. He can be counted on to work in each one whatever He wants . . . *if we will let Him do it.* It is completely possible, according to Galatians 5:7, to hinder people from responding to what the Holy Spirit is trying to do in their lives! By imposing ourselves, our will, and our standards on others, by boxing them into patterns that are comfortable to us, we can disrupt their freedom to discover, for themselves, how to be led, how to hear the voice of the Spirit, how to be sensitive to what He is doing in their lives. We *must* resolutely resist the temptation to resort to pressures of guilt or legalism to force people to respond in our predetermined ways! They must be free, or they will never know for themselves the power available through personal dependence on the Spirit.

Dependence Is Believing the Promises

One man was very uncomfortable with the concepts of church life I was sharing with a small group of people in California. His questions were tough ones and revealed considerable skepticism about the practicality of such a "hang loose" approach to church life. But after several hours of interaction he made a significant observation: "What you are talking about, basically, is an approach to church life based on *trusting the promises.*"

The teaching of Christ concerning the Holy Spirit, the historical accounts of the Spirit's work in both Jesus and the early church, the interpretations and exhortations of the writers of the New Testament letters, contain many specific and implied promises concerning what the Holy Spirit is doing and will do in the lives of Christians and in their life together. The difference between "putting up a sail" and "pulling on the oars," as I see it, is the difference between counting on the Holy Spirit to do what He has promised to do, and going about our life together as though there were no such promises.

Notes

[1]Robert C. Girard, *Brethren, Hang Loose* (Grand Rapids: Zondervan Publishing House, 1972), p. 68.
[2]Most of the New Testament epistles were written to respond to some problem in the church.
[3]Romans 8:9.
[4]Amplified Bible, Acts 2:4.
[5]1 Corinthians 3:12.
[6]Richard C. Halverson, *How I Changed My Thinking About the Church* (Grand Rapids: Zondervan Publishing House, 1972, pp. 63–67, Chapter 6, "Matrix of Mission").
[7]Ibid., pp. 64–65.
[8]Ibid. pp. 66–67.

4

"You Can Fly, But That Cocoon Has Got to Go!"

The life cycle of a silkworm, from egg to worm to moth, includes the stage at which the worm spins about itself a cocoon, composed of 400 to 800 yards of silk fiber, seals it from the inside and waits for metamorphosis. At the completion of the cycle, the adult moth will break the cocoon and fly away. The silkworm farmer does not allow most to become adults. At a key point in the cycle, he steams the cocoons to keep the moths inside from maturing. A few choice moths are allowed to mature, because they are useful for their captor's purposes. But most are not allowed to develop to adulthood, because if they do, they will burst their cocoons—breaking the fine silk cords that bind them—and go free, leaving a trail of broken cords which are useless to their exploiters. But if they are allowed to mature and escape, the reproductive moth may lay up to 350 eggs.

Could it be that most Christians are kept from maturing because their ecclesiastical "captors" cannot fulfill selfish purposes in free people, who, in moving from spiritual adolescence to productive spiritual adulthood, might leave behind in shambles, the secure-though-immature traditions that allow them to be more easily controlled by their exploiters?

It is a difficult thing to do, but preserving the freedom of the individual believer to make even wrong choices is key to developing people who know how to be personally responsive to the Holy Spirit.

Their freedom will make their brothers and sisters uncomfortable at times, but if they are ever to hear for themselves the voice of the Lord and respond personally to Him, they must be free.

In his letter to the Galatian church, Paul deals almost exclusively with the need for preserving freedom in the church, and the nature of that freedom.

In 3:2–5, he pinpoints the issue:

> I would like to learn just one thing from you: Did you receive the Spirit by observing the law, or by believing what you heard? Are you so foolish? After beginning with the Spirit, are you now trying to attain your goal by human effort? Have you suffered so much for nothing—if it really was for nothing? Does God give you his Spirit and work miracles among you because you observe the law, or because you believe what you heard?

The crucial question for the church is:

How does a Christian reach "perfection"? (v. 3) or, for the corporate perspective, How do the "works of God" get done in the church? (v. 5).

In Galatians 3 and 4, Paul lays a solid biblical foundation for teaching the things he teaches in chapters 5 and 6. His logical theological arguments rest solidly on God's past statements and actions, as recorded in Old Testament Scripture. (Since God never changes, the only way to be certain a new thing or new revelation is the work of God is to see how it squares with what God has done and said in the past. The Bible is the record of God's past actions and words.)

Paul's direct, practical response to the above questions begins chapter 5:

> It is for freedom that Christ has set us free. Stand firm, then, and do not let yourselves be burdened again by a yoke of slavery.

This response sounds strange and impractical to the modern pragmatic pastoral mind, accustomed to formulae and carefully delineated lists of "how-to's." It sounds contradictory to everything I was taught as I grew up in the church. And yet, the answer to the issue raised in Galatians 3:2–5 is freedom.

Behind personal prison bars built by the experience of sin and saturation with the thinking of the world, languishes the human self waiting for freedom, groaning to emerge and grow and express the beauty of the true humanness the Creator made for His own glory, true humanness He is newly creating in us through the Holy Spirit. The chief goal of the Spirit within is to emancipate that new Christ-related self and set it "flying."

The freedom for which Christ has set us free is: (1) freedom to become the strange and inimitable gift of the Holy Spirit to the church that the Spirit's will calls for us to be (1 Cor. 12:4–11); (2) freedom to discover what we really want to do, so that we can start having the time of our lives doing what God really wants us to do (Phil. 2:13); (3) freedom to get in touch with our renewed selves in Christ, so that by freely being ourselves, we can be what God wants us to be (Gal. 2:20); (4) freedom to help each other to get free, by calling forth the unique gifts of each other; by setting each other free to be the distinctive, Spirit-touched selves each of us is (Rom. 12:3–8).[1]

There is in Scripture, clearly stated, the promise of freedom. Jesus Himself proclaims our emancipation. In Luke 4:18 He announces that His ministry in the lives of people is going to set the captives and the oppressed free. In John 8:31–32 and 36 Jesus promises freedom that is definitely no mere illusion of freedom: the people who go on living in His word shall be "free indeed." In 2 Corinthians 3:17 Paul reveals that the gift of the Holy Spirit brings liberty with it. In Galatians 5:13 he further states that the believer's calling or commission is to be free.

"You Can Fly, But That Cocoon Has Got to Go!"

It is such good news that we can scarcely believe it—we keep falling away from it—because our world-shaped minds keep telling us it cannot be true. God, in His Word, carefully tells us what He wants from us. But nothing His Word calls for can come from our lives in the way that is pleasing to Him unless it is *real.* Only if what comes out of us is the free expression of liberated spirits, can it be a genuine expression of true love for God. Genuine holiness cannot be other than the free expression of free people doing what pleases God because they want to. If it is less than free—if coercion, pressure, or fear are the source of it—then it is not holiness, it is conformity—a mere work of the flesh.

God's relationship with His children is set deeply into a context of forgiveness, unconditional divine love, justification by faith alone, and superabounding grace that overmatches the totality of human sin.

Some people think that gives them a license to sin. But they reveal that they do not understand grace at all. If they really understood how much God loves them, and truly were trusting His favor toward them, sinning as a way of life would be impossible (as 1 John 3 says it is). If I know for sure I am loved, I don't have to keep testing it by rebellion. I am free to respond in kind—to love as I am loved. Sin becomes something God and I are working on together, to overcome it. And forgiveness, which is always there, is not the indulgence of a wishy-washy divinity, but a very important part of the process of my strong deliverance from sin.

Sin and its seductive partner, the mentality of the world, are a prison, a trap, a snare, a chain! They inevitably lock us into destructive life patterns, keeping us from experiencing the freedom that is rightfully ours because of Jesus Christ.

The world's approach to solving the problem of sin and its patterns of destruction is to become committed to a moral or philosophical system—a system of law often demanding superior self-effort, self-dependent action to produce better living (human goodness). True, God Himself established a system of law in the Old Testament, but He never expected law to overcome sin. He gave it to reveal sin (Gal. 3:21–22).

The problem with law, as a system of trying to please God and do God's work and solve the problem of sin, is that law itself is also a prison. It is a system of inhibiting bars and chains. A system of fear and guilt and burden, leading to inevitable failure. A slavery of conformity which robs us of spontaneity and cannot live with uniqueness. And so, it keeps the strange and wonderful new person, which the spirit is creating, from emerging in its rare beauty, zestfulness, and power.

Both sin and law are forms of slavery.

But now Christ has come and has told us that He has set us free from both!

Freedom and slavery are incompatible.

> Mark my words! I, Paul, tell you that if you let yourselves be circumcised, Christ will be of no value to you at all. Again I declare to every man who lets himself be circumcised that he is obligated to obey the whole law. You who are trying to be justified by law have been alienated from Christ; you have fallen away from grace. But by faith we eagerly await through the Spirit the righteousness for which we hope. For in Christ Jesus neither circumcision nor uncircumcision has any value. The only thing that counts is faith expressing itself through love (Gal. 5:2-6).

If I commit myself to live under obligation to the law (any set of impersonal, outer rules or standards or any external system of religion or ethics), seeking to be justified by my ability to conform to an external standard, thinking God can be pleased with that kind of holiness, or that such a commitment (represented here by the physical symbol circumcision) will produce what God wants in me or in the church, I show myself to be in real spiritual trouble. My whole relationship to God through Christ is in jeopardy. I have turned away from freedom of spirit back to the slavery of legal obligation and humanly-produced goodness. I have "fallen away from grace." Grace offers justification exclusively on the basis of faith in Jesus Christ, apart from any work of my own. I "have been alienated from Christ."

If a believer can choose the slavery of laws after having tasted the freedom of grace, he is stumbling in the beginning shadows of an imprisoning blindness that leads to spiritual disaster.

Paul has confidence that the Galatian believers are not going to make such a foolish choice (v. 10). But if they did (if they *could*) Jesus would be of no value to them. Salvation and freedom are only in Christ. Apart from Christ there is only slavery.

True righteousness is produced, and God's work gets done in free people, while still leaving them free. Here's how:

By faith
we eagerly await through the Spirit
the righteousness for which we hope.
For in Christ Jesus . . .
The only thing that counts
is
faith
expressing itself ("working"[2])
through love. (5:5–6)

When the work is the work of God, when accomplishment is God getting what He wants done in the church, and when in the doing, freedom of spirit is preserved, there will be two essential elements in what is happening . . .

faith
and
love.

When these motivations are present, the worker is free and the work is God's, because the worker, even though he labors very hard, is not depending on himself, but on God, and he is not doing what he is doing from compulsion, guilt, or for selfish advantage, but because he loves.

71

SPIRITUAL LIBERTY IS A MATTER OF CHOICE

Three phrases in 5:7–10 communicate the truth that freedom in Christ is a matter of choice:

Verse 7—"Who . . . kept you from *obeying* the truth?"

Verse 8—"That kind of *persuasion* does not come from the one who calls you."

Verse 10—"I am confident . . . that *you will take* no other view."

While liberty is offered freely to all, each must choose to take it for himself. Christ lived, died, and lives to set us free. But the experience of freedom is not "automatic" for Christians.

The Galatian believers were confronted with a choice. Someone was trying to persuade them to reject the law of freedom ("faith expressing itself through love") in favor of bondage to the law of humanly-produced goodness. Paul expects freedom to be the winner, but the entire letter is evidence that, as Christians, we have a free choice as to whether or not we will live in the liberty of free people in Jesus. Choice, in fact, is intrinsic to freedom.

One of the major problems connected with getting free ourselves, setting other people free, and trying to free the church to express the emancipated new humanity the Holy Spirit is creating, is that God does not force people to be free. And we cannot force people to be free. I cannot even force myself to be free. Forced freedom is not freedom at all. You have to take freedom when it is offered by Christ. You will have to receive it. *You will have as much freedom as you take.*

Now, as in the days of the early Galatian church, the offer of freedom of Spirit is extended to every believer, but most Christians and most of the church continue deliberately to choose the safe, visible bondage of institutionalized systems, societal acceptability, and traditional structure. Freedom looks like a dangerous adventure into uncharted territory.

"You Can Fly, But That Cocoon Has Got to Go!"

There is great security within the cozy cocoon of the standing order. No matter that within those padded prescripts we never experience flight!

As born-again persons we can refuse to come out of hiding (even if we are surrounded by a supportive, affirming network of people who are genuinely ready for us to emerge). We can refuse to fly, to work, to minister, to express our true selves, to give ourselves value. We are able to do many things the body, the family, needs us to be doing—things we do not yet believe we can do, or that we do not want to do.

Often, people say no to freedom because they believe some sin, some weakness, some unresolved problem makes them unworthy to be free. So they needlessly, even selfishly, languish in a prison of broken bars. Often they say no to spiritual liberty to be someone special, to express their specialness, because they do not want to accept the responsibility that goes with true freedom. It's easier to stay in jail than to admit:

this I can be,
this I can do,
and that gives me *this* specific responsibility
with *these* specific people in my life.

In self-indulgent fearfulness many of us would rather say no to the freedom to express our uniqueness, our gift, than to fly with resonsibility.

Freedom comes in taking freedom.

THE RISK OF LIBERTY

You, my brothers, were called to be free. But do not use your freedom to indulge your sinful nature; rather, serve one another in love. The entire law is summed up in a single command: "Love your neighbor as yourself." If you keep on biting and devouring each other, watch out or you will be destroyed by each other.

So I say, live by the Spirit, and you will not gratify the desires of your sinful nature. For the sinful nature desires what is contrary to the Spirit, and the Spirit what is contrary to the sinful nature. They are in conflict with each other, so that you do not do what you want. But if you are led by the Spirit, you are not under law.

The acts of the sinful nature are obvious: sexual immorality, impurity and debauchery; idolatry and witchcraft; hatred, discord, jealousy, fits of rage, selfish ambition, dissensions, factions and envy; drunkenness, orgies, and the like. I warn you, as I did before that those who live like this will not inherit the kingdom of God (Gal. 5:13–21).

The risk of liberty is that some people misuse it.

Freedom to sin is not the freedom for which Christ sets us free. That would be a cruel contradiction, because when I sin, I am still surrendering myself to bondage, to slavery. It is the nature of fallen man to tend to use the teachings of freedom as a cloak for the works of the flesh. But sinning is never freedom. It is the old slavery returning to try to clamp us back into its broken chains. Self-indulgence, willful rebellion against or neglect of the clear teachings of Scripture, constitute deliberate choices to be a slave to destructive patterns of behaving and thinking that actually "con" us out of freedom and "consume" the people our lives touch.

Jesus:

I tell you the truth, everyone who sins is a *slave* to sin (John 8:34).

That is the truth.

If we are honest we have to admit that this list (Gal. 5:19–21) hits every one of us at some point. (It may help to see your sin on this list, if you will think of the mildest form of each item, rather than the worst or most open form.) Set as it is in the context of discussion of spiritual liberty, this is clearly a list of examples of using freedom "to indulge your sinful nature." (v. 13). These are the misuses of freedom.

Praise God, I am forgiven of these sins. Jesus died for *all* these ugly things. But forgiveness is just the doorway to freedom. Christ promised that He would set me "free indeed" from sin (John 8:36). By faith I know He has. And I am expecting that, as His process in me continues, I will more and more, even in experience, be freed from sin—completion coming at the first face-to-face sight of Him. The Spirit's process in me is leading me out from behind the broken prison bars into a fuller experience of freedom *from* sin.

Freedom is to be being changed from these patterns of destruction—not to remain hopelessly locked into them for life!

But . . . believers often misuse freedom in exactly the kinds of destructive ways spelled out in this ugly list.

The results are, they "destroy" each other (v. 15). And they miss "the kingdom" (v. 21). The New Society, the loving Spirit-led Jesus community, continues to elude the grasp of those who persist in these works that inevitably destroy fellowship, roadblock love, disrupt harmony, undermine mutual- and self-esteem, shatter confidence, and pollute purity—and destroy all the other things without which the kingdom life style cannot be experienced. The kingdom is never experienced in its full splendor and joy by those who go at it in the flesh's way. The way of the sinful nature self-destructs.

The question with which the church has always wrestled when confronted with the biblical teachings on spiritual liberty is this:

With such a potential for misuse, is it really wise to teach Christians that they are free?

Is it safe to tell people that they are truly and totally and forever forgiven, justified by faith completely apart from works?

Is that safe? Wise? Prudent?

Safe? No.

Risky? Definitely.

Looking at human beings abusing their liberties, reading this list of "acts of the sinful nature," and recognizing how much of this is the way people go . . . there is a persistent proneness to protest: "It won't work!"

Setting people free is not a hedge against anxiety, for spiritual leaders. Because people who are truly free and know it, do what they want to do. And there is always the danger that they will do the wrong thing. The destructive thing. The sinful thing. But freedom is so absolutely essential to true holiness and godlikeness that the risk must be taken.

In effect, the approach the church has taken is to try to keep it a secret that people are free. For safety's sake, we may tell them they are free, but then we spell out for them 613 rules for holy living. Anxiety born of holy motives to protect the flock of God tempts us to soft-pedal the teaching of freedom and to focus on something safer.

And what we reveal is . . . we have forgotten God! We have chosen to act like the Holy Spirit is dead.

AGAINST MISUSE OF FREEDOM

When Paul looked at the church he saw God in it, very much alive and active. When he spoke of freedom as the atmosphere for our life together he was counting on the fact that the Spirit lives in the followers of Jesus. And, as a result, he has woven into his teaching on freedom several significant assurances. At work in the body of Christ are spiritual forces that are in operation to accomplish Christ's plan to unfetter His followers. Seeing these forces should convince us to pursue forthrightly, without unnecessary anxiety, our calling to set each other free to be who we really are and are intended to be in the Lord Jesus.

Liberty is the atmosphere, the environment, in which the church and people can emerge as the special gifts of the Spirit they are.

Freedom Principle 1: *The principle of love.*

The only thing that counts is faith expressing itself in love (5:6).

. . . serve one another in love (5:13).

The entire law is summed up in a single command: "Love your neighbor as yourself" (5:14).

But the fruit of the Spirit is love . . . (5:22).

Were self-giving love to characterize relationships among believers and provide the motivation for their choices and behavior with each other, freedom's risk would be nonexistant. Misuse of liberty would be out of the question. Rules or "strings" of any kind would be unnecessary. The response to misuse of freedom is not to establish additional rules to protect against sin, but to nurture the development of loving relationships.

Freedom Principle 2: *The principle of the Holy Spirit.*

The Holy Spirit is doing two vital things in the church and in its members: (1) Verses 16–18, He is striving, working, fighting the battle within us, to bring our desires and choices into harmony with the desires and will of God; and (2) Verses 22–23, He is the source of fresh, new, godlike spiritual qualities being produced in us . . .

But the fruit of the Spirit is love, joy, peace, patience, kindness, goodness, faithfulness, gentleness and self-control.

One Peter 1:23 hints that at the moment of faith in Christ and receptivity to His Spirit, God's imperishable sperm impregnates the receiving heart. God's new life begins to grow inside the human personality, incarnated in a resurrected human spirit. Evidence of that deep inner miracle of newly created selfhood is the emergence of new desires, pushing their way like wild roses growing on a rubbish heap, making themselves known first in conflict between the old patterns and the new desires (like the conflict described in Rom. 7). New desires grow in the power of the Holy Spirit until, given the consent of the human will, they control more and more of life.

And the fruit of the Spirit sprouts on the living branch and grows into a sweet spiritual harvest. It is a rich harvest of fruit that grows from God's sperm of life planted deep inside the person.

The direction of growth and production of the fruit is from the inside out. The sweet harvest of holiness God wants grows in the loose soil of spiritual liberty—the free expression of free people doing what pleases God because they want to.

Christ can dare to set Christians free because He has placed His own Spirit within them. The believer may do whatever his new Spirit-quickened desires wish to do, because through them he is being led by the Spirit. The power of personal choice is still there, and the desires of the sinful nature still fight back. But the Holy Spirit does not allow the one whom He indwells to go on "in the flesh" without a fierce inner battle involving conscience and an ever-keener awareness of sin.

The believer can be set free because there is now something (Someone) inside him that is stirring in him a hunger for godlikeness. There is a new set of options open to him in every situation: the choice to bow as a slave to the cravings of the flesh, or to fly on butterfly wings of Spirit-freedom and to taste luscious Spirit-fruit.

Freedom Principle 3: *The principle of the cross.*

The "sinful nature with its passions and desires" has been crucified. *Put to death!* (5:24). The world, with its proud systems of humanly produced goodness (law) has been crucified, as far as we are concerned, with Jesus on the cross.

When He died, Jesus disarmed the flesh of all its fire power by forgiving its sins. At the same time, He lifted the frustrating burden of trying to please God by conforming to external systems. His execution paid all the penalties such systems could lay on us, thus robbing them of their right to condemn us. And besides this, He fulfilled the highest of their demands with His love.

Our slavery came to an end there. The power of the sinful nature to control us is voided by the cross. The claims of Satan (mastermind of all the world's systems) are no longer legitimate.

Our response is to deliberately disavow sin's reign in our lives and the lives of our brothers (Rom. 6:11). Instead of testifying to the inevitability of sin in ourselves and our fellow believers, we are now free to trust in the inevitability of liberty from sin and to confess confidence in the power of the crucified Christ to set us and our brothers free.

Freedom Principle 4: *The principle of mutual responsibility.*

> Brothers, if someone is caught in a sin, you who are spiritual should restore him gently . . . Carry each other's burdens and in this way you will fulfill the law of Christ (Gal. 6:1–2).

The life style of the body itself is a guardrail against the misuse of freedom. We can live together in freedom if each of us will simply take responsibility for the other. Our freedom allows us to choose to carry each other.

Restoration of the brother who has misused his freedom (who sins) is not his responsibility alone, but ours together. Restoration involves forgiving the brother his sin (Mark 11:25). It may involve confronting him about his sin. Matthew 18:15–17 outlines the steps which we are to take to help the sinning brother to face it and to be renewed. In the final step the whole church is brought into the restoration process. Restoration also involves regularly meeting together for the purpose of stimulating each other to be loving and to do good (Heb. 10:24–25; 2 Tim. 4:2). Finally, restoration involves reconciling ourselves with our brother wherever strained relationships are in the picture (Matt. 5:23–26).

All of this presupposes a life lived in community, loving relationships, and a functioning body, where the members are caring for each other. It assumes that the church is a loving family and is acting like a family.

Freedom functions best in an atmosphere of loving commitment of a group of people to carry responsibility for each other.

Freedom Principle 5: *The principle of accepting responsibility for oneself.*

But watch yourself, or you also may be tempted . . . If anyone thinks he is something when he is nothing, he deceives himself. Each one should test his own actions. Then he can take pride in himself, without comparing himself to somebody else, for each one should carry his own load (6:1b, 3–5).

I am responsible . . .
   for the spiritual choices I make,
   for honestly evaluating my own spiritual life,
   for my own actions and reactions,
   for the burden of my own faults, weaknesses, and sins.
Several months ago I came to the startling realization, referred to earlier, that I had been trying to evade responsibility for my own disobedience by blaming the people close to me, I wanted them to change before I would respond to what God was saying to me! I saw that I alone was responsible before God. And that my own choices were hindering my spiritual progress and that of the church. I had been trying to force my load onto others.

We can live together in freedom if each of us can see ourselves as personally responsible for our own personal responses to the inner strivings of the Spirit.

Freedom Principle 6: *The principle of interaction.*

Anyone who receives instruction in the word must share all good things with his instructor (6:6).

The Greek word translated "share" is the word *koinonia.* In the Galatians' context it is strong affirmation of the power of the all-believer priesthood to assure the soundness and life of the church.

Remember the Galatian situation. A teacher is trying to influence the church to forsake its liberty in Christ for a return to producing "holiness" by human effort inspired by the law and its rituals. (It's the kind of thing that can happen when you let anyone who wants to, share and teach in the church. That was the style of the early churches. It could as easily have been someone on the other side of the issue—some libertine, misusing his freedom and teaching others to do the same. Potentially, the whole church might be led astray!) Paul is simply suggesting, in verse 6, that those who listen to whoever is teaching must not just sit there and swallow everything every "teacher" wants to lay on them. All are, in the broadest sense, "teachers."

All believers are priests. Priests don't just listen. Priests "share the good things" the Lord has given, even with their teachers. Priests interact! Share! Communicate! Speak up!

The apostle believes firmly in the power of the Holy Spirit to correct and instruct the church through the sharing, the interaction, of any group of Christians who will talk to each other. Freedom can be guarded from destructive misuse if those who are taught will share their good things (insights, truths, questions, confrontations, debate) with those who teach them.

Freedom Principle 7: *The principle of reaping and sowing.*

> Do not be deceived: God cannot be mocked. A man reaps what he sows. The one who sows to please his sinful nature, from that nature will reap destruction; the one who sows to please the Spirit, from the Spirit will reap eternal life. Let us not become weary in doing good, for at the proper time we will reap a harvest if we do not give up. Therefore, as we have opportunity, let us do good to all people, especially to those who belong to the family of believers (6:7–10).

The universal law of cause and effect applies to every level of the created universe—spiritual as well as physical. It is true that, in keeping with higher laws—redemption, propitiation, and forgiveness—God has turned back the inevitable eternal effects caused by our sins: separation from God, death, an everlasting holocaust of sorrows. But God has not set aside the law of sowing and reaping for the Christian. When we engage in destructive behavior, God, for our sake and the church's, normally allows us to reap what we sow, in order to help us break the pattern of destruction and bondage. It has nothing to do with forgiveness. From His side, God has forgiven every sin. But before redemption, in creation, the law of cause and effect, sowing and reaping, was woven into the tapestry of the universe. God sometimes intervenes and changes the process in behalf of believers (when some higher purpose of His is involved), but normally, the process moves from sowing to reaping.

Free believers have many choices they are free to make. We can choose, in any situation, to go with the flesh and its desires. Or, we can choose to go with the Spirit and His desires. Either way there will be a harvest: destruction (spiritual and physical sickness, poverty, slavery, etc.) or life (all the fruit of the Spirit, spiritual liberty).

The corrective power to the misuse of freedom is obvious. In addition to the body's restoration efforts, and all the other forces operating to assure against freedom's exploitation among the saints, there is this universal law (of sowing and reaping) that God uses so effectively to reshape believers into the image of His Son.[3] This is further proof that God Himself can be trusted to make His new "operation emancipation" work.

The summarizing statement of Paul's monograph on liberty that puts it well in perspective, it seems to me, is Galatians 6:15. We are reminded again that the life in Christ is neither a matter of living by laws (i.e. "circumcision") nor living without laws (i.e. "uncircumcision"). It is infinitely above and beyond anything so earthy. There is God! There is the transformation going on from within—the work of the Creator renewing for Himself a new people. Creating a new race with changed values, changed commitments, changed ideals, changed desires, changed self-images. Changed to be responsive to God.

> Neither circumcision nor uncircumcision means anything; what counts is a new creation.

The creative Holy Spirit lives in every believer. With the

kind of loving support and stimulation a close-knit spiritual family can provide, and without the diverting confusion of inhibiting restrictions and expectations arbitrarily imposed from the outside, the living Spirit within can be trusted to bring forth the priceless personal strangeness, uniqueness, beauty, and special impact of each member of Christ. The liberated uniqueness of each person is the primary gift of the Spirit to the church, to complete its expression of the multifaceted splendor of Jesus Christ.

Notes

[1]Gordon Cosby, *Handbook for Mission Groups* (Waco: Word Books, 1975), pp. 70–85, chapter 2, "The Calling Forth of the Gifts."
[2]NASB.
[3]Romans 8:28–29.

5

New Containers
for New Ingredients

Awareness
Is a troublesome thing.
It is not an
Off-again, on-again
Take-it-or-leave-it state of affairs.

A new awareness of Life
Is like a whole new blend of ingredients,
Rising up,
Sparkling,
Pushing its way to greater power.
And even if we ever so politely
And gently
Concede
To try to house it in old containers,
It will someday
Explode. [1]

Jesus talked about the problem of old containers and new ingredients in Mark 2:22 . . .

No one pours new wine into old wineskins. If he does, the wine will burst the skins, and both the wine and the wineskins will be ruined. No, he pours new wine into new wineskins.

Wineskins are structure. They represent organization,

commitments, settings, habits, *modus operandi,* thinking patterns, mindsets. Structure is important in the church. The why and how of our meetings, the principles we follow, our priorities, habits, and forms, the "traditions" that develop, the way we organize ourselves, are important.

Because . . . according to what Jesus says, our wineskins can either *lose* the "new wine" or *keep* it!

What Is the New Wine?

Key in on the context. Mark 2.

In the first 12 verses Jesus shakes His hearers with a radical "new" concept when He, a man, says to another man: "Your sins are forgiven."

"Only God can forgive!" they groan, running it through their preconceptions. Devout men suffer future shock because their concretized thinking can't handle the new wine.

He does it again in verse 14. He calls a known sinner, a social outcast (Levi the Publican) to become one of His closest followers! And then Jesus goes to the man's house and eats and drinks with the town's notorious group of turncoats, church dropouts and other assorted sinners. In fact, according to the narrative (v. 15) these "characters," "misfits," and "lost souls" are the ones who are following him. He is building his church out of such "trash"!

Future shock sets in again. The religious leaders cannot handle it. This bunch of rabble hasn't been to church since two years ago last Hannukah!

"These are the ones I came to heal," He insists.

They shake their heads. It does not fit their preconceptions. The new wine slips away again.

Then (vv. 18–20) someone notices that Jesus and His friends do not observe the special fast days. While the Pharisees and John's disciples are going without food, quite somber and serious, the motley crowd with Jesus makes every day a celebration. They eat and drink and laugh together like life was a forever birthday party.

There it goes again. Future shock.

"Why?" they ask. "Why don't Your followers cooperate with the fasts called by the constituted religious authorities?"

Jesus' response: "You can't fast when you're at the Lord's wedding party. When the Bridegroom is with you, you have to celebrate!"

The Pharisees' old wineskins are completely unprepared to handle the new wine.

Jesus explains to them why they are struggling so much with Him and His words and His friends' actions. Verse 21. Here's an old shirt shrunk by many washings. Worn thin and weak. A new patch is being sewn on. The patch has never been shrunk. It is still strong. When it gets rained on or washed, the new patch will shrink and, being much stronger than the old cloth, the new will tear the old apart!

There comes a time to stop patching up the old garment and start all over with something completely new!

Before the end of the chapter we find Jesus doing it again. While He and His disciples are strolling along together on a Saturday afternoon, He lets His disciples pluck a few heads of wheat to nibble as they walk. It's the Sabbath day! Now, every good Jew knows the Sabbath day is holy and that no work is to be done. So the Pharisees set up a howl.

"That's unlawful. Working on the Sabbath! Why are You letting them do it?"

Problem: the Pharisees are operating under a definition of Sabbath prohibition they received from a previous generation of learned religious *men*. If the new wine is anything it is a new life lived under the authority of the Lord, not men. And the Lord never intended the Sabbath to become the stilted burden religious men had made it.

So Jesus sets the record straight. And He concludes with the ringing declaration of His authority, "The Son of Man is Lord even of the Sabbath."

With one gush of new wine He explodes their traditions. New wine—offered, but getting away because the wineskin of their mindset and of their prior commitments was too brittle to contain it.

Some rather astounding, sweeping, and now nearly forgotten recent revivals have illustrated the truth Jesus stated twenty centuries ago, that you cannot put new wine into old wineskins or it will spill and be lost.

A church I visited in the Northwest was still talking about a "revival fire" that had been kindled there during the visit of a team of spiritually ignited laymen from Saskatoon, Canada (site of the beginning of the "Canadian Revival" of 1972). Nearly the whole congregation had been touched and, for a time, renewed. There were lasting effects to be seen in the new converts who'd been won and in elder Christians who had made new commitments to Christ. But by the time I got there (just a few months after the climax of the revival) most of the reports I was hearing were past tense.

At the height of revival, groups of Christians met every night of the week to sing, share, pray, worship, confess personal needs, and to restore broken relationships with each other and with God. They were a spiritual family, and spontaneous expressions of love and caring overflowed. Witnessing was a way of life—something almost "natural." It was a laymen's movement; pastors flowed with it.

But church structures, polity, and regular church meetings changed only imperceptibly, if at all. Time pressures, family responsibilities, and even church duties gradually curtailed the "extra" meetings where the revival had thrived. Revived people who had, for a fleeting while, been deeply involved in vital spiritual ministry and a dynamic body-life experience, found themselves sitting and listening again. They were going through the same, tired religious motions, and were confronted with the same manipulations and "Christian law pressures" that are so much a part of "normal" modern church life. No outlet. No room in the structure for the shared life. The professionals were busier than ever planning it all, saying it all, doing it all *for* the congregation.

And the new wine dribbled out the cracks in the old wineskin and was gradually lost under the dreary shuffle and shallow chatter of a departing Sunday morning congregation acting more and more like they did before revival came.

What is the new wine? The new wine is a new life style with Jesus Himself as the living, throbbing center. The new wine is a new life lived totally in response to Jesus Himself. The labels on the bottles all read "Jesus is Lord! He is King!"

THE THEOLOGY OF THE WINESKINS

I stated earlier, wineskins represent structure, organization, *modus operandi,* patterns, settings, times, and places. A group is a wineskin. A meeting is a wineskin. A method is a wineskin. A pattern of thinking or a mindset is a wineskin.

The church, made up of structured and structure-oriented human beings, will have structure. And structure is important, because the structures we put together can either lose the wine or keep it.

The wineskins that can contain and keep the new wine must have one special quality about them: flexibility.

In first-century Israel (and even today in parts of the middle east) wine was kept in skins. When these skins were new, they had a certain amount of elasticity. As they grew old they became hard and unyielding. New wine is still in the process of fermenting. As it ferments it gives off gasses These gasses cause pressure to build up in the bottles (wineskins). If the skin is new it will give, yield to the pressure. Stretch. If the skin is old and hard and dry, the action and changes taking place in the new wine will cause the whole thing to explode! The skin will be ruined. The wine will be lost.

New wine—the new life in the Spirit, the personal and corporate life lived in response to Jesus Himself—is going to produce changes, pressure, fermentation.

The church as a body needs to be free to move, unencumbered by the inescapable chains of many prior commitments which lock the church into patterns that are spiritually unproductive, which require no word from the Lord for their function and which perpetuate themselves purely on the strength of human habits and comfort. The church must be free from its marriages to things that once were useful but now stand in the way of spiritual growth by giving us familiar settings in which to hide. If the Spirit is to shape the church the way He wants to—if the Spirit is to give us power and enable us to become what God wants the church to be—then we must not be settlers protecting ourselves in comfortable human patterns. We must be sojourners, pioneers committed to folding up our tents and moving when the God of Abraham says Go!

A church controlled and empowered by the Spirit requires a free people and a free church. Free to move at the impulse of the Fermenter.

READY FOR THE ROAD

Hebrews 11:8 says Abraham went out not knowing where he was going. Another great verse in that same chapter tells about Jacob: "By faith Jacob, when he was dying, blessed each of Joseph's sons, and worshiped as he leaned on the top of his staff." William Barclay comments: "With the very breath of death upon him the old traveller still had his pilgrim staff in his hand! To the end of the day, with the evening now upon him, he was still ready for the road."[2]

We are called to see ourselves as alien to all the nailed-down structures of earth. Sojourners. Pilgrims. Adventurers. Explorers. Ready for the road. For change. For moving. For growth. Free enough, flexible enough to contain the dynamics of life. Structures that can contain new life must serve the new wine, enhance it, develop with it, or the new life will tear down (or blow up!) the old structures and the new wine will be lost!

As a congregation, we have made an honest attempt to let

the biblical principles being developed in this book guide our life together. And people have moved toward freedom. O.H. (Our Heritage Church) people do not fit into boxes. They do what they want to. They do not necessarily respond according to my expectations. They are alive to God. Jesus Christ is real to them. The Holy Spirit is clearly at work in their lives. They are terribly imperfect, and it shows. But there is no question that they belong to Him (and He is responsible for them.)

He is doing a new thing with them. Unlike anything I ever imagined when we began this "renewal pilgrimage." I was expecting God to produce something that more nearly approximated the culturally preconceived ideas to which I clung, as to the shape of the church's ministry and life. Instead, what is emerging is something strange and unfamiliar.

The life of the church as it has evolved does not center primarily around meetings at the church building, although the Sunday meeting is still an important event. The church family embraces a number roughly two-and-one-half times the regular Sunday attendance, most of whom have a living relationship with Jesus Christ and are involved in a ministry of life to each other and witness in their world. Their point of contact with and identification with the church may involve one or a combination of these three things: (1) the Sunday meeting, (2) a "little church" (small group) in a home and /or (3) regular personal interaction and relationship with the other members of the church. Primary identification for some is with one of the "pockets of community" that are developing in our midst. At whatever level their involvement focusses, all would identify themselves as part of the "O.H. family."

It is possible to have visited a worship service and to not yet have been "to church." Because the church, as it is developing, cannot be contained in a wineskin so arbitrary and limited as a Sunday "service."

There is new wine flowing. And new wineskins, new flexible and reshapable structures, must be found to contain it, or it will inevitably be lost.

How flexible are our wineskins? Or how hardened and rigid? How free to move in response to the movement of the Lord?

What if you went to church some Sunday and the whole congregation moved together to the park for worship? What if some weekend, just to be more of a family, the "usual pattern" of the meeting were completely set aside and the whole time were spent playing together? What if, for a while, the congregation were divided into groups which, instead of gathering at the church building, met in designated homes with designated leaders, coming back together after a month to share what had been learned and to celebrate new growth? What if, in response to the teachings of the Lord, your congregation moved out of its expensive buildings and rented another church building or a restaurant for its meetings and gave the money to the poor? What if the entire congregation moved out of town for a weekend to some sylvan setting? What if, in the interest of the development of the priesthood of believers the pastor took a secular job so that all the church's ministers would be "laymen"? What if, in order to function more like a caring family, the church asked its own needy to turn down their welfare checks and food stamps because, in the name of Jesus' love and the kingdom community we intended to see to their care ourselves?

What if . . . ?

Surrounded as we are by the rigidity of our ecclesiastical traditions, I believe that there is the serious need for leaders to inject some new experiences into the life of the church at its most traditional points—new experiences aimed at breaking up old comfortable patterns, softening the barriers to change, and introducing the new idea that change is part of being the church. (Like oiling leather to keep it from cracking—to keep it flexible.) I think it may be right for us to deliberately do something now and then for the specific purpose of keeping church structures from hardening into traditions—traditions that so often become comfortable idols we confuse with the reality of God!

Having said this, I am aware that the kind of flexibility the church needs must come at a far deeper level than that of structure alone. The deepest, most significant call for new wineskins, for responsiveness to new life, for pliancy in the hands of the Spirit, comes in concentration on the most basic questions of our life together:

Are we loving one another?

Are we serving one another?

Are we laying down our lives for one another?

Are we laying down our lives for the world?

The new wineskins we need will not emerge primarily through concentration on structure itself, change, renewal, or community. They are more likely to develop from a healthy, intense focus on God and on each other.

Who can say what fresh, dynamic shape the church might take if the Spirit were not bound to work within the narrow strictures of our culturally predetermined ideas, values, and patterns, dictated by the world's pressure to which we so thoughtlessly continue to bend. If we were free enough to allow Him freedom to shape us to His will, what strange, wonderful, unpredictable configurations might emerge?

Notes

[1] *The Gift,* page 52 Gordon and Gladis DePree, Zondervan.
[2] *The Gospel of Mark,* page 56 William Barclay, Westminster Press.

6
Future Shock: Renewal-Style

The greater . . . danger is to mistake culture for Scripture, to be blind to those things in church and society which displease God and should therefore displease us, to dig our heels and our toes deep into the status quo, and firmly to resist that most uncomfortable of all experiences: Change.

—John R. Stott[1]

We love to dream of being a church like the one in Jerusalem, A.D. 33 . . . when the church was an effervescent volcano of transparent sharing, loving fellowship, daily celebration, exuberant giving, miracles, intimacy, self-sacrifice, compassionate care, oneness, gladness, childlike simplicity, praising God, evangelism, and explosive growth (Acts 2:42–47).

Is that what one may expect of a twentieth-century church that has been moving toward renewal for several years?

Perhaps.

Is that a description of Our Heritage Church in Scottsdale, Arizona, after nearly a decade of struggle with the challenge of New Testament principles?

Well . . .?

Let me make one thing clear. Ours is definitely a church in process.

We have had hundreds of visitors the past few years. We

have welcomed them. They are still welcome. But there have been times when going through certain phases of the process, the thought has crossed our minds that it would probably be better for us to have hung a sign on the door that read . . .

NO VISITORS.

The public is not usually invited into the labratory where important experiments are being conducted. Nothing is finished that can be displayed. The sign on the door keeps everyone out but those involved in the experiments. When the polio vaccine was perfected . . . *then* Dr. Jonas Salk opened the door and showed the world a vial of perfected syrum.

But we have left the door open—even though it has meant that sometimes uninitiated witnesses have been there to see us get the needle in some unseemly part.

The church is *in process* . . . being made well.

One thing the Book of Acts does not do is to leave us a complete file of Sunday morning bulletins and the minutes of every meeting. But even the few details that are given reveal that though the Holy Spirit was present at their meetings and they knew it, *most* meetings of the early church were not foot-stompin', arm-raisin', highly entertaining affairs that sent you away feeling "worshipful," warm, and comforted.

Sometimes (usually) they were downright disturbing.

Take the ten meetings held between Acts 1:13 and 1:26. Nothing happened in that whole series that was more exciting than a church election.

And how about the meeting at the beginning of Acts 2? What would most pastors do if a tornado roared through the sanctuary, a ball of fire exploded in the middle of the meeting, and the whole church suddenly started speaking in tongues! So that it was reported throughout the community that they all left the meeting drunk!

94

The meeting in Acts 4 was totally devoted to hearing the frightening news that the city council had just banned the gospel. The Holy Spirit shook the place, and then He sent them all out to break the new law!

And the Christian today who thinks the New Testament church was always just a happy gathering of childlike souls rejoicing in the Lord has not looked at the minutes of the meeting in Acts 5. Two people dropped dead because they weren't being honest with the Holy Spirit! When they left "church" that day, the early Christians were not comforted—they were terrified! They were dead serious, not chattering with giddy exhilaration. God's order for that meeting was an intense, unnerving experience. And as a result, the "unbelievers" stayed away from the church in droves. (It was no small problem in those days making the church "attractive" to the community.)

Everyone is impressed with the fellowship the early church shared. And it is pretty impressive. How they freely gave anything and everything to meet the needs of the brothers and sisters. But how thrilling would the koinonia of the Jerusalem church have seemed to one living among the Greek-speaking believers described in Acts 6:1, whose needy were being skipped in the daily distribution of food because they were not native Jews?

We have heard how "accepting" and "open" the early church was. How convincing would the Christian community's openness and acceptance have seemed to a member of Cornelius' household, Acts 10? These Gentiles had to practically tear the church door down to get in. God Himself had difficulty convincing argumentative Peter to relinquish his prejudicial stubbornness. He had to give him the same vision three times to get him to reluctantly accept the Gentiles. The church was still arguing about their loss of "ethnic purity" as late as Acts 15.

Depending on where one was standing and when he was looking he could have touched the original church and found it quite *un*exciting at some of its moments. If anyone came to it, as most churchgoers in the twentieth century do, expecting to hear a good sermon and some nice music or see a good show, expecting one's family's needs to be met, one would have to have been disappointed. In fact, by the standards of Christian modernity, there weren't any "good services" in the Book of Acts. Nearly every time a meeting is described something disturbing, stretching, or confronting is going on.

The New Testament church is a quality of life that is there whether the Jerusalem Christians are sharing all things in common or the Grecian widows are being neglected daily. Whether the Corinthians are sharing in a wide-open meeting where many spiritual gifts are freely exercised or are being dressed down for tolerating incest in the membership.

The New Testament church is an authentically catalytic happening that is *changing lives.*

The members of the early church are not "pious saints" sitting around looking holy and acting religious. They are initially unchanged human beings who have been touched by the living Jesus and have been put together into a relationship with God and each other that is intended to lead them through a process that will eventually effect total change.

And since they are all in process, New Testament church life is a volatile syncretism of seemingly inconsistent contrasts—all at once—

divine power and human weakness
exhilarating victory and desperate struggle
amazing miracles and unanswered prayer
favor with the people and terrible persecution
wonderful conversions and violent rejections
explosive growth in Jerusalem and Ephesus and tiny
   struggling fellowships in Smyrna and Philadelphia
sharing and neglect
faith and discouragement

fantastic breakthroughs of Spirit power and agonizingly
   hard work
spiritual insight and doctrinal ignorance
openness and prejudice . . . . . .
But something is there that is
real,
     alive,
         life-changing.
A new order is being established in the very heartland of
the poluted old order. A new society is being led forth, in
which people and relationships are changing
                        changing
                        changing.
Everyone is imperfect and no one can remain the same.
Everyone and everything in the church is in process.

The New Testament church can do miracles (as the Spirit
wills), but it isn't enough. It is being changed so that it can
do the impossible: love in the face of hate, esteem others
more important than self, give one's own life for a brother.

The New Testament church can have great spiritual experiences (as the Spirit wills), but it isn't enough. It is being
changed so that it can experience greatness.

The New Testament church can speak in tongues (as the
Spirit wills), but it isn't enough. It is being changed so that it
can speak the truth in love.

The New Testament church can grow explosively (as the
Spirit wills), but it isn't enough. It is being changed so that it
can grow up into the fullness of the stature and personality
of Jesus Christ.

The New Testament church can preach Christ to its whole
world (as the Spirit wills), but it isn't enough. It is being
changed until it reflects Christ and demonstrates His living
reality to the whole universe.

*The New Testament church is the people who are being
changed.*

We all, with unveiled face beholding as in a mirror the glory of the Lord, are being transformed into the same image from glory to glory, just as from the Lord, the Spirit (2 Cor. 3:18, NASB).

The people who gather to Jesus as the congregation of believers who lovingly call their part of the body, "O.H.," are the church in process.

They, together and personally, are the people who are being changed. Every lame man is not walking and leaping. Every scale is not gone from every eye. All the widows may not be fed. Every vision may not be completely obeyed. Close scrutiny will uncover a rag-taggle bunch of unfinished believers . . . being changed.

THE WAY WE WERE

In that desperate moment when our church's first pastors were making their personal commitment to follow a course toward radical reformation of the church, we found ourselves reasoning like this:

> We will lose most of our people and may lose our jobs . . . but then, the way they are and the way we are, what do we have to lose?[2]

That fearful and admittedly pessimistic statement and that question rocked gingerly on our minds in the earliest stages of the church's renaissance process. It has turned out to be quite prophetic. Our losses have been that great. Loss of my job would have been less costly than the personal price paid to stay. But the question is still a valid one. Without the costly changes in the church, leaders and members would have remained locked in their perpetuating patterns of spiritual and relational immaturity and bondage. And that unquestionably would have been the greater loss!

The church *must* be changed! Not only in our tiny folicle of faith and fellowship, but wherever institutionalization has built structures which "protect" its people against practical confrontation with the kingdom call for personal and corporate change (Matt. 4:17).

The Great Commission not only calls the church to go everywhere preaching and baptizing, but also to "[teach] them to obey everything I have commanded you" (Matt. 28:19–20). That half of the project (mostly untouched by modern evangelical hands) is the toughest because it demands in both teachers and disciples openness to the deepest imaginable change; on the level of the basics of human personality. It demands an intensely penetrating and continuing confrontation with Christ's truth (John 8:31). In terms of structure, it demands a style of life and ministry that brings the members of Christ face to face with themselves, their impaired relationships, the worldliness of their value systems, and the stubbornly shallow level of their commitments. Face to face, that is, with the need to be changed, and with the demanding and hopeful possibility of change. Until the church is that kind of society, the Great Commission is just another proof text quoted out of context!

There must be change in the whole of how the church sees itself, how believers see each other, and how they see their life together. There must be change in the way we come together and what we do when we are together. There must be change in the way we feel about each other and in the quality and extent of the interaction that takes place between us. There must be change in how we see ourselves in relation to the world. And there must be change in the standards by which we measure success, prosperity, power, and love.

CHANGE: LIFE STYLE OF THE KINGDOM

In Matthew 4:17, Jesus' whole message is summed up in nine words: "Repent; for the kingdom of heaven is at hand."

The preaching of the good news of the kingdom is bound inseparably to the preaching of repentance. The Greek word is *metanoia*. Its meaning goes deeper than confession of specific sins or giving up sinful habits, though both may be involved in repentance. *Metanoia* means "the transformation of the basic structures of one's life."[3] Repentance is the reorientation of all of life to the kingdom style.

Radical change is required in those who want to come into Jesus' new society. God's new nation, the kingdom community, is a totally new and different thing. Former ideals, structures, viewpoints, goals, patterns, have nothing to say to the new community. It is so contradictory to the familiar old community (the world), that responding to the invitation to follow Christ into the new requires far more than a single moment of change (i.e., the new birth). Much more, we are called to embark on a continuing process of being changed (i.e., from glory to glory).

The most fundamental challenge we face is submission to the kingship of God. As long as even the most insignificant aspect of one's life is consciously or unconsciously "held out" for independence, self-sufficiency or disobedience, the metanoia-process is incomplete. It is a lifelong process.

"Choosing to be changed" is an absolutely necessary characteristic of the kingdom mindset. Unless I am willing to be changed in the basic structures of my life, I will not be living in true submission to God as King.

By the same principle, the church itself must be engaged in a continuing *metanoia* of its own, until nothing of this world holds any place of authority or priority, but everything in the church is in existential submission to her King. So steeped is she in the world's mentality, that she could never make *one* great and final decision to be changed and expect it to be enough. Change must become a cardinal characteristic of her life style. A friend and constant companion.

What Has Changed at O.H.?

Since that first trembling, desperate commitment to change, a sort of rudimentary spiritual alchemy has been taking place.

Future Shock: Renewal-Style

Alchemy: noun, a process of transforming something common into something precious.[4]

Change.

There has been a decided shift in priorities. As founding pastor I had taught the church by sermon and example that its chief reason for existence was evangelism. During my "desperate days"[5] I became counter-convinced that the purpose of the church is to reflect the splendor and beauty of Jesus Christ. Numerical success was everything in the early days. Now, if anything is everything, it is *love.*

Building warm, tight relationships has replaced organizational structuring on the priority list. For instance, when leaders meet (which they do at least weekly), maintaining the quality of their fellowship is the first order. All other matters of church life can wait for us to deal with relationships. There is a developing experience of shared leadership which in practice places the responsibility for shepherding (tending, feeding, guarding, guiding, and gathering) the church on a group of mature and gifted Christian men, who function together in fellowship and by consensus, as the "Pastoral Team." The first responsibility of this team is to be "together."[6]

Necessarily, church programming has changed. God's process has moved us away from the busy, involvement-oriented corporate style to something quite simple and flexible. The value placed in relationship-building has made the development and encouragement of small groups a major focus. These "little churches" range in size from six to fifteen persons. They meet to share life experiences, Bible study, and conversational prayer—aimed at getting to know Jesus Christ and ourselves better and helping each other to grow as persons and as followers of Christ.

The Sunday meeting ("Celebration") is designed to give maximum opportunity to believer-priests to minister to each other, to receive growth-producing teaching, and to join together in worship . . . all in an atmosphere of reality. It is

101

more like a family gathering than a presentation to an audience. It is extremely informal, largely spontaneous, and sometimes disturbingly true-to-life.

A most basic renewal is taking place in the church's perception of itself. The church formerly saw itself in almost purely institutional terms—"an organization to be built and run." It is nearly impossible to overcome this perception without a personal "revelation," a "conversion experience" in one's perception of the church. There must be a "reformation" that frees the mind to "see" the church as a living organism (the Body of Christ), as an inseparably united spiritual family ("brothers, sisters, mothers, children," Mark 10:30). It's coming. Less and less we are seeing the church as something we "attend" or "join." More and more we speak of it as something we *are* together, a family into which we have been born. It is hard to replace old habits, to give up old perceptions, but restoration is taking place.

As the church has struggled in the process of corporate reformation, I have struggled with personal reformation.

My priorities have shifted, too. My family, the personal needs of people and the building of the church as a "new society" have superseded the drive for success and the call to be an organizational grease monkey. In the process, I am struggling to learn an honest, giving life style with my family and with the church. I have had to wrestle with many fears. I have had to make time for people.

My ministry has suffered deep reprogramming. It has been extremely difficult to let go traditional pastoral control over the ministry of the church, in order to allow other believer-priests to minister. However, there are real joys inherent in the changes: (1) growing personal freedom to let God reshape my ministry according to His revealed priorities, gradually replacing bondage to ecclesiastical peer opinions and false guilts; and (2) growing confidence in my unique spiritual gifts, with freedom to concentrate my time and energies more and more in the areas of my giftedness, instead of wasting personal resources trying to conform to the expectations of the preconceived "pastoral image," which nearly always fail to take into account personal uniqueness.

I see evidence of metanoia everywhere in the church.

I can see it in the way we are beginning to live together as His family. A nonjudgmental acceptance of each other in the face of a high level of exposure to each other's weaknesses, failures, and idiosyncrasies is impressive, even though imperfect. We are becoming increasingly able to offer to each other the personal freedom to think for oneself, to be led by the Spirit, to decide, and to act in freedom, with support. We express a growing willingness to listen to each other talk, and to try to care. There is a growing number of concrete expressions of love—touching, listening, giving, sharing, forbearing. Small "pockets of living community" are being drawn together here and there, so that interaction, confrontation, and support can be a daily experience. We have developed a willingness to come together, not because the program or the preaching is the best we can find, but, because we are committed to each other.

There is a hard-won willingness to receive ministry from each other (nonprofessionals). It is no longer necessary that we be entertained. There is often great joy (even hilarity) in the simplicity of congregated spontaneity. And many are learning to hear God's voice in whatever anyone shares.

Our belief in the sovereignty of God is becoming firm. More and more we can see Him in the realities of our lives, gathered or scattered. We are coming to value the real. And increasingly, our responses to each other and to God, our service and works, are flowing out of the reality of dynamic relationships.

There is a deepening hunger for wholeness. And, in several of us, an aggressive treasure hunt for it is going on. This leads to a refreshing honesty about sin and personal need. Self-disclosure and transparency are coming into full bloom

103

in the lives of people who are making the choices to know and to be known.

Spiritual maturity itself is an unfinished state, a relative condition, a dynamic circumstance always reaching beyond itself for unrealized perfection. While unsynthetic growth toward maturity never happens without change in life's basic structures, not all believers who speak loudly of their desire for spirituality will give themselves willingly to a process that involves significant personal discomfort, or shakes the security found in familiar patterns.

FUTURE SHOCK: RENEWAL-STYLE

Growth itself is joyous, exhilarating, and wonderful. It is the process that leads to growth . . .

the pruning (John 15:1)
the winnowing (Matt. 3:12)
the chaff-burning (Matt. 3:12)
the shaking (Heb. 12:27)

. . . that is painful. But when the reformation is from God, the evidence of true change is exciting and inspires deep praise.

An agonizing aspect of our corporate wrestling match with the principles of the biblical church has been the loss of people, who were with us for awhile and then gave up on us for one reason or another and found their way to another church. To anesthetize our minds against the pain caused by this stream of attritions and because many are still dear friends, we lovingly refer to them as the "Our Heritage *Alumni* Association."

Several crucial issues have served as watersheds, to sift from the larger group a committed core, in a fashion not unlike the mustering of Gideon's army. The following is a partial list of our failures. These are painful stories to tell. I do not know that any of them could have been averted, given the dynamics of who we are, the dire necessity for alteration of the church, and the limitations of our knowledge and experience in the methodology of change. From the crucible of our "future shock: renewal-style,"[7] we offer the benefit of hard lessons learned the hard way—in hope that someone else who chooses to walk this way may avoid, where possible, some of the potholes in which we've nearly broken our legs!

The Change-to-Teaching Ministry Doldrums

Until I began to "see" the church, I saw myself as an evangelistic pastor. For me, this meant that every sermon was a clever rehash of the elements of the gospel, designed to entertain, intrigue, and attract churchgoers, and to lead to a basic decision about Jesus Christ. And I was quite good at it.

Then the truth dawned on me that I was giving my congregation nothing but milk. If they were ever to mature beyond spiritual babyhood, they needed meat—biblical teaching that could lead them forward toward full stature in Christ.

I asked the Lord to change my preaching to teaching. And, I began immediately working out my commitment to become a teacher, an equipper of saints.

The process was agonizing. Many of those early efforts were obtuse and dull. No fun at all! For me or the congregation. But it was a process we were forced to endure and to come to the kind of ministry that builds disciples. Many people could not bear the strain of adjustment.

From the "Teaching Watershed" we learned:

(1) It is essential to continually explain the biblical reasons for changes being introduced, so that members of the congregation have a solid basis for understanding that it is a worthy struggle.

(2) Leading a congregation into change demands complete openness with them about the leader's personal struggle to respond to the biblical imperatives concerning his

ministry—the agony the process involves for him—so that they have opportunity to choose to support him in his struggle and to feel they are part of it.

(3) No matter what good reasons we have for changing the public ministry of the church, some people are going to find in the process more discomfort than they are willing (or able) to bear, and they will break ranks.

The Goals Fiasco

I had been teaching New Testament church principles for eighteen months. They were being applied in visible form in a few small groups that had been started. And, as much as I understood how, I was applying them to my working ministry. There had been one-on-one and leadership group discussion of them.

The change and potential change was threatening to some. In some cases opposition was open and vocal. One man considered it his duty as a church officer to come to my study most Friday afternoons for six months to remind me how I was misleading the church. Even though I learned many important things through them, I dreaded these Friday harangues more than I can describe.

Through an unusual set of circumstances, Audrey and I spent two weeks on spiritual retreat in Darmstadt, Germany, with the Evengelical Sisters of Mary. This, we soon discovered, was sovereignly arranged preparation for the storm into which we were about to walk. Upon our return, I presented to the gathered leaders my "Goals for the Ideal Church,"[8] a document upon which I had been working for several months. It was the clearest statement to that date as to the direction I felt the church must go.

Within a few weeks, nine church officers (including my "Friday afternoon Paul Revere") had resigned and left the church with their families.

From the "Goals Watershed" we learned:

Future Shock: Renewal-Style

(1) If possible, local leaders should be "brought along" through a group process of researching biblical goals for the church. I did not understand that process, so I rushed in and "dumped" my own goals on them. They choked and ran. And who can blame them?

(2) Since the church, by nature, is a "network of relationships," in the renewal process there is no substitute for the development of healthy key relationships, expecting church direction to grow out of what the Spirit does in the context of genuine fellowship. It is almost completely ineffective, even wrong, to create policy *ex cathedra* and win approval by majority vote or by some form of dictatorship, however passionate the vision.

The Charismatic Cataclysm

When various so-called "charismatic gifts" began to spring up in the fellowship, I became extremely nervous. I was tentatively willing for God to do anything He wanted to do, but I was concerned that teachers outside the body were being too influential in shaping the body's theology about these things. When an "unauthorized" group of members began to meet for the apparent purpose of introducing and exercising the more controversial of these gifts, I felt that some solid biblical teaching was in order. So, I entered upon a seven-Sunday series on "The Sevenfold Holy Spirit," describing the breadth of the Spirit's ministry, as taught by Jesus and the apostles, and seeking to set the gifts of the Spirit firmly within the context of the whole scope of biblical pneumatic theology. I thought it was very good. I also thought it was quite conciliatory and accepting. On the sixth Saturday, however, an unofficial spokesman for the group called to tell me they were "all" leaving the church, because I was presenting "false teaching." And fifteen of some twenty or more "charismatics" left at that time. Thankfully, some stayed. Others later returned.

From this "Charismatic Watershed" we learned:

107

(1) With all my conscious efforts to be accepting and biblical, I was full of fear, prejudice, jealousy and nonacceptance (borne of long years of antipentecostal teaching in the churches in which I was nurtured). And it came through in my dealing with this matter. If peace is to come in the church between charismatics and noncharismatics (perish the terms! for they are current revelations of our carnal divisiveness) each must be willing to listen to the other, to learn from the other, to submissively answer to the other for attitude and theology, and to accept responsibility for the other. Both are armed with Scripture and experience. Both are saying, "Jesus is Lord" (which no man can do, without the Holy Spirit—1 Cor. 12:3).

(2) In dealing with any issue that has potential for dividing the body, it is essential to interact personally, with an open heart. It is never enough just to make unchallengeable pulpit pronouncements.

(3) You can't win 'em all! Especially when some have their ears sympathetically tuned to teachers who are projecting prejudices and fears of their own, and into whose teaching you have no input.

(4) But you can win some! If you (a) refuse to accept the legitimacy of any kind of division between true believers, and teach the church not to accept it; (b) insist that the Word of God itself has the final answer to the problems of interpretation, and that it simply must be allowed to say what it says about spiritual gifts and Christian relationships, regardless of whose prejudices it strikes down; and (c) determine to accept and affirm each other, without the necessity of full agreement on matters of doctrine and experience (Rom. 14:1).

(More on this in chapter 12)

The Shared Leadership Shock Wave

As long as we talked about the development of a biblical spiritual leadership team for the church, there was great ex-

citement about it. The congregation approved the constitutional changes that opened the way for the development of
such a team, by unanimous vote. And, again by near-
unanimous vote, the first "elders" were chosen. Eighteen
months later, after more teaching and discussion, and a
deepening commitment on the part of these men to their
ministry, it was necessary for me to be away from the church
for a period of ninety days. The elders, it was decided,
would "pastor" the church, as a team, while I was absent.
My leave was prepared for by a month of Sundays devoted
to further teaching on shared leadership, answering questions, and seeking to assure the congregation that its need
for shepherds would be filled by these growing, eager men.

Many people dropped out during my absence. It was
strange having "laymen" lead the services. It was even more
difficult to listen to "untrained" men teaching and preaching. It was a stretching experience. And some people could
not find in themselves the flexibility of spirit needed. More
left after I returned and reaffirmed that I was irrevocably
committed to the shared leadership concept. In numbers,
this was the most costly of all our watersheds.

From the "Shared Leadership Watershed" we learned:

(1) "Unanimous" votes do not mean everyone understands what is happening.

(2) It is fairly easy to talk about changing the church, but it
is an entirely different matter when the rubber meets the
road!

(3) In this case, much trauma might have been spared,
had the leaders taken more time for a more gradual process
leading toward the change. In addition to teaching, interaction, and assurances, it would have been helpful to have
had a series of short-term experiences with shared leadership, each followed by further teaching and full congregational discussion about the experience. This might have

laid a more solid foundation of realistic expectations for the actual change.

(4) During the period of preparation and the early phases of the change, many people needed personal attention to help them deal with the discomfort of the process. The elders could have been more sensitive to individuals who were having problems with the change, going to visit and interact personally with them.

(5) Naming a man "elder" doesn't automatically turn him into a pastor.

(6) Even with the most thorough preparation and personal attention, some people will not (or cannot) adjust to new faces in leadership, new voices in teaching (especially nonprofessional faces and voices), without great trauma. The fact must be faced that, given the option of sticking with the struggle or going to another church that is not demanding such adjustment of its people, many people will opt out.

The Sunday School Panic

In pre-renewal days, Our Heritage was a church built around a Sunday school. Fantastic attendance contests twice a year kept it growing. Classes were closely graded. The pastor spent about one-third of his time just keeping the Sunday school staffed, functioning, and growing.

Then came the discovery of long-neglected biblical principles of church life. Pastoral priorities began to undergo radical shifting. Madison Avenue tactics of church growth gave way to concentration on the spiritual maturity of believers. Much time previously spent concentrating on Sunday school was now being given to study for maturity-producing teaching. Pressure tactics necessary to keep a full Sunday school staff gradually gave way to the slower process of waiting for spiritual motivations and discovery of spiritual gifts. Small Bible study groups began, then flourished, for adults and youth, gradually replacing the youth and adult Sunday school classes. We became committed to bringing adults to spiritual maturity, expecting mature parents to reach and teach their own children.

We taught at length from Deuteronomy 6, etc., that the responsibility for the spiritual nature of children was given by God to parents—not the church—and that parents alone are in the position in the lives of their children to communicate a living faith. And they can and must do it. We offered a simple training course to parents who wanted help getting started with their children. Two creative experimental programs in childhood spiritual education sought to give parents usable tools and specific opportunities to be personally involved in their children's spiritual training, with the support of other parents. ("Sunday School: Family-Style" and "Family Clusters"—they will be described later.)

We are presently without a Sunday school. Our elders and parents are struggling with the need for a carefully thought-out approach to childhood nurture that meets real needs and is consistent with biblical principles.

From the "Sunday School Watershed" we learned:

(1) Instead of seeking to move the church's ministry to children, *en masse,* from the traditional to the parental, we might have done better to have moved with those families who were ready to experiment, giving those who were not ready more time to watch and to "catch" the spirit of renaissance. We were admittedly idealistic and impatient.

(2) Some parents need far more thorough instruction and constant close support to help them catch the truth that they are divinely called and uniquely equipped for the task of transmitting the faith to their children. For them, the shock of losing the "Sunday school crutch" is too great, unless there are parents and others close-by filling the vacuum with their positive input. The parents who have stuck with it, have come to see themselves as their children's chief spiritual teachers and models, and are comfortable in this role, even in the absence of any specific church program.

(3) Some traditional church programs (like Sunday

school), even though they violate important biblical principles, are so thoroughly engrained in the culture and so deeply imbedded in the minds of people, that many find it "impossible" to overcome the guilt, fear, and discomfort involved in participation in change where those programs are concerned.

(4) Some Christian parents do not want to take responsibility for the spiritual nurture of their own children, and simply *will not do it.*

(5) The change needed in the church's approach to children is more basic than introduction of another new educational program. There is a need for the whole extended church family—every member—to see the importance of children to the body and the truth that their nurture is the responsibility of *all,* a responsibility that calls for each adult to cherish the body's children, to learn to interact with them, and to seek to build personal friendships with them. In the context of these Christian adult/child relationships, modeling can take place and a living faith can be transmitted.

The Personalizing-the-Church Struggle

It started when I began to share my weaknesses and fears. It took strong forward strides at the commencement of the first small groups. As the number of groups grew, so did the personalization process. Then we stopped to talk to each other in the middle of the church services—nose to nose. Later the meeting was opened to questions after the sermon. Then we added spoken prayer requests and prayed specifically for them in the meeting. Other kinds of sharing and speaking out were encouraged. Occasionally the congregation was divided into small groups to share and pray. The need to develop deeper personal relationships was urged. The personal interaction, the sharing and praying and even the preaching became more honest and revealed personal needs. In the process of a few short years we could no longer go to church without having to listen to someone speak, with unpolished elocution, about something personal and real, and often painful, in his or her life.

We weren't talking about "going to church" anymore. We were talking about being responsible for each other. But the commitment inherent in simply being there began to be greater and more personally demanding. If you wanted to, you could go in and listen and go out and do nothing about it. No one would doubt your love or ask you why. But, when a need was shared, you found yourself faced with a series of decisions:

(1) Am I going to listen to this?
(2) Am I going to care?
(3) Am I going to pray?
(4) Is there anything I can do to help meet the need?

No one put that on you. No one but the Holy Spirit.

One man said he believed the personal approach and the teaching concerning sharing what we have with each other in need was biblical (he had been involved in helping some of the body's members who needed financial assistance), but he was not willing to continue exposing his $20,000-a-year salary to the kinds of decisions he felt he might have to make if he stayed.

Another man decided to leave after he had tried to build relationships with several people in the church and only a few of them responded. None to his satisfaction. He was not willing to keep trying. He had been "burned" by what he saw as unfulfilled promises inherent in our process of personalization.

And then there was the man who said he was hesitant to bring his friends to a church where the content of the gatherings was so unpredictable and where anyone might say something that would cause irritation or discomfort or have to be explained. He found the personal sharing depressing. He wanted to hear only positive, exciting things in church. He left.

From the "Personalization Watershed" we learned:

113

(1) Contrary to popular opinion, the world is not standing on its toes of anticipation, ready to jump at the chance to make the personal investment necessary to get involved in each other's lives.

(2) The hardest thing in the world for us to do is to really love each other. Most Christian love-talk is just talk. When it comes to laying down our lives, or our public images, or our statistical reports, or our budgets, in order to communicate love to someone in terms that are experienced as love by the recipient, most of us are quick to cop out.

(3) The way of love takes longer.

In each of these areas we were endeavoring to respond to principle, not to any prior experience of our own, nor to anything we had seen working successfully for any other church. We acted on the best reasoning and in the best spirit we had, as Christians, often having no idea where it would lead, or how high the price would be. We acted in faith that, if we obeyed the God-given vision, Christ would build His church, His way.

HELPING THE BUTTERFLY TO EMERGE... GENTLY

(Most of the basic principles in this section were developed by Dr. Larry Richards, an elder in our church, for his lectures in the Dynamic Church Seminars.[9] With his permission I have appropriated Larry's principles and ideas and freely combined them with my own.)

Change in the church is not so much a "crisis experience" as it is a process. Sometimes it has seemed to me that everything was happening at once in our process of change, but the conversion has actually taken years. We move gradually, but inexorably, to basic change. Change in the church is best approached in terms of "growth"—gradual, normal advancement toward spiritual maturity and full health. Significant change in the life of the church can reasonably be expected to be part of healthy growth.

Move with members who are ready; don't try to move the

church en masse. One of the challenges of the renewal process is: how to change the church without splitting the church. It normally does not work to "legislate" fundamental change (at least at the beginning) and to expect everyone in the church to go along with it.

An acquaintance of mine decided that everyone in his Conservative Baptist Church ought to be in small groups. His board was convinced, too. So they arbitrarily divided the church into geographical groupings of twelve. It worked great . . . the first three weeks! After that, the dropout rate snowballed. Last I heard, no one was in small groups in that church.

You cannot make the church change. It is not a thing. It is a life. It can only be changed voluntarily from the inside. And it is not a matter of rejecting or even ignoring those who are not hungry for change. It is simply the positive matter of moving with the ones whose spiritual stomachs are growing. If something real begins to happen with them, it could become contagious.

Move on multiple levels; don't rely on any single method or approach (such as small groups). Beginning a new program of small groups is not the absolute key to renewal of the church. Groups are a powerful tool, but the need for change is so deep it infects nearly every facet of the church's life.

Move gradually through "experience modification"; don't try to move people simply by introducing concepts. Words are not enough. If they are not accompanied by some definite modification of the "church experience," renewal will never happen. People need positive experiences that can help them to understand the concepts.

In his seminars, Larry Richards suggests four levels on which modification of the church experience can be introduced.

(1) *Pastoral modeling.* There is no point in trying to move the church toward change (renewal, spiritual growth), if the

115

leader is not famished for renewal himself.

As a leader, I should ask myself what kind of church I want and how badly I want it.

I want a church experience (for myself and my congregation) in which everyone can be free to be himself. I want church life to be characterized by openness, honesty, bearing one another's burdens, loving and supporting each other. So I've been trying to learn to let those things characterize my life. I have begun to share my weaknesses, struggles, and personal needs, openly, and to go to people in the church with my problems. I have begun to let a lot of organizational "stuff" go to be with people. No point in sitting around praying for someone else to break the ice, to be the example. I know I'm "it."

I want a team of local spiritual leaders who will live their lives together in loving care for each other, serving as each other's support team (and mine). So I have spent the last four years giving my whole life to these men—what I feel, what I think, what makes me glad and sad, where I hurt, my family problems, my burdens and hopes and dreams and frustrations and my love and time and listening ear. Praying as I do it, that they will learn to be that way together.

Modeling cannot be done "at a distance." It requires involvement in the lives of people. And it requires allowing people to get personally involved in one's life. It's costly, time-consuming, and inefficient (like Jesus consuming twenty-four-hours-a-day, three years of his short life with those disciples), but it's the only way "modeling" ever gets below the level of pulpit pronouncements.

Modeling: "What I want to see in others, I ask God to do in me."[10]

(2) *Introduction of "non setting-structured" experiences.* A "setting-structured" experience is an experience in which the attitudes, actions, and content are all predetermined to some degree by the setting in which it takes place. The Holsteins all come home at milking time. When the barn

116

door is opened, each one goes every time, to her own stall. You see it in church every Sunday. People returning to their own "stalls." (I have to admit that even I sit in approximately the same place each Sunday!)

Now try to introduce change. Change the order of the hymns, or the placement of the sermon, and some people will be uncomfortable and upset. People resist change in the church because it doesn't fit what they have come to expect in that setting.

It is a problem of confusion about security. Church-goers are terribly secure with the structure of the church as they have known it all their lives. Some have believed that, of all the institutions of earth, the church was the one that would not change, but would remain the "citadel of security" in a generation bombarded by scary changes. But security for the believer does not rest in structures—not even the structures of the church. Our security is in a living relationship with the living God! If every earthly structure changes, our God stands unshaken and secure.

Challenge: since there is this confusion about security, how can change be introduced in such a way as to reduce the upset and discomfort caused by such change?

Possible response: Introduce new growth-producing experiences away from the settings that presently structure church experiences. At first, don't touch the old structures. Renewal doesn't have to do with structures anyway. Renewal is new life and changed people.

Examples of "non setting-structured" experiences . . .

Retreats are not new, but they can be used to spark renewal. No one expects a retreat to be the same as "going to church." So a weekend experience—away—can be designed to introduce interaction, relationship building, "body life," etc. Before returning to the old settings, explanation can be made as to what they have been experiencing on the weekend, relating their experience to New Testament church-life concepts. A "church renewal appetizer" which could start them asking for more. All without disturbing the existing structures . . . yet.

A pastor in Minnesota wished to break down the "distance" between himself and his church people—wanted to know them and be known by them. His starting point was an informal weekly "dessert" in the setting of his home, to which the members were invited, a small number at a time. In these evenings of unprogrammed, informal, personal interaction the distance was shrinking.

(3) *Gradual change of "setting structured" experiences.* There is significant potential for newness and body development in many places in the church structure as it presently exists. There are, for instance, small groups all over the church: committees, boards, classes, clubs, choirs, auxiliaries, etc. Can change be brought to these existing wineskins as "phase I" of total renaissance in the church?

It's possible.

Sunday school classes, for instance, can be changed to provide opportunity for personal interaction, leading to freedom, reality, and life. The simple method of giving class members something to discuss in pairs or in "buzz groups," occasionally. Larry Richards' book *Creative Bible Study* gives a pattern to follow that can take a group from "sitting-and-listening" to the "active-participation" level in a year.

Larry also tells of a wise pastor who introduced significant change into the experience of his congregation starting with the midweek service. He announced a special six-week series of Bible studies on Christian fellowship. For six weeks when the saints gathered on Wednesday night, after an opening song he passed out a "study sheet" containing questions about a preselected Bible passage to be discussed, and divided the whole group into small groups. Each group was to discuss the questions, share personal prayer requests and pray for each other. At the end of six weeks it ended as promised, and the meeting returned to "normal"—in spite of the clamoring of some for the groups to continue. Later, another series was conducted similarly. Again, it ended amid even more expressions of yearning for the "new style" to continue. After other such series, the midweek service attenders were led in an evaluative discussion of both approaches—the new and the usual. This led amicably to the establishment of continuing small groups. Members were offered a choice between the regular Wednesday meeting at the church (which continued) and the groups meeting in homes. The results: most chose the groups, the number of those involved in Bible study and prayer increased as the groups grew, and real renewal began in that church.

We took our "Sunday Morning Worship Service" congregation through a four-year process that turned the meeting and its participants upside-down. I'll tell the story in chapter 11. The process of positive change in our church board's "setting structured experiences," which brought it from the typical to the personal, is told in chapter 10.

Given the *vision* and the *time,* the church's "setting structured" experiences can be led to renaissance.

(4) Finally, *introduction of new "setting-structured" experiences.* Shiny new meetings, methods, "ministries," which are added on a more or less permanent basis, can bring missing essential elements of the shared life into the church.

When we began our first small group and committed ourselves to small group life as a continuing "program" of the church, we were introducing a new setting-structure to the church experience. People who involve themselves regularly in one of these groups find themselves regularly in a setting which structures into their church experience such positive elements of group life as interaction, relationship-building, etc.

In one church of Larry's acquaintance, the pastor and a key layman, sharing and praying together about the spiritual needs of the church, concluded that everyone in the church was either a sheep or a shepherd. They decided to ask the members of the congregation one Sunday morning which each thought he was. The next step was to give a small group of "sheep" to each "shepherd" (and vice-versa). Each "shepherd" was asked to gather his "sheep" to a regular meeting in his home in which they would all share the happenings of their lives together and pray for each other. In refreshing simplicity, the church was being renewed.

Living communities of various forms and purposes, family spiritual education innovations, continuing methods of helping people to get involved with people in ministering ways—all offer opportunity for new settings which can help to structure fresh church experiences.

THE FRUIT OF THE SPIRIT IS . . . PATIENCE

I've heard Larry Richards say often, "Expect the process of renewal in a church to take fifteen to twenty years."

Patience, the fruit of the Holy Spirit,[11] does not come down from heaven like a gentle rain to trusting souls who sit and wait. I *never* prayed for patience. I was given a "vision" of a twentieth-century church tasting a first-century quality of church life and, in desperation, began to follow the vision. I have felt extremely *im*patient. Anxious. Angry and frustrated at the slowness of the process—or the pain it involved. And . . . after a while . . . I felt caught in the process God had begun. I wanted to get out. But couldn't. I wanted to run away. But couldn't.

I have given up a thousand times. But when I turned to go back, I found I could only go on toward more and deeper changes. My human nature has longed to return to the security and acceptability of my old way of ministry. But the Spirit has dragged me—sometimes kicking and screaming—into the next step in the process.

Ask me at any point along the ten-year trail we've been on, if I was experiencing the fruit, patience. I'd tell you immediately and resoundingly, No!

I have never *felt* patient. I have not long-suffered sweetly

or nobly or well. In the flesh I have said again and again,
No more!
This is it!
I've had it!
I quit!

But here we are. Ten years into a renewal process. Scarred and weakened. But still going.

The flesh has warred and lusted against the Spirit. But the Spirit is ultimately the winner.

Viewed on the surface, you might miss it. But lift a pruned twig or two, and you may be able to catch a glimpse of the patience-fruit the Spirit has grown there among the fleshy foliage.

Notes

[1]John R. Stott, "The Conservative Radical," *Post American* (now *Sojourners*), Nov.–Dec., 1973.

[2]Robert C. Girard, *Brethren, Hang Loose* (Grand Rapids: Zondervan Publishing House, 1972), p. 62.

[3]Andrew Greeley, *The Jesus Myth* (Garden City: Image Books, 1973), pp. 44–45.

[4]*Webster's New Collegiate Dictionary* (Springfield: G. & C. Merriam Company, 1977), p. 27.

[5]Girard, *Brethren Hang Loose,* pp. 29–62.

[6]See chapter 10 for a full description of how the "Pastoral Team" functions.

[7]Helpful insights into how change affects people may be gained from Toffler's *Future Shock.*

[8]Girard, *Brethren, Hang Loose,* pp. 99–106.

[9]Dynamic Church Ministries (formerly "Step 2"), 3161 West Sheryl, Apt. B-23, Phoenix, Arizona, 85201. The basic outline of this section is from Larry Richards' lectures, as are many of the ideas, which I have freely paraphrased and combined with my own without further footnoting.

[10]Ibid.

[11]Galatians 5:22.

7
Reviving the Priesthood

There is thoroughly entrenched in our church life, an un-biblical two-caste system. In this two-caste system there is a clergy-caste which is trained, called, paid, and expected to do the ministering. And there is a laity-caste which normally functions as the audience which appreciatively pays for the performance of the clergy—or bitterly criticizes the gaping holes in that performance (and there always are gaping holes).

No one expects much of the lower or laity caste (except 'tendance, tithe, and testimony). And everyone expects too much of the upper or clergy caste (including the clergy themselves!).

The greatest problem in the whole business is the fact that the Bible's view of ministry[1] totally contradicts this system. So we are found in the awful dilemma of trying to fulfill the ministry-ideals of Scripture with an unscriptural ministry system that is totally inadequate for the job! And, no matter how high we raise the requirements for the clergy, it will never be adequate to approach the kind of production and life envisioned in the Bible!

I am not saying there is no need or place for a full-time, professional ministry. When I speak of the clerical system, I am speaking of the approach to ministry in the church that depends nearly exclusively on professionals; and thus stifles the ministry of the universal priesthood of believers.

The clergy of God are the people of God.

When the word "clergy" (κλῆρος) is used in the Bible in reference to people, it is not referring to a limited office of ministry in the church.

The word's original meaning is "a lot." It is the word used when the soldiers cast lots beneath the cross for Jesus' clothes (Mark 15:24) and when the eleven cast lots to determine who should be the successor to Judas (Acts 1:26).

When the word is used to describe people, it is a reference to the people of God. Peter, in 1 Peter 5:3, warns his fellow elders not to lord it over "the clergy." The word means: allotments, portions, shares, inheritances, estate, property.

In 1 Peter 5:3 it is a way of saying (1) that the believers under the ministry of an elder are God's possession, God's inheritance, or (2) that the elder's portion or allotment is the believers God has entrusted to him for which he is to care. The point made is that no man is to manipulate and control these allotments (the flock) as though they were his own. They belong to no man. They are *God's.*[2]

The controversial Roman Catholic historian-theologian Hans Kung unexpectedly declares:

> From a theological point of view, then, "clerus" means the share in eschatological salvation which God gives to *each* individual believer in the communion of all believers . . . We must then conclude . . . that the particular "share" (clerus) of the Lord is precisely not just the clergy, but the whole people of God; and Christ is the "share" (clerus) not just of the clergy, but of the whole people of God. The word "*clerus*" too, therefore, belongs to the whole church and not just to those who hold office in it; and while the New Testament can support the use of the term as applied to individuals, it is fundamentally the property of the whole church.[3]

It is unfortunate (tragic) that this word for God's special

people (all believers) has come to be applied only to an exclusive group within the church. It is an indication of what has happened to the ministry of the church.

Every person in whom the Spirit of Christ lives is sacred, holy sanctified for divine service. But through a long process of human decisions, that sacred possession, the true clergy, has been desecrated and subjugated—taken off the throne and out of the holy place and chained to the pew! The church has nearly totally restructured itself to function without the ministry of the believer-priest.

Church historian Philip Schaff concludes:

> In the apostolic church, preaching and teaching were not confined to a particular class, but every convert could proclaim the gospel to unbelievers, and every Christian who had the gift could pray and teach and exhort in the congregation. The New Testament knows no spiritual aristocracy or nobility, but calls all believers "saints," though many fell far short of their vocation. Nor does it recognize a *special priesthood* in distinction from the people, as meditating between God and the laity. It knows only one high-priest, Jesus Christ, and clearly teaches the universal priesthood, as well as universal kingship of believers. It does this in a far deeper and larger sense than the Old Testament (Exodus 19:6); in a sense, too, which even to this day is not yet fully realized. The entire body of Christians are called "clergy" ($\kappa\lambda\widehat{\eta}\rho os$), a peculiar people, the heritage of God.
>
> On the other hand it is equally clear that there was in the apostolic church a ministerial office, instituted by Christ, for the very purpose of raising the mass of believers from infancy and pupilage to independent and immediate intercourse with God, to that prophetic, priestly, and kingly position, which in principle and destination belongs to them all. . . . But these ministers are nowhere represented as priests in any other sense than Christians generally are priests with the privilege of a direct access to the throne of grace in the name of their one and eternal high-priest in heaven.[4]

Brethren, Hang Together

In order to come into the freedom and richness offered by Christ in the full experience of His body's life, the church today finds itself fighting against eighteen centuries of stubborn church tradition. It was between A.D. 150 and 200 that the clerical system began to crystalize in the church, and the every-member priesthood began to have its functions diverted into a gradually rising one-man ministry for the local churches.

The "gnostic heresy,"[5] had plagued the church since before John wrote his Gospel and letters which were aimed at floodlighting its errors. In the mid-second century of the church, the excesses of the "Montanists"[6] began to trouble some churches. Early in the second Christian century, fear dictated some of the moves church leaders began to make to "secure" the church against the inroads of these heresies. In a struggle for unity and for control, leaders began to mistrust the Holy Spirit's ability to bring correction and sound teaching through a plurality of local teachers. So, one by one, the functions of the believer priests began to be given to one strong spiritual man in each church. At the same time, as metropolitan churches spawned new churches in nearby communities, some of these local leaders expanded their sphere of leadership to include the surrounding congregations. And, before long, "bishop" was no longer a local, but regional church office, with increasing influence. It happened so gradually, so almost naturally. By early in the third century, the hierarchical system was already clearly taking shape.

The church was fairly well ready to accept the changes that were forced upon it when Emperor Constantine became a Christian and decreed that Romans should become Christians, and pagans flooded the church—unregenerate pagans—after A.D. 300. The body had already largely given up its dependence on mutual ministry, the every-member priesthood. And now it accepted to its own further detriment, the decree-converted heathen, who were utterly dependent on leaders who did everything for them. How else could it be? Most of the new "Christians" had not received the Holy Spirit—so no spiritual gifts were there in the congregations to challenge the legitimacy of increasingly powerful ecclesiastics whose egos thrived on new power.

From there it was only a few steps to a return to an Old Testament-style priesthood, and from there to the papal empire and the dark ages.

When the Reformers came (most notably Luther) they decried the excesses of power of the unscriptural church hierarchy. They "revived" the biblical notion of the priesthood of all believers, and called the church back to personal, individual "justification by faith alone." They changed many important things—corrected many important errors. *But they retained a modified version of the clerical system of ministry in the church.*

John Wesley, who came 200 years after Luther, caught the vision of the body and put its principles into operation in the formation of his "Methodist societies" around "class meeting"[7] life and "lay preachers." But his spiritual posterity let it die.

The Plymouth Brethren, and others like them caught some of these principles and have given somewhat rigid adherence to them.

But for the most part the last generation of Christians handed down to us the same clergy-dominated church structure they received from their ancestors. It's a structure which bears little similarity to that simple, powerful, Spirit-dependent, mutually-ministering body of first-century Christians.

The clerical system—the whole approach to church life which makes distinction between clergy and laity—is not only different from the biblical approach to ministry in the church, it is in direct contradiction to revealed principles.

In practice, if not in theory, the clerical system grossly

violates the principle of the priesthood of all believers. It does this in that it

    (1)   places one man above the other members of the congregation,

    (2)   allows one man and his gifts to dominate,

    (3)   inhibits the free exercise of gifts in the church,

    (4)   sets up a priestly caste which alone is authorized to administer the church's ordinances,

    (5)   makes the saints think that when it comes to the work of God the professionals can do it all and do it better,

    (6)   makes the saints perpetually dependent on professional leaders,

    (7)   gathers people to a man instead of to the name of the Lord Jesus,

    (8)   produces one-sided interpretations of Scripture,

    (9)   thus, perpetuates the tragic division in the body of Christ,

  (10)   inhibits the cleric's own personal freedom to be the Lord's free man, by making him responsible to please those who are paying his salary, and

  (11)   obscures the truth of the headship of Christ.[8]

WHO ARE THE PRIESTS OF CHRIST?

As the New Testament unfolds the blueprint for ministry in a local church, it is discovered to be a ministry of all believers to each other. The unique characteristic of life in the church is mutuality. Everything in the church has the stamp of "one another" on it.

In the Old Testament just a chosen few were priests. But even from the Old Testament era it has been God's plan that His people be a people not merely represented by priests, but that they be a people with such constant, open access to God that they know themselves and become known as a "kingdom of priests" (Exod. 19:6).

In the New Testament, every person who receives Jesus

Christ and acknowledges Him as Lord is given the gift of the Holy Spirit (Acts 2:38), is called to a special vocation in life (Eph. 4:1), equipped by the gifts of the Spirit for ministry (Rom. 12:4-8) and thus *ordained* a full-fledged ministering priest in the church of God (1 Peter 2:5, 9). When the Holy Spirit baptizes a person into the body of Christ, whether hands are laid on him or not, that spiritual baptism into the body is an "official" ordination ceremony. The High Priest is Jesus Christ. *All* believers comprise His "royal priesthood."

THE AUTHORITY OF THE BELIEVER-PRIEST

The office of believer-priest carries authority with it—the authority of Christ Himself. Paul was thinking about the ministry of continuous spiritual renewal believers have to each other, when he concluded his description of mutual ministry in Ephesians 5:18–21 with the instruction . . . "And be subject to one another in the fear of Christ."

No matter how small a person's gift is, it is important to the body. When a member of Christ is ministering with his gift, other believers are expected to be willing to be ministered to by him. The church is given people gifted as leaders, but there is an important sense in which *every* believer-priest leads the others. Each believer-priest supplies a unique ministry that is essential, if the body is to see and experience the fullness of what is involved in its being the complete earthly expression of the living Christ.

Even the most gifted, most spiritual, most mature, most knowledgeable must be willing to submit to the ministry of the weakest Christian operating with his gift. Always the body must receive that ministry as though it came directly from the Lord—just as it receives the ministry of the gifted, the stong in the faith—just as it would receive the ministry of Christ Himself!

If we are not willing to submit to the ministry of all—if we will submit only to the ministry of the eloquent, polished, and pleasing, we reveal in ourselves a set of worldly, carnal motives, pride, and a troublesome lack of discernment of the Lord's body.

IMPORTANCE OF THE BELIEVER-PRIEST

This truth is vitally important to the experience of spiritual unity: every believer is unique, gifted according to the will of the Spirit (1 Cor. 12:11) and indispensable (1 Cor. 12:21) to the life of the body. Each brings his "special" ministry to the body just by being himself. Paul indicates in 1 Corinthians 12:25 that failure to see this truth is a basic cause of disunity in the church. The church begins to approach the kind of unity that convinces the world of the reality of the living Christ, when it begins to recognize the inherent, God-given high value of the ministry of each and every believer-priest.

No professional or team of professionals has been ordained, who is able to reveal Christ alive in the world. To no less than a functioning royal priesthood, utilizing the unique ministry of every truly born-again believer, has the full revelation of Jesus Christ been committed.

A SPIRITUAL HOUSE FOR A HOLY PRIESTHOOD

If this is true, one of the most important goals toward which the church can aim is to be the kind of spiritual environment in which believer-priests are helped to discover their uniqueness, and are freed to develop and engage in their special ministries for the edification of themselves and the body.

In NASB's marginal reading of 1 Peter 2:5, it looks like that's what the apostle is encouraging:

> . . . you also, as living stones, [*allow yourselves* to be] built up as a spiritual house for a holy priesthood, to offer up spiritual sacrifices acceptable to God through Jesus Christ.

That is how we are to see the church—"a spiritual house for a holy priesthood." We are to cooperate in the development of the proper setting for the life and growth of each Christian as priest and minister.

The church has no business trying to provide a setting for anonymity! A place for people to hide, remain private, live to themselves. The church's function is to be an environment in which *every* believer is provided the opportunity, the encouragement, and the freedom to be, in his own peculiar way, a minister of the gospel of Jesus Christ, a priest among priests, offering spiritual sacrifices to God and bringing God into focus for people.

The church setting needs to be the kind of atmosphere that moves people outside of themselves and into the kinds of close relationships in which spiritual ministry is the normal exchange between people. The church is to be an environment in which it is possible to know each other well enough to be serving each other's real needs. The church is to be a setting for the exchange of burdens and helps as well as ideas. It is to be a "spiritual house for a holy priesthood." The commitment that holds it together must be horizontal as well as vertical. The church setting must help believers to move beyond self-interest and commitment to preacher-heroes, aesthetics, programs, and services, to mature servanthood, priesthood, and the ministry of Christ as a personal calling that engages each one's total energies.

Somewhere in church life there must be opened up wide places where there can be mutual ministry (interaction) among the members of the body. It is as indispensable to the health and growth of the church as preaching and teaching, prayer and worship, or evangelism. The church must do more than talk about the priesthood of all believers. It needs to see the priesthood idea as more than a clever lever to press reluctant workers into service for the institution. The believer-priesthood is not another program that can be added to the church to supplement the ministry of the professional pastor. The believer-priesthood *is* the biblical ministry of the church. If ecclesiastical professionals have a place, it is simply as believer-priests, themselves, with special gifts to be used in the process of "[preparing] God's people for works of service" (Eph. 4:12).

When the light on this first began to dawn on us, we immediately were confronted with the need to rethink everything our church was doing, including all our meetings. It became painfully apparent that there was no place in our church life for interaction, nowhere for the development of the kinds of relationships where mutual ministry could take place between priests.

Restructuring was necessary.

The accepted life styles of materialistic secular society opposed the kind of daily mutual ministry toward which we must be moving. Suburban America is a society of fences and private tract homes into which each family retreats, locks the door, pulls the drapes, and sits down to watch television for the next forty years, hoping no one interrupts.

The "New Society" (the kingdom community, Christ's New Testament dream of the church) contradicts and challenges this pattern. The society into which we are called is described in Romans 12 as a community of people who are . . . .

giving themselves to God both physically and spiritually,
refusing to conform to the thinking and style of the world,
evaluating themselves as dependent on one another,
evaluating one another as necessary,
ministering to one another with gifts God has given,
really loving,
abhorring evil,
choosing good,
devoted to one another,
outdoing one another to show respect,
diligent in ministry,
warm-hearted,
enthusiastic about serving,
encouraging one another in hope,
helping one another to persevere through life's troubles,

132

praying together,
sharing to meet the needs of the saints,
practicing hospitality,
blessing one another even when hurt by one another,
rejoicing together,
weeping together,
practicing oneness,
spending time with ordinary people doing ordinary things,
looking to one another for wisdom
living at peace with one another,
    etc.
"One another . . ."
"One another . . ."
"One another . . ."
"One another . . ."

Too long the church has just gone along with the world's way of not relating to one another. The church has decided not to disturb the status quo for fear of offending people who want to keep their privacy and loneliness. But we have been called to reject that life style—to move into Christ's new society. To be a house for priests! A society of ministers! A family of new people who really care for each other!

When the church gathers, as the New Testament tells it, it is the happy gathering of a loving family at the supper table. Its ministry when gathered is described in Scripture like a smorgasbord, a potluck supper, what the church used to call a "love feast" or "agape." It is not one expert cook preparing one dish for everyone. It is each person bringing to the supper what he or she has prepared—the thing each does best. All who have something to share bring it as an offering to God and the others. Those who have abundance to share make up for those who can bring little. All share, all eat, all are fed. It is not all filet mignon and pecan pie, and we don't expect it to be. Some of it tastes better than the rest. Some is better prepared, more nourishing, more enjoyable. Some are just learning to cook.

133

But we're there together. Sharing. Loving. Listening. Celebrating. And it's good. We're growing in the realities of the living Jesus. We're learning to be His body.

What then, brethren, is [the right course]? When you meet together, each one has a hymn, a teaching, a disclosure of special knowledge *or* information, an utterance in a [strange] tongue or an interpretation of it. [But] let everything be constructive *and* edifying *and* for the good of all" (1 Cor. 14:26, Amplified).

All of us together are God's specially called clergy. We are in the process of being built into a house of priests.

As I was thinking about this, my imagination carried me away into the story of *The Wizard of Oz*. Near the end of the book, the Tin Woodman, the Scarecrow, and Timid Lion are disappointed. Their dreams of being what they wanted to be had all hinged on the power of the "wizard" who has just been discovered to be an ordinary old man running an audio-visual device.

But the wizard proved to be equal to the occasion, in spite of it all. What he said to the Scarecrow and the Lion interested me. The Scarecrow had dreamed of having a brain. The wizard responded with something like, "Scarecrow, there are people the world thinks of as brilliant, and they have no more brains than you do. What they *do* have is a *diploma.*" So the wizard solves the problem by giving the Scarecrow a diploma.

The Timid Lion thought he lacked courage. To him the wizard said something like: "There are people the world thinks of as brave, who have no more courage than you do. What they *do* have is a *medal.*" So he proceeds to pin a hero's medal on the lion, thus solving the problem.

I borrowed the wizard's words and applied them one weekend to the congregation of our church. I said, "There are people the world thinks of as priests and ministers, and they are no more priests and ministers than you are! What they *do* have is an *ordination.*"

After having said that, I proceeded to ordain the whole congregation!

I simply explained that ordination is a traditional ceremony of the church which recognizes the call of God and the gifts God has given, and formally acknowledges the ministry a person already has committed to Him. God has already ordained the person for ministry. The church simply officially recognizes what God has already ordained.

"God has already ordained you ministers and priests," I said. "The moment the Holy Spirit put you into the body of Christ by the new birth, your call to priesthood began. I intend for us to formally confess that Royal Ministerial Calling today—by an act of ordination.

"If you think that your lack of ordination keeps you from being a real minister and priest, after today, you will no longer have that excuse."

The ordination ceremony we used appears below.

The truth is, no ordination ceremony is necessary to put you into the ministry. Every believer, indwelt by the Spirit of Christ, is already called, appointed, ordained, commissioned a priest in the church of God.

A SERVICE OF ORDINATION FOR BELIEVER PRIESTS

Presentation of the Candidates

I present all those here assembled who have received Jesus Christ as Savior and acknowledged Him as Lord, to be ordained as believer-priests and ministers in the church of God.

Brethren (addressing any ordained ministers or elders present), these are they whom we propose, God willing, this day to ordain priests and ministers. They are lawfully called to this function and ministry, and they are qualified for the same. Satan would accuse them of impediment and weakness and inability, but in the name of God, we deny the validity of all such accusations to restrain them from their ministry. Revelation

---

1:6 declares, "[He]has made us to be a kingdom and priests to serve his God and Father—to him be glory and power for ever and ever! Amen."

Examination of the Candidates

So that these elders (if present), this congregation, and the angels may witness your confession, you shall answer positively the following questions:

Have you personally received Jesus Christ as your Savior, and do you acknowledge Him as your Lord?
Answer: I have.

Have you been called of God to the office of believer-priest in the church of God? (You have!)
Answer: I have.

Will you give yourself diligently to this high calling?
Answer: I will.

Will you seek to minister to your brothers and sisters in Christ as well as others the Lord gives you, as He gives you the gifts and the strength to do so?
Answer: I will, by the help of God.

Act of Ordination

The Lord pour upon you the Holy Spirit for the office and work of believer-priest in the church of God. Be a faithful minister with the gifts He has or will give you, in the name of the Father, the Son and the Holy Spirit.

(Have each elder or minister lay hands on each believer-priest as he says the following. Or have each believer-priest put his hand on the shoulder or head of the person next to him, while the following statement is read.)

Take authority to minister as a priest in the church of God. And let your ministry of life strengthen the church.

Benediction (Hebrews 13:20–21)

May the God of peace, who through the blood of the eternal covenant brought back from the dead our Lord Jesus, that great Shepherd of the sheep, equip you with everything good for doing his will, and may he work in us what is pleasing to him, through Jesus Christ, to whom be glory for ever and ever. Amen.

A PRIEST OF GOD FOR MY BROTHERS

The foreign-looking letter in the church mailbox bore several strange stamps with the national designation "D.D.R." The writer's name was Rainer Richter. It was written in German.

I read very little German. So, letter in hand, I drove out to Canaan in the Desert, the U.S. home of the Evangelical Sisters of Mary from Darmstadt, West Germany—to see if one of the sisters could translate for me.

Sister Josepha was astonished. "This letter is from *East* Germany," she told me. "It is a miracle it even got out of the country."

She translated:

I have just read your message "Let Loose, Brother" and was very blessed by it. The Spirit of God is surely working the same in all the world—among you as well as among us here in the body. We here also have experienced, as you have, what a blessing "letting loose" is. What I read by you was for me to a great extent not new, but in my special situation now, much of what you write struck me anew . . . During my theology studies the Lord took me into the school of "letting loose," and I am, like you, very thankful for the teaching through our mutual brother Nee. As you can imagine, I have taken note of this way which the Lord has led me with much attention and joy—the way of God with you and your congregation.

At first I thought this meant that *Bruder, Lasst Los*[9], the German edition of my book, *Brethren, Hang Loose,* had come into his hands, but the word Rainer Richter used indicated that what he was reading was not the whole book, but a portion of it, brought into his country past the border guards.

The message of that book takes on increased relevance for an iron curtain church. The church *must* maintain a very low profile. Under constant pressure and scrutiny by an unfriendly government, it must be ready any day to function without highly visible leaders. The urgency of pursuing the development of the "all-believer priesthood" is intensified. The buildings of thousands of iron curtain churches have been confiscated, turned into warehouses, museums, etc. Faced with this possibility, the truth is more readily grasped that the church is not a building but a people whose spiritual growth can be facilitated by the interaction of their lives, even totally apart from specially designated buildings. If the church survives at all, it will necessarily revolve around a living, active, ministering every-member priesthood. Nearly everything visible and public is undependable. Against such a backdrop the message that the Spirit of God is dependable, that Christ Himself is personal Head and Savior of the church, and that the church needs nothing more to fulfill its mission than "its Living Lord Jesus Christ filling the lives of surrendered people," becomes extremely practical.

My East German brother is not just writing a letter of thanks. He says:

> I was especially excited about what you would write about the "Universal Priesthood" of the church. And on this point I received the urge from the Lord to write you this letter. . . . On a retreat several years ago the Lord opened my eyes about "Universal Priesthood" in His Body. . . . Surely Luther was right in his special emphasis toward the Catholic Church that every believer can administer the Sacrament. Even a mutual serving of the believers in the gathering of the congregation through the gifts of the Spirit (1 Cor. 12) would probably not deal completely with that which the Lord says in 1 Peter 2:5. . . .

Peter tells us there that we Christians are being put together as a "spiritual house to be a holy priesthood, offering spiritual sacrifices to God through Jesus Christ." In 1 Peter 2:9 he calls us "a royal priesthood."

Luther discovered this, and urged radical change in the church of his day. "Every believer can administer the sacrament," he taught. Most protestant churches cannot go along with that! But "offering spiritual sacrifices to God through Jesus Christ" involves much more than the Lord's Supper. Rainer Richter goes a step further: he speaks of "mutual serving of the believers" through the exercise of the spiritual gifts in the congregation. But even that, as surely a part of the priesthood ministry as it is, does not deal completely with what Peter is teaching.

> On that retreat with brothers and sisters from all of East Germany, the Lord showed us the following: Jesus Christ is once and for all our High Priest (and Sacrificial Lamb) who once and for all presented Himself for us to God as an offering for sin.

That's basic to grasping the rest of what he says in his letter. Jesus Christ is our High Priest. As part of His one-and-only high priestly ministry, He is also the Lamb that was sacrificed *for us.* Jesus negotiated our peace with God at the price of His own blood.

> From Him we learn: a priest is the mediator between God and man. So the ministry of a priest of the believers is above all a quiet ministry of every one born again; a ministry of prayer in which we bring before God the Father the sacrifice of Jesus in its fullness for all who belong to Him through Jesus Christ: Jesus, the Offering for sin, the Sacrificial Lamb which went to death for sin which I see in my brother and for my own.

What is this ministry of prayer by which we bring the sacrifice of Jesus before the Father in behalf of our brothers and sisters?

One example of what it involves is the Acts 7 description

of Stephen falling to his knees amid the hail of murderous stones and praying, "Lord, do not hold this sin against them!"

Another is Jesus' own prayer for His executioners: "Father, forgive them, for they do not know what they are doing."

By virtue of the fact that the Holy Spirit lives in him, the Christian is never out of the presence of God. Thus, prayer is as much a matter of desire and attitudes as it is words spoken (Rom. 8:26, 27). If that is so, we are serving as priests for our brothers and sisters, offering to God spiritual sacrifices through Jesus Christ—in fact, offering to God the *sacrifice of Jesus* in its fullness—when we extend to them the benefits of the cross. When I forgive my brother his sin; when I cover his fault with my love instead of my judgment; when I restore him, bring him back into fellowship; when I pray for his forgiveness and offer it to him myself—because Christ has already provided this forgiveness and blessing in His high priestly sacrifice—I am ministering for my brother the sacrifice of Jesus.

The New Testament priesthood is rooted in and illustrated by the dramatizations of Old Testament worship. The specific picture is dramatized in the service of ordination for Old Testament priests, in Leviticus 8. (Rainer Richter refers to this chapter in his letter.) Leviticus 8 describes the first priestly ordination under Mosaic law. Each part of the ceremony pictures something significant about the new and living style of ministry that would be brought into being by Messiah when he arrived 1500 years later.

The Lord's instruction to Moses is to gather the whole congregation of Israel to the tent of meeting. Moses tells the congregation that what he is about to do is exactly what the Lord has commanded. Aaron and his sons are brought forward. These are God's chosen priests. The dramatization begins. Aaron and his sons are washed with water—symbolic of the baptism into the body of Christ by the Holy

Spirit (1 Cor. 12:13). Then comes the donning of the priestly clothing—each item symbolic of some part of Christ's high priestly ministry. The special robing of Aaron and his sons pictures the wonderful reality of our having been clothed with Jesus Christ (Gal. 3:27). This robe marks us clearly as priests of God.

Next, oil, the Old Testament symbol of the Holy Spirit (Zech. 4) is poured on the head of the priest: *we* each are universally indwelt, anointed by the Holy Spirit for priestly ministry. At the commencement of the sacrifices, Aaron and his sons lay their hands together on the head of the bull and then on the ram, so that their sins become identified with the offering. Priests are those for whose sins atonement has been made and received.

The letter continues:

> Jesus, the Burnt Offering, fragrant to God—His righteousness, His love and meekness, His obedience . . . are intended for the brother next to me—Him (Jesus) I bring as a complete offering before the Lord for my brother, because the Lord sees my brother wholly in Jesus . . .

In Leviticus 8:22–30 instructions are given for a beautifully symbolic part of the ordination drama which shows how we minister the "spiritual sacrifices to God through Jesus Christ," how we minister the fullness of Christ to each other.

The ram of ordination (margin: "filling") is presented. The priests-elect lay their hands on its head. Moses kills the ram. He daubs a bit of the ram's blood on the right ear lobes, right thumbs, and right big toes of the priests-to-be. God, who ordains us His priests, intends to set apart *everything* about us for ministry. Our ears, for listening to our brothers. Our hands, for reaching out to aid our brothers. Our feet, which He has turned from running away, to going where He sends. His priests are to see themselves as totally belonging to God.

As the choreography of ordination moves on, Moses cuts

the ram (representing Jesus and His sacrifice) in pieces. A variety of unleavened cakes and wafers is added to the cut-up sacrifice. One by one, Moses, acting for God, places the pieces into the hands of the priests. Together, each of them lifts his piece of sacrifice to the Lord in a "wave offering." One by one, Moses takes the sacrificial portions from each priest and returns them to the altar. There, the sacrifice is burned.

> The whole sacrificial animal is presented to God. Bit by bit I fill the hands of my brother with this consecration sacrifice of Jesus before God (Lev. 8:25–28).

Each action and all of it together forms the single, comprehensive act of offering the sacrifice to God. It is not just when the parts are burned, but also when they are shared and received—that whole interaction between them is very much part of the act of worship.

Peter again (with italics added):

> You are a royal priesthood . . . offering up *spiritual* sacrifices acceptable to God through Jesus Christ.

We are in the picture drawn in Leviticus 8. We are God's anointed priests to each other, offering spiritual sacrifices to God. We come together wanting to know and experience the fullness of God's sacrificial Lamb, Jesus. My brother holds out his empty, needy hands to me. I share, we share, what we each have of the sacrifice of Jesus. We talk, tell, converse, interact, exchange our lives in Jesus with each other, until we have given away all that we are and have in the Lord. "Bit by bit," before God, as an offering to Him, I fill the hands of my brother with this consecration sacrifice of Jesus—until his hands are full of Jesus! He holds the sacrifice of Christ and can offer it, in his turn; to God for his brothers and sisters.

What tremendous joy to receive and give in this kind of exchange that brings to both of us, to all of us together, the fullness of Jesus the Lamb!

None of the priests in the Mosaic liturgy held the whole sacrifice. Together they held the sacrifice in full. The wonderful limitation of the believer-priesthood is that to know and experience the fullness I will always need my fellow priests.

> Once a drudge of an "accuser of the brothers" I become a "priest of God" for my brothers. God has shown us this as an essential step to "reformation of the church". . . . I greet you united in our Lord Jesus Christ.
>
> Yours,
> Rainer Richter and my wife Elizabeth

(On the day I was preparing this section, a second letter came from Rainer in response to one of mine. It contained warm expressions of oneness in Jesus, and an invitation to come to East Germany to "praise the Lord together" and to converse with the brothers and sisters about the priesthood of believers.)

Notes

[1] For a quick resume of the biblical view of ministry, see Exodus 19:5–6; Romans 12:3–8; 1 Corinthians 12:4–7; 14:26; Ephesians 4:11–16; 1 Peter 2:5–9; Revelation 1:6; 5:9–10.

[2] This New Testament term seems to be restating the Old Testament concept stated in Deuteronomy 4:20 and 9:29.

[3] Hans Kung, *The Church* (Garden City: Image Books, A Division of Doubleday & Co., Inc., 1976), p. 494.

[4] Philip Schaff, *History of the Christian Church,* Volume II. A.P. & A., pp. 60–61.

[5] The Gnostics, among other serious errors, denied the incarnation of Jesus Christ.

[6] The Montanists were quite biblical in doctrine, but were extremely emotional, legalistic, and self-righteous, calling themselves "the spiritual church" in contrast to the rest of Christendom which they referred to as "the carnal church."

[7] The Methodist class meeting was a small group of about twelve mem-

bers, which met weekly to support, share, correct, and otherwise minister to each other. They were quite effective in keeping the spiritual lives of their members vital.

[8]Some points on this list were paraphrased from William MacDonald, *Christ Loved the Church* (Kansas City: Walterick Publishers, 1956), pp. 52–54.

[9]Robert C. Girard, *Bruder, Lasst Los* (Stuttgart: Christliches Verlagshaus GMBH, 1974).

8
Wherever Two or Three
Hang Together

"You shall be to me a *kingdom* of priests."

The mountain shook and smoked as Moses stood "mouth-to-mouth" with God[1] for the unveiling of an eternal strategy. Peter says the promised is fulfilled in Jesus (1 Peter 2:5–9). With the intimate God-man relationship offered in Christ, we have become

a nation,
a royal race,
a new society,
a community . . . of priests.

Community.

A word being revived among believers today. A concept arousing latent hunger for relationship, intimacy, support, interaction, and changes in life style. A reality expressed in "living communities" springing up like dandelions here and there in and outside the meticulously groomed lawns of the established church.

Tiny communities, like the one in Hawaii where my family and I lived with eight other people for ten weeks last summer. A predominantly Catholic community in Michigan, reportedly numbering about 10,000. A "household" in California where some fifty people share everything "in common." An "extended family" of two families who live in two houses down the street from me, in Arizona, in which

145

each family keeps its own things, but makes everything available to each other. Tightly bound and disciplined communities, like the Evangelical Sisters of Mary in Darmstadt, Germany (with tiny communal branches in other parts of the world) whose discipline includes the practice of celibacy.

In nearly every city, they are sprouting and growing.

The Book of Acts, in its early chapters, includes an account of the church as the *community* of God. Their common life was built directly on the relational teachings of Jesus. With no time-hardened church traditions to circumscribe the movement of the freshly-diffused Holy Spirit among them, they set a pace for shared living that, by its placement where it is—early in the account of the Spirit's outpouring—forms part of "the promise of the Gospel" . . . an aspect of promise as yet unfulfilled for most Christians.

The untapped potential of living our lives together is tremendous. Close living maximizes the opportunity to share deeply in the gift of redeemed personhood and the gifts of the Holy Spirit. Sharing is possible at a level which greatly increases stimulation toward spiritual growth—formation in us of the likeness of Jesus. Community can be an excellent setting for learning to be lovers in Jesus' style, givers, healers and the healed, change agents and the changed. It can be the scene of significant spiritual support and demanding accountability. It can be a "household" into which deeply troubled people may be introduced to an experience of healthy, caring family life—often the missing ingredient needed to facilitate emotional healing. Community with a high degree of material and emotional commonality probably offers the only possiblility for experiencing the Acts 4:34 miracle, "no needy persons among them."

Community living offers the potential, as described by one Episcopal bishop, "not of living in the world and going to church; but of living in the church and going to the world."

I have been careful to say "community *can*," not "community *does,*" for I have known people who spoke much of community and who even came to live in close physical proximity, who experienced little, if any, of what I have described, because they shared so little of themselves in common with each other.

It must be said again: *the whole church, as described in the New Testament, is a life style community.* I do not mean that all Christians lived in the same house. They did not. Personal ownership was not ended. Many voluntarily sold possessions so as to give, but no "law of the church" ever dictated an end to personal ownership. Christians spent time together every day, but often had time alone. Their houses were open to each other. Their food and all their possessions were voluntarily available to meet each other's needs. They shared day-by-day the common happenings of their lives, as well as the spiritual teachings and insights the Lord was giving. They saw and experienced oneness. They assumed full responsibility for each other—spiritually, emotionally, materially. As Ron Sider puts it, they accepted "unconditional economic liability for and total financial availability" to each other in Christ.[2]

KOINONIA EQUALS COMMUNITY

The now-familiar, much-used New Testament word for Christian fellowship—*koinonia*—implies more personal involvement between brothers and sisters than coffee after church or warm feelings of nostalgia at the Christmas candlelighting service. *The Analytical Greek Lexicon* defines *koinonia* (Acts 2:42, etc.):

fellowship, partnership, participation, communion, aid, relief, contribution in aid.[3]

Its root word is *koinos* (Acts 2:44, etc.):

common, belonging equally to several . . .[4]

In verb form, the word is *koinoneo* (Rom. 15:27, etc.), meaning:

to have in common, to share, to be associated in, to

147

become a sharer in, to become implicated in, to be a party to, to associate oneself with *by sympathy and assistance,* to communicate with *in the way of aid and relief.*[5]

Time and dulling church tradition have watered down the word "fellowship" until it no longer aligns with the New Testament concept. The word "community," defined as living in close relationship and sharing what we are and have in common, comes much closer.

In the New Testament church, whether they lived in each other's homes (as in Jerusalem[6]) or lived in their own homes and "urgently pleaded . . . for the priviledge of sharing (*koinonia*) in . . . service to the saints" (as in Macedonia[7]), the spirit and life style of community was one of the things that set Christians apart from their pagan society.

Even as late as the third century, Tertullian, in his *Apologeticus,* contrasts the life style of the Christian community with that of the pagans of his day. To his pagan peers, he writes:

> That especially which love works among us, exposes us to many a suspicion. "Behold," they say, "how they love one another!" Yes, verily this must strike them; for they (pagans) hate each other. "And how ready they are to die for one another!" Yes, truly; for they are rather ready to kill one another. And even that we call each other "brothers," seems to them suspicious for no other reason, than that, among them, all expressions of kindred are only feigned. We are even your brothers, in virtue of the common nature, which is the mother of us all; though you, as evil brothers, deny your human nature. But how much more justly are those called and considered brothers, who acknowledge the one God as their Father; who have received the one Spirit of holiness; who have awaked from the same darkness of uncertainty to the light of the same truth? . . . And we, who are united in spirit and in soul, do not hesitate to have all things common, except wives.[8]

The writings of both friends and enemies of the church of

the early centuries contain significant passages concerning the mutual love and care of Christians for each other. One enemy, Lucian, who saw Christianity as nothing more than an "innocent fanaticism" says, in an "intelligence report" to the emperor:

> It is incredible to see the ardor with which the people of that religion help each other in their wants. They spare nothing. Their first legislator has put into their heads that they are all brothers.[9]

A number of early writings tell how believers saw the Lord Himself in the faces of each other, and how they saw personal mutual care as direct ministry to Jesus.[10]

> It belonged to the idea of a Christian housewife, and was particularly the duty of the deaconnesses, to visit the Lord, to clothe Him, and give Him meat and drink, in the persons of His needy disciples.[11]

In the centuries that followed the paganizing of the church under Constantine with the help of those who welcomed his "conversion," mutual care became an institutionalized thing. And personal relationship with and responsibility for one another eroded. The church became more and more impersonal, and "community" became an organizational word, with less and less of the beauty and sweet fragrance which still clings to the Acts 2 story of *koinonia*.

Yet, the Bible still holds it out as a promise. A promise with no time limits on it that would lock it into those early days, out of reach for the church of the twentieth century. The living church is community. Not just a "pocket" of it here and there, tantalizing or scandalizing the rest of us (depending on one's perspective). But *the church, the whole body of Christ is intended to be a life style community.* A dynamic scene of nourishment and healing and support and growth and love and care and joy-in-relationship.

How can it be?

149

I have no final answer. But I would like to suggest a place where it can *start*.

THE LITTLE CHURCHES

It's Tuesday night—or Wednesday—or whatever night or day the group has chosen to meet. The agreed-upon time has arrived. The doorbell rings. By ones and couples they gather in the host's living room or family room. There's the usual chit-chat, sharing top-of-the-head interests of the day and week, news of mutual acquaintances and absent group members. Coffee or tea is served—members seem to unwind a bit when they get a steaming cup in their hands.

The leader calls the group to prayer, or simply catches the direction of the conversation and capitalizes on it to lead into a more specific kind of personal sharing or the study of the Word. Bibles open to the chosen passage. (There are, perhaps, a half-dozen translations around the circle.) This group of three to a dozen people begins together to discover God's plan for their lives. Together, in the open Bible and in each other's open lives, they are coming to know Jesus Christ more intimately. Together they work through spiritual questions, hang-ups, and daily problems connected with being Christ's followers in the world.

None is the authority. No authority is needed. Except the Holy Spirit, speaking through His written Word and the letter He is writing on Christ-filled human hearts. This is the church. Getting to know Jesus Christ, by sharing together what He is doing as well as what He has said. They are getting a taste of what it means to be a community of priests.

Such Little Churches as these have a profound effect on the life of our church. Nothing we have tried to do in our struggle toward new life has been more important in sustaining spiritual renewal, than making small groups a primary focus of our life together. About seventy percent of our members plus a significant number of others are involved in group life. The essential ingredient the small group is able to add to the life of the church is interaction. Interaction can lead to relationship. Relationship can lead to community.

They meet to fulfill a threefold purpose: (1) to get to know Jesus Christ better, (2) to help each other grow, (3) to learn what it means to be part of the body of Christ.

Committed to listening to each other without resorting to judgment of what is shared, and to count very little to be beyond the bounds of things "proper to talk about," we approach the dynamics of group life with a stout, four-legged *confidence.* (1) There is confidence that the Holy Spirit lives in His people, and can be trusted to lead them singly and in groups, and to communicate to them the desires of the Head of the church, Jesus Christ. (2) There is confidence in the ministering capabilities of the royal priesthood of all believers, and that the simple interaction of Spirit-indwelt priests can lead them toward spiritual maturity. (3) There is confidence in the power of the Word of God, to teach, reprove, correct, train in righteousness, and equip the people of God for whatever is God's work. (4) There is confidence in the effectiveness of the body's functioning, the intercourse of gift with gift, member with member, to provide a setting for authentic growth of love and spiritual unity. There is confidence that these dynamics combine in a living way, in the Christ-centered small group, to build up the community of God.

The form of the meeting is simple: (1) sharing the experiences of life, (2) sharing Bible study, and (3) sharing prayer.

The sharing of life experiences is a key process in moving toward the common life. Keynotes of this sharing are honesty, freedom to talk about anything, freedom to choose one's own level of self-disclosure and a friendly group that is willing to listen and value what is shared. Deep personal hurts and high personal joys (as well as what happens between low and high) are shared and lived through with the group. The idea is to share our common life as family.

The Bible study is, for most groups, a sharing experience

rather than a lecture experience. A few groups have someone who prepares questions for study in advance, and/or provides a few minutes of prepared input before opening the meeting for free-for-all interaction. Others study the Bible in an unprogrammed manner—approaching the Word like a committee whose assignment is to ascertain the passage's meaning and to apply it to their lives. Using either method (or some alternate approach) their purpose is not to correct each other's doctrine, but to help each other to discover Jesus in the Word and to learn how to walk with Him in living life.

The shared prayer is most often in conversational style and grows out of the things we've unearthed in our study and personal sharing. Sometimes open-eyed and a process of interaction itself, the prayer time may include tearful confession, quiet or noisy praise, serious God-focussed interaction about someone's specific need, expressions of mutual affirmation and caring, and even guffaws and giggles.

The meeting normally lasts two to two and one-half hours. Some run longer.

CHILDREN IN THE GROUPS

Children are included in some groups, for part of the meeting, then they go to another part of the house to play. One group assigns one of its members each week to be with the children and to plan activities for them. They pass this task around among the members. Other groups welcome children, who spend the entire time playing within earshot. Some groups simply leave the children at home with a sitter (usually a relative). Another idea would be to take all the children to one group member's home, other than the meeting place, and to assign to a different group member (or team) each week the task of caring for them. In our group the children are welcome and wander in and out as needed.

Leadership

Group leadership most often rises from the group itself, or revolves around the host. Some groups pass leadership around. Others operate without designated leaders. Group leaders and/or representatives gather with the elders two or three times a year for communication and instruction. The weekly congregational meeting (with plenty of opportunity for sharing) provides a more frequent opportunity for interaction between groups.

Basic training for group leaders is personal experience as a member of a healthy group. (There are other good styles of group oversight that involve a more disciplined approach to leadership development and greater frequency of meeting. We have deliberately chosen to give our groups a great degree of freedom and to keep the structure of management extremely loose. This necessitates a strong, continuing emphasis on keeping the network of personal relationships healthy.)

Termination

We have no formula for terminating groups. They last as long as their members are committed to meet. We have no rules that keep people from moving from group to group if they wish (with the exception of the Yokefellow groups which are closed), though there is strong encouragement through teaching and counsel, to stay with one's group even though a particular combination of persons may present taxing personality adjustments. There is great potential for growth in situations that require a certain amount of "stretching." However, some groups are unhealthy and unedifying and should be abandoned and allowed to cease. We allow these things to happen without leadership interference.

Size and Division

According to psychologist Howard Clinebell, "seven to twelve members, plus leader or co-leaders, is an optimal number for a growth group. There is a greater chance of achieving a sense of caring and community—i.e., becoming a true group—if the number of relational bridges which must be built is relatively small. Groups of less than five, however, provide too few opportunities for the growth-stimulus of encountering a variety of personalities, life experiences, values, and perspectives. And the absence of one or two members depletes the interaction severely."[12]

Unless a group is "closed," members sometimes bring friends they think might benefit. And the number grows. It's good to plant the seed of division early in the group's life, encouraging members of a growing group to discuss among themselves how best to divide when they pass the "optimal number." Dividing a family is a painful process—and often that is exactly what a healthy group becomes. Since our groups are largely free from ecclesiastical control, and we have never tried to force change or outside leadership upon them, sometimes a group will ignore the appeal to divide. The result is that the interaction is diluted. It becomes increasingly difficult to significantly involve introverted members in the presence of more people. As the group grows to twenty or more members, dialogue (two or three people doing most of the talking) replaces the free-flowing, immediate style of interaction and its equality of opportunity. New members added after that may be excited about the group (even though it is too large it may be more personal than anything they've ever experienced in the church), but with twenty or more members, it is no longer a true small group experience. Lacking small group experience, new members often do not comprehend the value of more intimate units, and thus will more likely resist attempts to divide. Soon you have something whose lacks you were trying to overcome by starting the group—a congregation—which, ironically, if it is to effectively minister to its members, will probably need to establish some small groups!

There are constructive ways to divide growing groups. And believers, mature in their understanding of the value of small groups, can approach division with evangelical enthusiasm. For instance: (1) The group may decide to conduct a missionary venture by commissioning two or more of its family units to begin a new group in another location. The shock of division can be softened by commitment to bring the old and new groups together periodically—say, monthly—for a potluck dinner or other gathering. (2) The church's leaders may request that group members who have leadership gifts consider accepting assignments as leaders of a new group. (3) Members of several groups, who live in a particular geographical area, may be invited to form a new group in their area.

I do not wish to leave the impression that we have found a satisfactory formula which we carefully apply to the matter of group division. Our approach has been to teach and exhort concerning the positive principles of group life (including the principles of size) and to leave the matter of growth, division, and termination to the members and the Spirit.

PROBLEMS

If a problem (doctrinal, relational, etc.) develops in a group, there are a number of possible courses of action. The Holy Spirit can be depended on to indicate which is the right course in each situation. Here's how we have handled such situations:

(1) If the problem indicates a lack in the body's doctrinal understanding, the congregational meeting (worship and teaching service) provides a natural setting for sound, corrective biblical teaching.

(2) If the network of personal relationships in the body is intact, one or more elders will have functioning relationships with the group leader or members, and can communi-

cate to the group through that relationship. Correction by this means often takes place almost naturally.

(3) One of the leaders of the church can be sent to the group's meeting to share with the whole unit the exhortation, instruction, etc., that may be needed.

(4) Since God uses such problems to refine the group and to help it to grow in its own capacity to handle problems, often the best course is for leaders to pray and wait, remembering that the group already has powerful spiritual forces working within it.

A middle-aged man began attending one of our "little churches." It was a group of fairly young Christians. They welcomed him. He was talkative and stimulated discussion. But it was not long until they became aware of some unsettling biases. He was dogmatic and legalistic. And soon every meeting of the group was a heated discussion of the man's erroneous ideas. After about six weeks of this, the group which had lovingly welcomed and openly listened became uncomfortably aware that the man was not there, as they all were, to learn with the others, but to teach his private interpretations. What had been a helpful and loving group had become a tense weekly debate. And they did not like it.

My first reaction had been fear that this false teacher might lead some of these young believers astray. But as I watched, I saw how they were growing amid the conflict. They had deeper convictions than at first, and were becoming intensely committed to the truth. They were studying their Bibles like they never had before. So I prayed for them. And encouraged them to do whatever *they* felt was right. I advised them to confront the man with their true feelings about what he was trying to do. I worried, but I could see God working.

Finally, the men of the group, on their own initiative, set up a confrontation with the man, and invited me to join them. The meeting confirmed what had been suspected of his motives, and he was told, "If you are not ready to come to the group meetings as one who needs to learn from the other members and not as a closed-minded pitchman for your own dogmatic doctrines, then you must not come back to the group again!" It was a very difficult thing for the group members to do, for they had opened their hearts to the man and his wife, but it was the necessary course.

The man never returned. He sent a few "anonymous" letters as parting shots, but we have not seen nor heard from him since. Most of the members of the group have become strong Christians with significant personal ministries.

ARE GROUPS "INGROWN"?

I am often asked if the little churches tend to be "ingrown."

> *ingrown,* adjective: having the direction of growth or activity or interest inward rather than outward.[13]

Does a healthy family tend to be ingrown? If unashamedly spending time together developing relationships with each other, focusing on nourishment and growth of members, seeking to meet real needs of members and seeking to provide a loving base of acceptance and support from which to live their lives in the world, is being ingrown, then they are ingrown, and they should be. For they are providing exactly the kind of nurture needed by the members of any healthy family.

The truth is that by the very nature of the group process they are learning to reach out beyond themselves to touch the lives of others, and to give themselves away. There is nothing ingrown about learning these arts in the positive, responsive context of fellowship with spiritual brothers and sisters. The thing that happens in a healthy group is that what its members learn of relating and loving and sharing within the group, often profoundly effects how they function in *all* their relationships. Sharing life together leads to sharing life outside.

At this point an important distinction should be made. In

our approach to group life we do not perceive these groups primarily as task groups or mission groups assigned to specific unique ministries. Rather we see them as growth groups assigned to provide nurture, fellowship, and support for believers.

VARIETY, THE SPICE OF LIFE

The spirit of the community has developed in a variety of group styles in our local church. The central thrust of group life for us has been the continuing spiritual growth group. It has "sprung up" in forms that have drawn together, in ministry to each other, groups of women, men, divorcees, singles, junior high students, high school students, college and university students, electronics plant employees, and even O.H. alumni. Most of our little churches, however, are heterogeneous groupings involving most of the above in a wide range of ages and life situations. We are convinced that the heterogeneous group has the best potential to meet the real growth needs of its members.

In addition, two kinds of special purpose groups have functioned with effectiveness: (1) Family Clusters and (2) Yokefellow Groups.

The Family Cluster was an experimental attempt to draw together three or four sets of parents with school-age children, to form a childhood nurture group, in which parents were helped to grow in their role as the chief shapers of their children's spiritual lives. Initiator-coordinator George Eberly recruited families for each cluster and spent the first five weeks leading the group meetings, and teaching parents some of the fundamentals of how children of various ages learn. After the period of orientation, the parents themselves shared responsibility for leading the one-hour meetings. The coordinator supplied each group with material and ideas. The approach was to briefly introduce a biblical concept at the beginning of each meeting, and then to involve parents and children together in activities designed to illustrate and apply the concept, and as family units, to read and discuss Bible passages pertaining to it. (For instance: when the concept to be taught was "I am made in the image of God," the biblical passages had to do with characteristics of God which are, in other passages, said to be the characteristics of people. The activities were designed to teach the meaning of "image," and included such things as taking Polaroid photographs and making crayon sketches of each other, asking: "How is the sketch [or photo] unlike the person whose picture it is?" and "How is the sketch [or photo] like the person?" etc.)

A Yokefellow group is a closed circle of people who have committed themselves to meet for a minimum of twenty-two weeks, to go with each other into an indepth search for understanding of themselves. The program was developed by Cecil Osborne (*The Art of Understanding Yourself,* Grand Rapids: Zondervan, 1967), and is serviced from his Burlingame Counseling Center (19 Park Road, Burlingame, California 94010). Members pay a minimal fee to take a personality test. Personalized slips, each dealing with one facet of test results, are mailed to the group's leaders biweekly, to be distributed to each member. The meetings, as we have experienced them, consist of voluntary responses to the test slips and the instructions they contain for dealing with the personal problems revealed; struggling together to an understanding of the sources of these problems; sharing of past and present life experiences that relate to the problems; affirming and supporting one another to provide a loving atmosphere in which the risks of self-disclosure are more readily faced; sharing insights, biblical and personal, that have helped us to understand and deal with the problems; and praying for each other. The group commitment also includes daily prayer for the other members, as well as personal "homework" involving reading assignments (in the Bible and other books), personal projects designed to deal with the issues raised by the slips, and specific praying based on what each is discovering about himself.

Members of these groups (both Yokefellow-style and spiritual-growth-group-style) testify to greater self-understanding, significant spiritual growth, healing in areas of long-standing spiritual problems, new freedom to feel and to be oneself, and a more intimate and affirming level of fellowship with other group members. To know and to be known in our weakness and then to be loved, is itself a life-changing experience.

In theory, we dream that all our groups will lead to these same results. And some do. In the ideal of community, there is freedom to openly expose oneself in a fellowship of people ready to listen (without harsh judgment), love (without hypocrisy), share themselves (without defensiveness) and walk together toward deepening healing and surrender to God (without pretension or pressure). It *can* happen, if we can agree to let Scripture say what it says, respond to each other as Scripture exhorts, and trust the Holy Spirit in each other—without resorting to legalistic pressures for conformity and self-protective measures for security.

The little churches: "islands of caring and growth in . . . the lonely sea which is our world."[14]

We do not believe that our approach to building "beginning community" in small cadres of Christians is the only approach. Another wineskin may be as good or better. It is also true that merely getting people to meet in small units is not automatic assurance that they will break into a sharing life style. Some smaller units are so impersonally structured and so rigidly controlled that they continue to stifle the sharing of life. Interaction in such groups, if any is permitted, is often on a purely ideological rather than intimate level. And relationship-hindering walls never are permitted to crack.

COMMUNITY-SPROUTS

If a group is healthy it doesn't meet long before a deep

bond of camaraderie, even love, develops between participants. They pray for each other. They bear each other's
burdens (and bear each other as burdens[15]). They forgive
each other sins. If they are close, they sandpaper the rough
edges off each other. They support, encourage, affirm, rebuke, reprove, and correct each other. They become each
other's counselors. Deepening friendship develops. They
keep in touch between meetings. They help each other in
practical ways, even participating in one another's material
needs. Best of all, because they are sharing His reality and
exposing His working in their lives, Jesus Christ becomes
inescapably real. By their exposure to His life in each other,
by sharing living evidence of His availability for involvement
in daily life, they are helping to keep each other renewed in
the Spirit.

In short, they experience a primal form of Christian community.

The Church at Wakefield's House

They all lived in the same general area of the city of
Phoenix, about ten to fifteen miles from where our church
meets. One by one they found each other in the congregational meetings, and other contexts (for some were involved in other churches). They wanted to begin meeting to
study the Bible and to share their lives. Of course, we encouraged and welcomed it. They decided to meet at
Wakefield's. Thursday nights.

The meetings begin with a family potluck dinner, each
week. Children and adults are together in a time of singing,
sharing, and prayer. When the group turns to Bible study,
the children go to another part of the house to play, or to
the backyard to swim. Often special Bible studies and other
directed activities for children are provided. Bible study for
adults and youth revolves around a prepared list of study
questions which are handed out at the close of each meeting, for the following week. Incorporated in the study list are

questions designed to stimulate personal sharing related to the passage under consideration. Dr. Norm Wakefield, host, prepares the study sheets and leads most of the meetings.

The group has grown in love for each other, and in numbers—many from outside the O.H. family.

It soon became apparent to them that God and they had more in mind than an outpost Bible study group of a church a dozen miles away. Because of the distance and the ecclesiastically cosmopolitan make-up of the group, they determined that they were (or at least ought to be) a fledgling church. Their part of the city needed the new kind of church they could be.

They decided (with the blessing of mother church) to experiment with the idea. So, in addition to their Thursday meetings, they began to assemble as a congregation on Sunday evening. O.H. people could continue to gather with the mother church, too, as long as they wished. Children, since the group has nearly as many of them as adults, are given a special place. The new church seeks for ways to involve them and their parents in meaningful interaction in and beyond the meetings. The new church has two elders: Norm Wakefield and Ted Sellers.

When last I talked with Norm, a few days ago, they were struggling with how to respond to the growth that was filling their house to overflowing twice each week, without resorting to building a church building. (Dividing a congregation is even more challenging than dividing a small group.) Some of the options being considered are: (1) establishment of a sister house church in the same general area. Spiritual resources could be shared between the two groups, by frequent exchange of teachers, and regular retreats that would bring both congregations together. (2) Purchase, by one of the members, of a home with more space for meeting. (3) Rental of a restaurant or other facility. And . . . Arizona weather is such that, most of the year, meetings could be held out-of-doors. The greatest point of struggle seems to be

the challenge of refusing to respond to growth in any way
that would result in dilution of the level of interaction and
fellowship. At present, the group is moving toward discovery
and development of more pastor-gifted leaders. Their dream
is to begin a sister house church when there are at least two
leaders who are equipped to serve as its elders.

A POCKET COMMUNITY

There is a tiny, intense module of living community happening right down the street from me, where the Wilkes and
Fergusons live. A growing relationship and deepening commitment grew between these two families (both a part of our
local church and very much dedicated to the renewal process). They decided to be closer together, geographically, so
that what they believed was mutually beneficial (sharing of
their lives) could be a daily experience, a whole-life experience. So they sold their homes (one in North Scottsdale and
the other fifteen miles of city driving away in Tempe) —
homes each family had occupied for several years—and
purchased a house and three adjacent lots in Scottsdale.
The Wilkes own the house and one lot. The Fergusons own
the other two lots, and on one of them they built a home.
Rod Wilke supervised the construction of Fergusons' house.
The remaining lots are intended for expansion of the community. They share yard equipment, cars, a swimming pool,
and everyday's ordinary happenings. At least once a week
they share a meal together. Most weeks it's more than one.
They are available to each other whenever needed. And
while they maintain ownership of their possessions, all things
are considered the property of the members of the community. (In addition, they readily make what they have available to the larger community, the local church.)

About a year ago they took into their extended family a
very troubled young woman. She was in such a deep state
of depression that she would spend days in bed, simply because she could not face life. Subconsciously rejecting even

the sound of her own voice, she was unable to speak above a whisper. A psychiatrist felt that a loving, supporting family could provide the best opportunity for building self-esteem. In fact, without it, they could see little hope. After a year in this environment, she was able to speak, got a job teaching school part time, and was becoming a valued member of the church.

It was not to be a totally happy experience (though we have not yet seen the end of the story). An old psychosis returned, leading to intense verbal abuse and even occasional violence to those who were near her, and it seemed necessary that she be removed from the community to a psychiatric hospital. The families battled a deep sense of failure and inner conflict. The struggle to arrive at consensus about what to do in this situation produced a temporary strain between them that tested their commitment to each other. The community survived. And promply took into their midst, a very lonely young man.

With whatever limitations and lacks may be apparent, in terms of size, discipline, human weakness, and level of commonality of goods, this "pocket of community" is providing a good, visible model for the entire local church, of what it may mean to live our lives together. That is tremendously important, since one of the greatest hindrances to bringing the kind of change needed in the church is the lack of models to follow.

COMMUNITY AND ABANDONMENT

There is yet a line between what is being experienced in most of our little churches and the full experience of New Testament *koinonia* (i.e., to live in common) as described in Acts 2 and 4 and 2 Corinthians 8. It is the line of abandonment.

> abandon, verb: to give up with the intent of never again claiming a right or interest in.[16]

Acts 4:32–35 offers a cameo of the early church "over the line":

Wherever Two or Three Hang Together

All the believers were one in heart and mind. No one claimed that any of his possessions was his own, but they shared everything they had. With great power the apostles continued to testify to the resurrection of the Lord Jesus, and much grace was with them all. There were no needy persons among them. For from time to time those who owned lands or houses sold them, brought the money from the sales and put it at the apostles' feet, and it was distributed to anyone as he had need.

Some of us make an occasional excursion over the line, but we usually slip back to a safer distance—where the air is less threatening and our possessions and privacy are more secure. As a temporary condition, it is all right. God understands our reticence to pioneer in such a no-man's land. But He still holds in mind the dream of His people living in complete oneness, valuing each other more than anything, needing each other more than pride of possessions, clinging to each other as though they were seeing in one another's faces the face of the Lord.

I do not believe the fulfillment of this prophetic dream depends on *everyone* moving next door to or in the same apartment complex with everyone else. But clustering is desirable. And such pockets of community should and will spring up, more and more, as economic, emotional, and spiritual needs demand, and as the Spirit moves people in that direction. But for the whole church to live as the Acts kind of community, it is essential for individual and corporate priorities and schedules to shift radically . . . until time is found for groups of us to spend time together more often than weekly—daily, if possible. Until more meals (not elaborate entertaining affairs, but simple family meals) are shared together. Until strangers are more enthusiastically welcomed into our homes, etc.

Abandonment means we have come to see each other as kin, have committed ourselves to build that relationship at almost any cost, and have relinquished claim to all we have, in order to assume unlimited liability for and total availability to the other members of Christ's body.

It can start wherever two or three hang together.

BOOKS ON GROUPS

Gordon Cosby's *Handbook for Mission Groups* (Waco: Word Books, 1975) is an excellent source of direction concerning task-focussed groups. Its value goes well beyond group life, in that it well-defines the church's primary task as the calling forth of the uniqueness of each person. David Mains' description of the "modules" at Chicago's Circle Church, contained in *Full Circle* (Waco: Word Books, 1972) may also be helpful for mission groups.

A sound, clear handbook for leaders of nurture groups, written from the viewpoint of the professional psychologist is *Growth Groups* by Howard Clinebell (Nashville: Abingdon, 1972). The first three chapters are a practical guide to answers to questions about basic group dynamics. In my book, *Brethren, Hang Loose* (Grand Rapids: Zondervan, 1972, pp. 123–152) is given a picture of the history and function of "The Little Churches" of Our Heritage Church.

Two books detailing the philosophy and function of the Yokefellow Groups are *The Art of Understanding Yourself* by Cecil Osborne (Grand Rapids: Zondervan, 1967) and *Prayer Can Change Your Life* by William Parker and Elaine St. Johns (New York: Cornerstone Library Publications, 1957).

Larry Richards has authored several books that either deal directly with group life (especially groups for Bible study) or provide growth-stimulating biblical studies: (1) *"69 Ways to Start a Bible Study Group and Keep it Growing"* (Grand Rapids: Zondervan, 1972). (2) *Becoming One In The Spirit* (Wheaton: Victor Books, 1973), (3) *Born to Grow* Wheaton: Victor Books, 1974), and (5) the *Bible Alive* series, a twelve-volume teaching/learning tool covering the whole Bible, published by David C. Cook. In addition, he has published three major works which include sections showing where Bible study groups fit into the whole scheme of church life and Christian education, and giving sound instruction on their use: (1) *A Theology of Christian Education* (Grand Rapids: Zondervan, 1975), (2) *Creative Bible Study* (Grand Rapids: Zondervan, 1970), (3) *A New Face for the Church* (Grand Rapids, Zondervan, 1971).

The *Serendipity Books,* by Lyman Coleman, are an overflowing reservoir of ideas for relational games and Bible studies designed to introduce groups to a relational meeting style. A few of our groups have used these studies as "curriculum" on occasion, but their normal use with us has been as leaders have dipped into the Coleman idea-bank to find the right tool to bring a group back from the conceptual to the personal.

Stimulating books on "community" are Graham Pulkingham's *They Left Their Nets* (New York: Morehouse-Barlow Co., 1973, distributed by Logos International, Plainfield, New Jersey), Ronald Sider's *Rich Christians in an Age of Hunger* (Downers Grove: InterVarsity Press, 1977), and *Life Together* by Dietrich Bonhoeffer (New York: Harper and Row, 1954).

In addition to these books, the monthly magazine, *Faith at Work* (11065 Little Patuxent Parkway, Columbia, MD 21044) includes a regular section called "Ideas for Groups."

Notes

[1]Numbers 12:8.

[2]Ronald J. Sider, *Rich Christians in an Age of Hunger* (Downers Grove: InterVarsity Press, 1977), p. 103.

[3]*The Analytical Greek Lexicon* (Grand Rapids: Zondervan, 1970), p. 235. I have deleted Scripture references from the definitions, for easier reading.

[4]Ibid.

[5]Ibid.

[6]Acts 2:44–46.

[7]2 Corinthians 8:4.

[8]Phillip Schaff, *The History of the Christian Church,* p. 167.

[9]Ibid., p. 168.

[10]See Matthew 25:31–46.

[11]Schaff, *Christian Church,* p. 168.

[12]Howard Clinebell, *Growth Groups* (Nashville: Abingdon, 1972), p. 21.

[13]*Webster's New Collegiate Dictionary.*

[14]Clinebell, *Growth Groups,* p. 14.

[15]Dietrich Bonhoeffer, *Life Together* (New York: Harper and Row, 1954), pp. 100–103.

[16]*New Collegiate Dictionary.*

9

No Needy Persons
Among Them

Ten dozen trembling disciples unexpectedly found themselves the center of the city's attention. They had burst out of the upper room with strange, unlearned syllables tumbling out of their mouths, telling the flocking international crowd the marvels of God's working. And with liberated native tongues they convincingly preached the resurrection and return of Jesus Christ.

People listened. Trusted the living Jesus. And upon believing received the gift of the Holy Spirit.

All who believed—some 3120—were magnetically drawn together by hunger to know Him on whom they had believed. They gathered to hear apostles repeat the words of Jesus. They heard what He had done, what He was now doing, what He had claimed, and what He had promised.

In response, they loved each other. Jesus was living His "new commandment" in them. In the Spirit, they discovered that they were a family. A very poor family.

The family came into being in a context of poverty and deprivation. To begin with, the city of Jerusalem had more than its share of poor people. Impoverished beggars flooded the temple area, hoping to take advantage of the heightened generosity of feast-goers (who believed it to be especially meritorious to give alms in the Holy City on feast days). Older people, many of them poor, came to the city in unusual numbers to wait for death or the Messiah. Rabbis migrated to the Holy City—unpaid teachers living on contributions—followed by their religious students, who also were unusually poor.[1] When the gospel exploded in the heart of the city, among the people who gladly received it were hundreds of the penniless and mendicant.

Then add to these "residents" hundreds of uprooted pilgrims, who had come for the Feast of Pentecost, found Messiah, and stayed on to become a part of the dynamic new community that quickly developed among His followers. In all probability many of these travelers, staying beyond their planned departure dates, ran out of money, and flooded the Jerusalem job market beyond its saturation point.

Surrounded by unusual need, the young church (without recorded hesitation) plunged into a life together of costly sharing. They accepted "unconditional economic liability for, and total financial availability to, other brothers and sisters in Christ."[2]

In the Spirit of Jesus, they opened their hearts to one another, and began to give. They were "together." Every day. The "apostles' teaching" was part of it. But time was also spent in "fellowship." The word is *koinonia,* (i.e. . . sharing, communication, conversation, interaction, giving, and receiving). They *interacted.* They were together in a way that exposed each to the others, where the real needs of real persons become apparent. This personal involvement made it impossible to shrug off the deprivation of those who had become members of one's family.

Necessity and love combined to produce a special spiritual adventure: *they shared all things in common.* When a need arose among them, they had not yet learned to say, "Tsk, tsk. Isn't that too bad. We'll pray for you." The thrust of the biblical narrative gives the impression that, if the resources to minister to the shared need were available, in pocket or purse, in an old sock, or stuffed in a mattress, the response was to cheerfully "shell out." Or, if the need was for socks or mattress, and extras were available, they were given. Or if the brother could not use a mattress because he had no room in which to put it, he was taken in and became part of the family. If the need was for money to buy food, to pay a fine, or to pay the rent, and there was no ready cash, some surplus item was sold to raise the cash (perhaps the old black and white TV set in the "rec" room, or . . .). And, if the need was as stubborn as it was in A.D. 32, when the minor surplus items were cleaned out, the next step was to put a "For Sale" sign on the summer cabin in the woods, or on the extra car. Then, because there were still unmet needs, many were led by the Holy Spirit to double up: they moved in with each other for an intimate and powerful level of *koinonia,* and one sold his house and gave the money away!

Private ownership was not looked down upon as "less spiritual" nor was the practice ended. People still "possessed" things (Acts 4:32). A rare phenomenon of early church life was that they sensed their oneness so powerfully that all came to treat the things they possessed as though they belonged to each other. Everyone was joyfully participating in some way in the loving community of goods (Acts 4:32–35).

And none was without a family. Loneliness was being effectively replaced by community. Insecurity was practically destroyed. They knew they were accepted and loved. The crippled, the blind, the retarded, the outcast, the epileptic, the eccentric—all found a home in the church. All were healed or in the process of healing.

As a result, "There were no needy persons among them!" Together, rich and poor, the spiritual family made its material and spiritual resources available. It was enough.

Was this a once-in-history happening never intended to be repeated? Or is it a vital though unfulfilled part of the promise of the gospel?

The fact is, the radical Jerusalem event came in *direct*

response to the teachings of Jesus.

JESUS ON MATERIAL THINGS

Jesus' thinking about material things is in direct antithesis to the usual way people (even Christians) view them.

He once said to His friends, "How hard it is for the rich to enter the kingdom of God!" (Mark 10:23). They were amazed. Under the Old Testament they had been taught, conversely, that material prosperity was evidence of God's blessing; poverty proof of God's punishment for the unspiritual. So He emphasized the point: "It is easier for a camel to go through the eye of a needle than for a rich man to enter the kingdom of God." He does not say it is wrong to be rich. He simply says that wealth and material security are hindrances to spiritual life.

On another occasion, Jesus warned that delight in riches and concern for worldly things has the dangerous potential of choking the life out of the seed of the gospel planted in a person's heart (Matt. 13:22).

The cadre of men around Him consisted of family men, business men, and wage earners. Each had the responsibilities, needs, and desires that are common to such men. Still Jesus said to them:

> Sell your possessions and give to the poor. Provide purses for yourselves that will not wear out, a treasure in heaven that will not be exhausted, where no thief comes near and no moth destroys. For where your treasure is, there your heart will be also (Luke 12: 33–34).

To the same men, and all who choose to follow Him, He said further:

> Give to everyone who asks you, and if anyone takes what belongs to you, do not demand it back (Luke 6:30–31).

Our evaluation of the comparative value of poverty and wealth is usually out of step with His. We can glimpse it in this preamble to His instructions to His disciples on how to handle material things:

> Blessed are you who are poor,
>   for yours is the kingdom of God.
> Blessed are you who hunger now,
>   for you will be satisfied . . .
> But woe to you who are rich,
>   for you have already received your comfort.
> Woe to you who are well fed now,
>   for you will go hungry (Luke 6:20–21, 24–25).

Jesus had the discomforting habit of talking in disdainful terms about our attachment to material things.

Wealth is trouble.

It gets in one's way when one wants to see the kingdom.

It hinders one when one wants to go with God.

To be poor is a great blessing.

> It can make one hungry for God.

> It makes it necessary for one to depend on God.

To sell what one has and/or give it away

> to feed the hungry, clothe the naked, lift the oppressed,
> is a great opportunity—
> good preparation for Christ's coming.[3]

When His enemies yelled "He is crazy!"[4] they did so with good reason. He stubbornly insisted on turning world-shaped value systems upside down.

Jesus compared the value of the human soul with all the amassed wealth, power, and glory of the entire world system and forthrightly declared: When you have a choice between keeping your soul and getting all the world can offer—better choose to attend to the needs of your soul. The whole world is not enough to pay what it's worth (Mark 8:35–37).

Since that is true, the great concerns of life are the spiritual concerns. Of concern for material things, Jesus, the radical, says, "Forget it!"

"Look," He says, "your Father in heaven is going to take care of you. He's going to see to it that you are fed, clothed, and watered. So, with a Father like that, you ought to stop worrying about food, clothes, drinks, and bills. Stop worrying about the future. Make one thing the all-consuming passion of your life—the kingdom-community of God and His righteousness—and all that you need will be added to you" (Matt. 6:25–34).

Not everyone is told to "sell all and give it to the poor." (Some are.) But care of the needy is to be part of each disciples' handling of personal possessions. Everyone in His spiritual family—even the poor themselves—are called upon to share what they have with needy others.

MODELING THE TEACHING

Not only did He preach the gospel of unconcern for the things of the world and of generosity, He was the full-color, wide-screen, multi-dimensional, living-breathing, moving picture of the concepts He taught.

The Old Testament prophets created anticipation that Emmanuel would be recognizable by His interest in the needy and oppressed. One Sabbath in Nazareth, at the commencement of His ministry, Jesus bowled over His assembled neighbors and relatives by reading Isaiah 61:1–2, and claiming to personally be its fulfillment. The passage announced that Messiah's ministry will focus on the needy . . .

the poor,
the bound,
the bruised,
the blind,
the spiritually and physically maimed,
the sick,
the sinful,
the alienated,
the rejected,
the separated from God.

Jesus Himself was a poor man. This impression is deeply stamped on the memory of the early church, and preserved in the Gospels. The night of His birth was spent in a stable. The offering made at His dedication was the offering the law allowed only for the poorest—two tiny squabs (Luke 2:24). His earthly father, Joseph, died before Jesus ministry began, leaving the eldest son with a fatherless family for which to care. One who boasted "I will follow you wherever you go," was warned, "Foxes have holes the birds of the air have nests, but the Son of Man has no place to lay his head" (Luke 9:57).

Walking through grain fields one Saturday, Jesus' disciples plucked heads of grain, rubbed them with their hands and ate the raw kernels (Mark 2:23). They weren't stealing. Deuteronomy 23:25 tells the poor in Israel that they may walk through a neighbor's field doing just that. They were not allowed to go in with a sickle and get rich at a neighbor's expense, but they could eat to keep body and soul together. It was a provision to keep the poor from starving to death. Jesus needed it, and took advantage of it.

All His travels were on foot. When He rode in triumphal entry into Jerusalem, He rode astride a borrowed ass. Many of His teachings came in the form of table talks while He was guest in someone's home. He received no salary for His ministry. He collected no store of savings or holdings. No one was ever excluded from His "services" because they could not pay. He was never given an honorarium for His message, His healing, His ministry of deliverance, His counsel, or His prophetic teaching. He never charged a fee. He never accepted one. As far as we know, His only possessions were the robe on His body and the sandals on His feet.

When He sent out workers He expected them to operate the same way. "You have received without pay," He reminded the Twelve in His commissioning, "Give without pay" (Matt. 10:8).

FULL GOSPEL BUSINESS

Concern for the poor, the deprived, the troubled, the sick, the neglected, and the alienated was definitely not incidental to Jesus' ministry. It was *why* He came.

He was headed for the cross. There He would reconcile mankind to God. But the language of His life style says that raising a man's spirit to new life, saving his soul from destruction and calling him to live close to God, without touching the situation in his home, the hunger in his stomach, the pain that is ravaging his spirit, the hang-up that is defeating him, or the failure that is crushing him, would be inconsistent and unthinkable. A person is not spirit only. He is a whole being—mind and body too. Sin, for which Jesus died, has touched *every* aspect of *every* person's life situation. Redemption is short-sheeted (a cruel joke) unless it also touches all of life as it really is.

The promise of the gospel is that God's cleansing action in Jesus Christ can and will save the whole man (1 Thess. 5:23–24). Total physical redemption waits for resurrection morning (1 Cor. 15). Until then, weakness, sickness, and failure will be part of our Christian experience. The surrounding world will remain our enemy. But the announcement of the kingdom, the victory and fulfillment to come, includes the good news that the world is to be given a glimpse of it now.

So Jesus preached, "Be changed, for the kingdom of heaven is near." And as He preached, He also touched, forgave, healed, liberated, and lifted. He said to the poor, "Come with Me and see the kingdom." Those who did not stumble over Him became part of the "advance contingent" of the kingdom on earth. They were formed, by the power of the Holy Spirit, into a community of love and sharing. Their needs were met. Working together they met the needs of others, until "there were no needy persons among them." *Through each other* the living Jesus offered them food when hungry, forgiveness when guilty, healing when sick, companionship when lonely, a place of belonging

176

when they didn't fit, a shelter when outcast, a coat when cold, love when hated, strength when weakened, protection when under attack.

The way they lived together was no strange, unrepeatable spiritual mutation, the expression of an early "lunatic fringe." It was a direct response to Jesus' teaching and modeling. It was and is His plan for the community of the people of God.

"NOW, CONCERNING THE COLLECTION"

When the New Testament church collected money, it was always (with no exception that I have found) to meet the needs of people. Paul, in several places (Phil. 4:10–19; 1 Cor. 9; 1 Tim. 5:18), discusses supply of the needs of Christian workers (apostles, elders, etc.). Giving to make it possible for gifted Christian workers to give more of their time to ministry, was an affirmed practice of the early church. This, however, was no departure from the principle that giving is to supply people-needs. Most teaching about money in the primitive church centered in a concern for the needs of the deprived.

Offerings for the poor became prominent in the Book of Acts. The whole point of "sharing everything in common" and "selling their possessions" was for "distribution to any-one who had need." The selection of the seven men to "serve tables" in Acts 6, was to care for this distribution. Acts 11:29–30 records that later, at a time of crop failure and famine in Judea, a significant gift from the predominantly Gentile church in Antioch was sent to the hungry Christian Jews there. When Paul was arrested in Jersualem, in Acts 21, he was there bringing a large sacrificial offering from the gentile churches to help the struggling Hebrew Christians buy food.

The care of needy brothers was a constant concern of Paul and the churches he founded. So much so, that Christian emergency relief expert Larry Ward draws the following conclusion for Christians of this decade:

> A church (whatever its denominational label) assumes responsibility for the poor and the hungry whenever it sets out to be a "New Testament Church in faith and practice."[5]

THE FAMINE OF '44

The recorded history of the primitive church contains this incident: A group of Christian preachers ("prophets") from Jerusalem came to the Roman city of Antioch to minister to the new and thriving church there. One of them, a man named Agabus, stood up among the gathered believers, and with special insight from the Holy Spirit, predicted that a severe famine would spread over the entire Roman world (Acts 11:28). Even before he shared his revelation, in A.D. 44, severe drought was already producing crop failures in a few scattered provinces. Agabus adds the dimension that it was going to be a world-wide problem.

Famine came. Thirteen years of it. Touching many parts of the empire and the lives of millions of people, between A.D. 41 and 54.

The church in Antioch listened to the Lord as He spoke through Agabus. They remembered the poverty already existing among their brothers and sisters in Jerusalem and Judea. This young, committed, heterogeneous band of Jewish and gentile, rich and poor believers immediately decided to sent help—a gift to feed their forever family members at "first church." The plan was for each of them to give to the proportion of his ability. Saul and Barnabas would carry this spontaneous expression of love and spiritual unity from the Antiochan brothers to the elders at Jerusalem—to meet the nutritional needs of the partners there.

The drama of human need and Christian response was to become the hallmark of the Christian community for the next three centuries.

Long after the worst of the famine was over and the empire's economy had begun to recover, the saints in Jerusalem were still in a desperate struggle to survive. Several years of severe drought had practically inundated food supplies in Israel. Food had to be shipped in from other parts of the world, then to be purchased by the Jews. If you were among the very poor, there was no money to buy the expensive imported food, and the persistent specter of starvation hovered over your existence. In addition, the poverty of the Jerusalem Christians was intensified by severe persecution and open harassment, which often included confiscation of property (Acts 8:1–3; 9:29; 12:1–5; 23:12–15; Heb. 10:34). Undoubtedly there were also subtle forms of job and business discrimination that created additional economic pressure. The result was that the Judean Christian community was left in desperate straits. They needed help to meet even the most basic of human needs.[6]

Paul carries the message of their need wherever he goes. Both his letters and the historical narrative tell of his continuing efforts to maintain a flow of funds to the Hebrew hungry.

His continuing concern triggers the Spirit-fired development in the apostle's heart and mind of the *New Covenant Theology of Giving*—active material *koinonia*. It runs through his writing like the ripple in a parfait sundae, and becomes concentrated in 2 Corinthians 8 and 9, his longest and most poignant appeal for Jerusalem-directed generosity.

During more than a decade of famine, one of the hardest hit areas was the province called Macedonia. And in A.D. 57 (the time of Paul's writing the second Corinthian letter) the Macedonian economy was still reeling from the effects of the prolonged food shortage. It's a detail that makes the story Paul tells in the first five verses of chapter 8 even more amazing.

Paul had been reluctant to accept a gift from people who were themselves struggling with hunger and privation, because he knew they were going beyond their ability to give. And yet, the Macedonians begged Paul for the privilege of making themselves even poorer, in order to save the lives of hungry fellow believers in Judea, and to experience community with them.[7]

Is this not another example of imprudent fanaticism? Does the Lord want His people to be so worldly unwise as to deepen their own misery to give for the temporal needs of people they have never seen and from whom they will apparently gain nothing in return? Generosity is not for the poor, is it? Is not this "Macedonian madness" an act of unthinking sentimentalism?

On the contrary, the apostle insists that this is the normal Christian life. Almost his next word (8:9) is to remind his readers of how their Lord Jesus set precisely that kind of example. The model for generosity is no millionaire philanthropist giving impressive amounts away while carefully protecting his own lavish life style, but the Son of God, who gave Himself poor, so that through His poverty we might be made rich!

The Macedonians cannot be dismissed as foolish or imprudent. They, like the first church in Jerusalem, were merely looking at the model.

HELLO, JESUS, CAN I HELP?

There is another important motivation that led the early church to assume responsibility and liability for each other. It was mentioned briefly in the preceding chapter, in connection with a historical quotation telling of the ministry of Christian women "to visit the Lord, to clothe Him, and give Him meat and drink, in the person of His needy disciples."[8]

Cyprian of Carthage came to Christ around the middle of the third century. After his conversion in his mid-forties, he sold all his land holdings and gave the money to the poor. Later as a church leader, he collected a hundred thousand sestertia ($3000) to purchase the release of Christians who had been kidnapped by neighboring Barbarians. He wrote that it was a great privilege "to be able to ransom for a small

sum of money Him, who has redeemed us from the domin-
ion of Satan with His own blood."[9]

The original Christians saw their care of poor and captive
brothers as direct ministry to Jesus Himself. They had heard
Jesus say it. It is preserved for us in Matthew 25:31–46. The
heart of the passage is verse 40:

> I tell you the truth, whatever you did for one of the least of
> these brothers of mine, you did it for me.

It could be called the principle of Incarnation. Or, if you
prefer, of Identification.

The way our Lord so completely identifies Himself with
His people is a great mystery. He and His people become
"one flesh" (Eph. 5:31–32). When a person believes on
Jesus as Savior and acknowledges Him as Lord, he is baptized (placed into) Christ and into His body and into His
Spirit (Rom. 6:3–7; 1 Cor. 12:13). God places him into
union with Christ. He is one with Christ. And Christ is one
with him. God no longer sees him as separate from Christ.
He is now seen and known as "in Christ." He is to see
himself that way. No longer separated. One with the Son.

It goes even further. At the same moment we enter into
union with Christ, we are baptized (placed into) His body.
We are immersed in a mystical union with one another. We
are, hence, to see one another as one with Christ. Our spiritual brothers and sisters are alive in and completely identified with Jesus, and Jesus is alive in and completely identified with them.

Now, with spiritual eyes, we are to see our brothers and
sisters in God's family—"the least" of them, the weakest,
most immature, and least worthy—as *Jesus!* Can this be
true? When I look at my brother I see his sin, his failure, and
his faults. I am irritated, prejudiced, and threatened by him.
He is inconsistent, uncommitted, selfish, and tries my patience. I do not find him lovable. And yet I am to see him as
Jesus coming into my life! That is exactly how far the Bible
takes the principle.

Matthew 25:40 and 45 is not the first nor last passage to speak it.

Proverbs 19:17—

He who is kind to the poor lends to the LORD.

Proverbs 14:31—

He who oppresses the poor shows contempt for their Maker, but whoever is kind to the needy honors God.

Matthew 10:40, Jesus, to His disciples—

He who receives you receives me, and he who receives me receives the one who sent me.

Matthew 18:5, Jesus to His disciples, on humility—

Whoever welcomes a little child like this in my name welcomes me.

Luke 10:16, Jesus to the seventy of His followers being commissioned—

He who listens to you listens to me; he who rejects you rejects me; but he who rejects me rejects him who sent me.

John 13:20, Jesus, at the Last Supper—

I tell you the truth, whoever accepts anyone I sent accepts me; and whoever accepts me accepts the one who sent me.

1 Corinthians 6:15—

Do you not know that your bodies are members of Christ himself?

Acts 9:5, Jesus, to Paul on the Damascus road—

I am Jesus, whom you are persecuting.

To persecute those who believe is to persecute Jesus. Jesus and His followers are inseparable. Touch a disciple and it is the Lord you touch. What is being done to the least of His friends, is being done to Jesus.

Not long after I began to see this principle in Scripture, the phone rang in the middle of the night. As I sat on the edge of the bed, forcing my sleep-weighted eyes to half-mast, listening to the troubled voice on the line, my vocal chords said the person's name, but my thoughts were saying, silently, "Hello, Jesus. What's the problem? Can I help?"

This insight constitutes a powerful motivation for responding to the needs of others—for giving, bearing, visiting, touching, healing, forgiving, sharing, caring, freeing, and for laying down one's life for fellow believers.

OUR GIVING PILGRIMAGE

I cannot share a glowing account of how our congregation has taken all these teachings and principles in hand, and has gone on to become the paragon of generosity—the twentieth-century fulfillment of all that the New Testament teaches about community, stewardship, and the eleemosynary arts. But it may be helpful to follow our trail of congregational responses to financial circumstances, the teachings of the Word, and what we have been hearing as the voice of the Spirit. I confess that our responses are not very close to "abandonment." But they demonstrate how God has seemed to deal with us in a continuing process of change.

From early on, we have operated church financial affairs on three basic assumptions, each based on Scripture.

(1) *God has promised that He will supply the church's needs:*

> My God shall supply all your need, according to his riches in glory, by Christ Jesus. (Phil. 4:19 KJV)

(2) *All giving is to be free from the pressure of guilt and carnal manipulation of any kind.*

> Each man should give what he has decided in his heart to give, not reluctantly or under compulsion, for God loves a cheerful giver. (2 Cor. 9:7)

(3) *When there is a financial shortage, God is trying to teach us something.* One day there was a shortage in the temple treasury (or they were afraid there might be one), so some "volunteers" came to Jesus' disciples for the "required" contribution. Peter, aware of the emptiness of the young kingdom community's common purse, came to Jesus

with the problem. Peter did not realize that what he had was not a problem at all but a wonderful opportunity for something special from God.

Jesus gave Peter two things from God. First, He used the opportunity to teach His disciples about their freedom from the demands of men, namely, that they were not obligated to contribute to the maintenance of the temple. On the other hand, they were free to contribute, in order to keep the door open to the hearts of their Jewish contemporaries who might be offended by freedom they could not understand. Second, Jesus gave Peter an opportunity to watch as God miraculously supplied something to give. At Jesus' instructions, Peter went to the sea and threw in a hook. A fish grabbed it. Peter reeled it in. When he opened the fish's mouth, the money necessary for the voluntary contribution was there (Matt. 17:24–27). The shortage had a purpose. The Lord had an important lesson to teach and He wanted to demonstrate His Father's ability to supply what is needed for His followers to be givers.

These assumptions have led us to reject some commonly accepted elements of typical church fund raising. Here are two examples:

"Storehouse tithing." "Normal" evangelical church life includes the use of strong encouragement, buttressed with some pretty hard-to-avoid Old Testament texts, to motivate members to bring to the church ten percent of all they earn for the purpose of financing local operation. In our local church we have chosen to place little or no emphasis on "storehouse tithing." The prime reason being that the New Testament places little or no emphasis on it. We think that is reason enough that the church should not. It is not that tithing has no place in the life of the Christian, nor that it is unbiblical. The gracious principles involved in tithing are carried over into the New Covenant, not as laws to be obeyed under threat of penalty, but as a spirit of generosity that is so liberal and self-giving that it can only flow from agape-love.

And ten percent is too limited a figure to describe the response of genuine love.

"Spiritualization." (Or perhaps more accurately "mythologization.") This is the process by which pastors, church treasurers, and pressured board members, seek to motivate people to give or to pledge, by making it sound as though giving one's money to "this church" is the highest act of personal commitment to God. As a reward for participation in the current year's fund drive, one is led to believe he will receive God's special blessing (and furthermore, participation may be the only way to escape the sickness, poverty, and despair God may allow to descend upon non participants!) Of course, I'm overstating the case—though I have heard appeals that were not far from that. It is common to tell Christians that their giving proves their love for Christ, their loyalty to the church, and their obedience to the Holy Spirit. The Sunday "collection" is spiritualized by giving it sanctified names, like "Worship in Tithes and Offerings." (We hope it will be worship. Failing that, let it at least pay the bills.)

In addition to these two, we have had serious questions about other things—the "annual stewardship drive," the "every-member canvass," and even the public passing of the offering plates. They all seem to carry nonverbal messages and rely on motivations which are not consistent with the basic biblical assumptions. Guilt as motivation, appeal to carnal desires, social pressure, and the implied threat of nonacceptance are too frequently a part of these accepted approaches to financial stewardship. Such pressures as these exclude love, stifle trust, by-pass the personal leadership and motivation of the Holy Spirit. The giving acts can just as readily flow from the "lust of the flesh, the lust of the eyes, and the pride of life," as from love, trust, and the Holy Spirit. If the New Testament is clear on anything, it is on the fact that the only works from our lives that have eternal significance—true spiritual value before God—are works that flow from love, trust, and the Holy Spirit.

So, in our mission to set people free to walk in the Spirit, we began early to question and to retreat from stewardship motivations that could lead to works (giving, etc.) without true spiritual value.

I invite you to walk with me through our "giving pilgrimage." Don't look for perfection along this trial—watch for signs of progress.

Our Heritage Church was started in the spring of 1965 by a pastor (me) committed to building a super-church. He was a trained manipulator of people, a "PR" man, who came to the pastorate after five years as a professional fund raiser. The church was "successful," programmed to the hilt, and over its head in debt from day one.

In the fall of 1967 (two and one-half years later), the pastor experienced the beginning of a dramatic and thorough personal reorientation away from "dependence on the flesh" (things done by human power and skill apart from the activity of God) toward complete "dependence on the Spirit." At that point he began to teach and to lead the church from the new basic personal conviction that all God wants the church to do and to be will be produced in it if we concentrate on keeping people alive to the Holy Spirit; the Spirit will do in and through them what God wants if we give Him room to do it. This, he believed, would include witness, evangelism, prayer, works—and giving.

This new conviction had an immediate effect on teaching related to financial stewardship. The pastor began to see his role as dealing with causes instead of symptoms. If people are not giving as they should the solution is not to create pressure or to manipulate the flesh to respond to the need, but to deal with the spiritual life of the congregation, their love, their dependence on the Lord, their capacity to respond to the voice of the Holy Spirit. If giving is in the Spirit's heart, then when people are alive to Him and filled with Him they will give, in response to Him!

No Needy Persons Among Them

The financial history of Our Heritage Church has been that we are always either barely making it or in real trouble. February and July are inevitably the worst months of the year. After the new conviction that the Holy Spirit had to do anything that really counted in the church, we were perpetually in financial difficulty.

Church board meetings were "wonderful" times spent wrestling with the specter of "certain financial disaster" that always hovered over the place. Fifteen hundred dollars in past due bills was not an occasional dilemma, but a persistent plague! Repeatedly someone would propose that the problem be solved by going back to the old "tried and true" approaches that had been so much a part of our previous church experiences: "every-member canvass" and all those other delightful methods of manipulating people. Some of us were determined to see what would happen if we were to deal with the problem on the basis of prayer and faith, leaving it to the Holy Spirit to move His people to give them a purpose of heart to be generous. Then, the church board would spend two hours debating church finances and five minutes praying about them. This ritual was repeated monthly.

A RADICAL STEP OF FAITH

I, for one, was getting tired of the hassle. After all, had not God promised He would supply our needs? We talked about faith easily. But it was foreign to the way we lived. No institutional church in its right mind deals with financial problems like the ones we were facing by praying and believing. You have to do something. Something that has worked for other churches. Something to put pressure on people. No matter how often we went back over the principle "God will do in and through us all He desires if we will concentrate on keeping filled with His Spirit . . . ," still, every board meeting was an agonizing wallow in the muck of shortages, needed cuts, those awful people who aren't doing their share, etc. ad nauseam. We often spoke of Philippians 4:19, but we never could quite believe.

As our local dollar gap widened, God began to speak through the stubborn crisis in a radical way. I shared with Ron Rogers (then assistant pastor) and with Audrey what I thought I heard Him saying. They confirmed what I was feeling and committed themselves to go along on a daring step of faith. It took two months to convince the board to go along. But, finally convinced that God had told us to do this thing, they consented. Beginning that month all other church expenses and obligations would be paid first; then if there was anything left, it would be divided between the two pastors' families, up to certain limits. We would trust God to keep His promise and to supply our families' needs from His riches in glory. Furthermore, we asked the board members not to share this plan with anyone outside the board meetings. And, finally, it was agreed that if there were financial shortages, shortages in salaries, etc., the board would respond, not with lengthy discussion as in the past, but by praying together about it.

It was an exciting experience! In the first place, the past due bills were all paid the first month and we were not behind again for two years. The two pastors received full salary only two or three times during that two-year period. Some months there was as little as $200 to be divided between the two families. But never before had I seen a church board take such loving personal interest in how I was making it financially. They cared. And they prayed. When the temptation to indulge in the old-style money-discussions got too strong, they elected a "financial projection committee," and turned all money matters over to the committee. The committee, in turn, was charged with one responsibility in relation to financial problems: they were to meet regularly to pray. That is all.

Each month we would share with the board how God was supplying our needs. And He was. In our family we even took in four nieces and nephews for three months of this time. We were amazed at how the Father, through His people, suppled the groceries needed. And the abundant supply of really good clothes for the children, kept us gasping with excited thanks-giving. People who had no idea of the situation we were in gave generously of food and other gifts. There was a phenomenal difference in family attitudes toward everything God provided. The prayers of both children and adults around our family table expressed a reality of gratitude beyond anything we'd felt before. All sensed our direct dependence on the heavenly Father and came to see everything as coming from Him. At the end of eighteen months both the Girards and the Rogers were amazed at what had happened. In both families, for the first time since we'd been married, all our bills were paid (at least up to date) and both had savings accounts containing several hundred dollars. (The fact that part of God's method of supply was through providing a job for Debbie Rogers, and the first royalties on my first book, did not dilute the sense of miracle.)

In the board meetings another miraculous thing happened. When we talked about faith there was a hopeful measure of understanding. We now knew what it was. We were all watching God work in response to our faith. So, about midway through those two years, the church leaders decided to take another step of faith, to move a bit closer to full dependence on the Holy Spirit in the lives of our people. At that point we stopped passing the offering plates in the meetings and placed them at the door. As I recall, there were three reasons for doing this at that time: (1) to give more time for personal sharing in the worship service, (2) to reduce the place of money in the church's public presentation of itself (the world is confused by the church's constant demand for money), and (3) to demonstrate in a concrete way our dependence on the Holy Spirit to move His people to give for the needs of the church without the artificial pressure of the passing plate.

DISCOVERING BIBLICAL PRIORITIES

As we were beginning to settle in, secure in our new habits of faith, financial crisis struck again. For some reason, the pastors suddenly found it nearly impossible to live on the "leftovers." Even normally good months of church giving turned sour—and then came February!

God was again preparing us to listen.

We now had a new team of leaders—our first contingent of "elders." And (joy of joys!) they began to ask: "What is God trying to say to us? Is something wrong with our present approach to church finances? To giving? To financial priorities?"

Together, we began to search the Scriptures diligently in the face of the financial pressure. As we dug into Old Testament and New our attention was called to the biblical priorities for giving and spending through the church. Priorities came to center stage in our research because in our study of the giving passages we were each discovering that the Bible actually concentrates on a set of financial stewardship objectives that is radically different from the goals that had been guiding our church's ministry to that time. The Bible's sharing focus seemed to contradict the financial priorities of nearly every church with which any of us had ever had to do!

In the Old Testament history of God's involvement with the Hebrew people, tithing is taught.[10] Two-thirds of the tithe went to the temple to provide for its upkeep and its staff of priests. But according to Deuteronomy 14:28–29, every third year the whole tithe was used by each local community to minister to the practical needs (food, specifically) of two kinds of people: Levites (priests, special "spiritual workers") and people with special needs (the passage lists aliens, orphans, and widows). So one-third of the tithe was to go to special workers and the poor.

190

But the tenth (tithe) was only the beginning of God's instructions on sharing. There was the law of gleaning (Lev. 19:9–10). Everyone who had anything was a farmer. When harvest time came the corners of the fields were to be left unharvested and nothing dropped in the process was to be picked up, so that the poor (without farms of their own) could come into the harvested fields and glean for their own needs.

There are repeated references to the individual's and the community's responsibility to care for those in need in specific ways. In addition to tithing and gleaning there was the revolutionary law of the Year of Jubilee (Lev. 25), the fiftieth year, when all the land was to be redistributed to the families who had originally owned it. Therefore the poor would not always be poor but would have a chance to know fullness and plenty.

There was the law of the Sabbatical Year (every seventh year), one of the provisions of which was that all the slaves were to be freed and sent off with enough material goods to have a chance at a new start (Deut. 15:12–18). Another provision of the Sabbatical Year was that all the land was to lie fallow "that poor of your people may eat" (Exod. 23:10–11). The volunteer grain was to be left to be gathered by the poor.

There were the laws of lending to the poor to help them through their crises (Exod. 22:25). There was to be no interest charged on such loans. King Solomon said, "He who is kind to the poor lends to the LORD."

The priorities are clear . . . even in the Old Testament.

The New Testament's concentration on the objects of Christian giving are even more disturbing. We studied every passage we could find on money and giving in the New Testament and discovered a startling consistency.

Jesus' teachings include a scarce handful of references to giving for institutional purposes (i.e., the temple), including the story we looked at earlier (money in the fish's mouth).

But to each reference like that one there are a score in which He speaks of giving to meet the needs of the needy and each other. In Matthew 10:10 He places Christian workers on the priority list. Human need is the focus of nearly all Jesus' teaching on money.

In the Book of Acts and following, the entire concern of the early church (when it comes to giving) is for meeting the needs of (1) needy people and (2) Christian workers. *All* the references to and teachings about giving in the early church concentrate on one or both of these priorities. The focus is on meeting practical people needs: housing and food, companionship and family, the need for evangelism and spiritual equipping through God's gifted men who sometimes receive full or partial support to free them for ministry.

As we compared our church giving patterns with these teachings, the biblical aims stuck out in our study like birds of paradise in a weed patch.

The response of the elder team to these discoveries was to take immediate beginning steps to realign congregational attention to the biblical objectives. First, they moved the pastors' support from the last thing paid to the top of the monthly payment schedule. Second, they began to grapple with the development of a "ministry of helps." It was a time of high unemployment in our church, and we began to try to respond to some of those needs. Many mistakes were made, but a process was commenced toward a new broader commitment to minister to human needs. A third level of response came when we sold our second parsonage and a significant amount of the proceeds were given to evangelical agencies involved in feeding the world's hungry. Fourthly, the elders developed and published a statement of "Financial Policy," which is reprinted here in its entirety:

A FINANCIAL POLICY FOR A LOCAL CHURCH

1. We recognize responsible giving as a normal expression of the Spirit of Christ indwelling each believer.

2. Giving is a gift of the Holy Spirit, and is to be the free

and cheerful expression of loving hearts. Therefore, we feel that receiving gifts should be completely voluntary without resorting to the kind of pressures that might create situations in which people give out of fear of embarrassment, nonacceptance, or judgment, or to be seen by man.

3. The New Testament method of stimulating giving involves:

 a. Teaching people to be responsive to the voice of the Holy Spirit.
 b. Creating a climate in which relationships of love and mutual care can develop.
 c. Sharing of information concerning needs corporate and individual, domestic and foreign, institutional and personal.
 d. Exhortation, teaching, challenge to give (2 Cor. 8; 9).

4. The Living Church is not of the world, even though it is in the world. In the course of being the church, it must handle the things of the world (i.e., money and all physical property).

5. The church is not a business. Other motivations and commitments are more important and sway its decisions and policies to a greater degree than financial profit or loss, capital gains, etc. Often the church is called upon to take "steps of faith" or to obey a command of the Lord or to follow a priority or procedure that calls for usually acceptable business procedures to be set aside in favor of biblical imperatives.

6. The church must, in all it does, provide all things honest in the sight of all men at all times.

7. The Holy Spirit speaking through a consensus of the body always has the final word on church financial and property matters.

8. The New Testament sets two things as top priority targets for Christian giving:

 a. Support of Christian workers.
 b. Ministry to human needs.

It is not clear from Scripture which of these two is first, so it is probably best to hold them on the same level. All other items fall below these two on the priority schedule.

9. In the disbursement of designated funds, we follow the

policy of honoring designated requests. We trust that the Spirit is leading His people.

10. Disbursements of undesignated giving (General Fund) follows the following schedule of priorities:

    a. Staff support and expenses (pastors, secretary, interns, and any other paid staff salaries, car expense, direct ministry expenses, etc.).

    b. Helps (assistance to meet human need, beyond designated funds).

    c. Arizona-New Mexico District Budget (at regular monthly rate set by the elders).

    d. Church building payment.

    e. Church property expenses (utilities, insurance, taxes, repairs, maintenance, etc.).

    f. All other church expenses.

11. The church treasurer shall handle all deposits and disbursements. He shall keep up-to-date records and present a written financial report (showing all income and expenditures) monthly. He shall meet with the elders at least once each month to keep them informed on church financial matters. He may meet with them at any time it seems necessary for mutual counsel on church finances.

12. The financial secretary shall help the treasurer count the offerings, and shall keep a record of identified contributions. He shall mail out cumulative receipts to all contributors annually.

13. A "Helps Task Force" shall be composed of at least 3 members who will disburse Helps Funds and give individual and family financial counsel. *First request for help*—if it seems to be a genuine need and funds are available, the Tast Force *may* give the financial help requested. They may also make known the availability of counsel, as described below.

Second request for help and each subsequent request—in order to meet the real needs, the Task Force will need to give, not just money, but "our own selves for your sakes." They will involve themselves with those being helped to give aid in bringing permanent solution to the problem (i.e., teach family money management, find employment, aid in bill consolidation, aid in changing buying habits, etc.).

(Adopted by consensus of the Elders and Deacons meeting Saturday, June 12, 1976, Our Heritage Church, Scottsdale, Arizona.)

The "schedule of priorities" (#10) has been extremely difficult to come to, in terms of practical disbursement of funds. In fact, we struggle and fail often, to follow *c* through *f*. But, in our process of becoming, it is good to have before us these objectives, and to have within us a persistent dissatisfaction until this *is* the way we live.

Some women in the church added to their response the development of a food cache, called "The Lord's Larder," and a free clothing and household items store, called "The Lord's Provision." Items from both are distributed without cost or hesitation, as requested. Contributions for both are sought regularly from members of the body.

A shift in individual giving patterns has followed. Three years ago, a congregational survey taken by the elders, disclosed that fifty-one percent of total giving was directed through agencies or on an individual basis *outside* the channel of the local church treasury. Most of this was given for missions, evangelism, and human need. Of the forty-nine percent that passed through the treasurer's books, most went for local expenses, with fifteen percent going to missions and people-needs. Last year, more than one-fourth of total giving through the church treasury was designated for specific people-needs, while the giving outside that channel continues. These personal stewardship adjustments make giving a joy, but at the same time give our church treasurer many new gray hairs, as certain traditional financial demands are left to "go begging."

If you have the impression that our giving/spending priorities are now fully in line with the biblical norm, don't be misled. It is not true. The process has only begun. But it has begun.

Brethren, Hang Together

THE NEW COVENANT THEOLOGY OF GIVING

Upon writing this "giving history," we found ourselves in another financial crunch. God was walking and talking money again.

Back to the Scriptures. Together we were led through a study of Paul's New Covenant Theology of Response to Need, 2 Corinthians 8 and 9. Six principles of response emerged for us, as we worked through these chapters.

First, *the model for gracious giving is the grace of God* (8:9). The one activity and quality really consistent with the nature of grace is giving. Not selling (even at a good price). Not rewarding. Not releasing under pressure. Giving . . . as Jesus gave.

Second, *generosity is the flow of God's grace through His people* (8:1–4; 9:14–15). New Testament giving involves the direct activity of God in the life of the giver. The final exclamation of the passage declares the life style of generosity to be an extremely precious "charisma" of God's grace to us, that we may freely exercise with joyous thanksgiving for the privilege.

Third, *if readiness is the mindset of the giver, it is acceptable* (8:12). Among the Greek meanings of the word for readiness is "alacrity of mind."[7] It communicates the idea of a mental aliveness, eagerness, and cheerful willingness. No need to get "psyched up" for the activity of giving—the readiness is always there.

One evening in the midst of work on this material, I was sitting at my supper table, rewarding myself for my hard work by watching a World Series baseball game on television. In a few minutes I was planning to go to a concert with my wife. The evening was neatly planned. (It couldn't happen to a nicer guy.) It was about that time God decided to show me how "ready" I was to be a giver and a lover.

The phone rang. On the line was a man with a family of ten people (and three dogs) who had just arrived in Scottsdale with $1.95 in his pocket, no place to stay, nothing to eat, and upon arriving had been told that the job for which he had come from Florida to Arizona was not available because the Boilermaker's Union was on strike.

Did my "liberal" spirit, poised and eager, leap briskly into loving action, rejoicing in the wonderful privilege of being able to help in Jesus' name? You can bet your Salvation Army referral phone number it did not! Sadly, I confess, I was angry with God for messing up my neatly planned evening, and for forcing upon me confrontation with a situation which required more faith and love than I felt I was ready to exercise.

I moved reluctantly to meet this family's needs out of sheer dogged, grudging obedience to the Lord's commands. (Lacking the readiness, I think we are called to respond, for Jesus' sake, by faith. But it's not fun like it could be. The joy is missing.) As the time of their sojourn with us (we turned the church's classroom building over to them for several days) moved on, I came to love them. And was genuinely thankful the Lord had come to us in such a way. But . . . I'm sorry, Jesus, at first the readiness was not present.

The freedom and joy of ready generosity is inhibited in its development and is undermined at its foundations by that spoiler of cheerful giving, the sin of *covetousness* (9:5, NASB). In a society characterized by greed for more and more, the Christian community must evaluate its economic priorities to see whose they are—God's or the world's. According to Colossians 3:5, covetousness is not as harmless as "looking out for number one." It is idolatry. Another God! Sparing, reluctant sharing, stinginess—failure to be godlike in generosity is (can it be?) the result of allegiance to idols!

An alacritous mindset is important because God is delighted to see His people having the time of their lives being channels for His grace of giving. The lexical definitions of the word for "cheerful" (9:7) include gay, joyous, and mirthful. The word is *hilaros,* the root of "hilarious." God plans for the church to be the dynamic community of hilarious givers. A family getting its "kicks" from generosity.

Fourth, *how much we have available to give is based on God's grace* (9:8–11). God supplies what He supplies to us, not for us alone, but for us *and* others in and outside the body of Christ. Each is given enough so that he may experience the reality of economic *koinonia.*

If one brother is blessed financially more than others, it is not because he is more spiritual or more deserving. It is not because he is better, smarter, more diligent or "lucky." (Some people are as smart and diligent as Getty or Onassis, and are far more spiritual, yet scarcely have enough to eat!) It is because God, of His own choice, for His own reasons, has caused His undeserved material favor to abound to one more than others. That brother is to remember that God has not "enriched" him so he can be more powerful, more influential, more comfortable, more secure, or more wrapped up in material things than other Christians. God has given him more, so that he may respond more readily to the needs of the Body of Christ . . . "and to all" (9:13 NASB).

Fifth, *the purpose of Christian generosity is that there may be equality* (8:12–15).[11] God is calling together a family who will have accepted economic liability for and financial availability to each other.

> It is a question of equality. At the moment your surplus meets their need, but one day your need may be met from their surplus. The aim is equality (8:14 NEB).

The roots of this teaching are in the Old Testament. It grows out of something God said to Israel at the time He promised that He would supply bread for them every morning of their desert trek (Exod. 16:12). Each day at dawn, as the dew evaporated, the ground was covered with a delicate, flaky wafer—manna. The Israelites were told to gather only as much as each family needed for *one day.* One "omer" (about four pints) per person would be enough, Moses said. Some greedy or anxious people tried to gather more than they could use. But when they measured what they had gathered, they discovered that each had no more than one omer per person!

He who gathered much did not have too much, and he who gathered little did not have too little (Exod. 16:18 and 2 Cor. 8:15).

Just as God has insisted on equal portions of bread for all His people in the desert, so now the Corinthians (as channels for God's gracious giving acts) should give "that there may be equality" among God's new people.

Equality in what? I do not believe this is a call for absolute economic equality. This would require a system of community in which sharing is forced on the basis of law. There is no biblical precedent for such a community, not even the Jerusalem event. Community of goods must remain a voluntary commitment. (This would not exclude the existence of Spirit-led "covenant communities" whose members choose to give up personal ownership.) Verse 14 uses a word that means "want" or "need." Romans 12:13 calls for believers to "share with God's people who are in need." Equality in the necessities. At least this would include food, clothing, and shelter. It could include such things as medicine and basic education. It may also include emotional and spiritual necessities such as love and community. A genuine no-one-claimed-that-any-of-his-possessions-were-his-own-but-they-shared-everything-they-had-attitude could lead to such equality.

Ronald Sider reminds us that we live in this world with a "billion hungry neighbors"[12] scattered across a globe whose distribution systems are geared to bring plenty of food to the rich (even in famine), but leave the poor even deeper in their desperate poverty. This raises questions which, against the backdrop of biblical teaching, are screaming for Christian answers.

199

Sixth, *personal and body giving patterns produce a specific harvest* (9:6, 11–14).

> Remember this: Whoever sows sparingly will also reap sparingly, and whoever sows generously will also reap generously (v. 6).

This harvest of grace-full giving includes: verse 11, enrichment in everything so that liberality can become a way of life; verse 12, needs of the saints are supplied, an overflowing "way-beyond-oneself" kind of continuing ministry to God, through thanksgivings stimulated by one's giving; verse 13, God is glorified, for the giver's obedience to the gospel and the liberality of soul-fellowship demonstrated in the giving act; verse 14, recipients pray for givers, and givers reap a harvest of loving concern from those to whom they give.

THE BEAT GOES ON

Now, we hear Him calling us to go beyond a mere "increase in giving." He is inviting us to become a "community of givers" who have adopted a giving life style. We find ourselves unable simply to address the shortage in the church treasury. Instead, we hear God saying that He wants us to grow up as givers. He wants us to move from the selfishness and parsimoniousness of our present reluctant and materialistic patterns (which are more responsive to our own covetousness than to the needs of others or the will of the Spirit), into a new way of life, in which giving is not an isolated activity which infrequently and hesitantly surfaces in our lives, but is, instead, a description of the way we are— the people we are becoming.

What will be our response? If the past is any indication, we will, led by a few insightful individuals in the body who hunger for full economic *koinonia* and are ready for full abandonment, move a few steps closer to the biblical norm. The insightful few will experience impatience at the slowness of the rest. The rest will stretch and grow. God's process in us will require further action on His part. More people's needs will be met as the operation of His grace persists.

Notes

[1]Ronald J. Sider, *Rich Christians in an Age of Hunger* (Downers Grove: InterVarsity Press, 1977, p. 102).

[2]Ibid., p. 103.

[3]Luke 12:32–40.

[4]Mark 3:21–22; John 10:20.

[5]Larry Ward, *There Will Be Famines.*

[6]Sider, *Rich Christians,* p. 102.

[7]The word translated "sharing," "participation," etc., in 2 Corinthians 8:4, is one of the *koinonia* words, designating fellowship or community.

[8]Phillip Schaff, *The History of the Christian Church,* p. 168.

[9]Ibid., p. 168.

[10]Ronald Sider deals effectively with these Old Testament laws, in *Rich Christians,* pp. 87–95.

[11]Ibid., pp. 107–112.

[12]Ibid., pp. 32–37.

10
Teamwork in Ministry

Dependence on the ministry of the Royal Every-Believer Priesthood does not leave the church leaderless.

There are certain God-given abilities listed among the spiritual gifts in the New Testament that are obviously the equipment of leaders. Most specific among them are gifts designated, in Romans 12:8, as "leadership" (Greek: to be set over, preside, govern, superintend[1]); and, in 1 Corinthians 12:28, as "administration" (Greek: government, director—root: to steer, direct—a related form designates: a pilot or helmsman[2]).

That it is to be a totally unique style of leadership, utterly unlike anything observable in earthly society, is emphasized by Jesus in Matthew 20:25–28. The authority structure of the church is established upon the principle of servanthood rather than "leadership" (as the term is understood in society). His leaders are to be an unusual breed of nonleaders He would rather call "servants." He defines His servant-leaders as follows:

verse 25—They do not "lord it over" people.

They do not achieve greatness by "exercising authority" over people.

verse 26—Their leadership style is totally unlike that of the world's leaders.

The greatness of their leadership is measured by their servanthood.

verse 27—The best leaders are those who always serve, not their own needs, but the needs of those in their care.

verse 28—Like Jesus, servant leaders are willing to give their lives to meet the needs of those in their care.

They pour not only their time and energy, but their very souls[3], into those they serve.

A further unique feature of Jesus' scheme of "servant leadership" is that, in the New Society (the New Testament ideal of Christian community), leaders are not to be seen or to see themselves as being in any sense "above" those they are called to lead. He talks about it in Matthew 23:1-12.

The church is a society of people, everyone of whom are in it by the pure, undeserved favor and loving kindness of God. He chose to place them into the body of Christ in complete contradiction to the fact that everyone of them was devoid of any personal merit, achievement, or goodness worthy of His choice. And when from the body's members, He chooses some for leadership, they are dependent for their ability for spiritual leadership on gifts (the word is "charismata"—graces) which He has given, again, completely apart from any merit, achievement, or goodness on their part. Church leadership is never to be "one above another."

The Lord solemnly warns these undeserving leaders He has chosen by grace, not to "lord it over those entrusted to you" (1 Peter 5:3); and "do not think of yourself more highly than you ought" (Rom. 12:3), and to "consider others better than yourselves" (Phil. 2:3), and, when tempted to receive from others some elevated title or to be viewed by others in some elevated way, to remember, "you are all *brothers*" (Matt. 23:8).

In fact, He goes so far as to put to rest the whole idea of

exalted positions of "leadership" in the church with the startling instruction,

> "And do not be called leaders[4]; for One is your Leader, that is Christ. But (instead) the greatest among you shall be your servant" (Matt. 23:10–11, NASB).

The most sought-after position in the church is *servant*. Others may call me "brother" or perhaps "servant" (if it's true). But I must not covet the designation, "leader."

These are difficult instructions from the Lord, given the present deep entrenchment in today's church, of the world's system of leadership. Never having observed or experienced Jesus' dream of "brother-servant-leadership," today's Christians are looking for leaders who will "lord it over them." They almost instinctively seek to elevate to an above position anyone God seems to have gifted, in an eager quest for shiny heroes they can idolize. They mistakenly refuse to accept leaders as brothers or as equals.

One is your leader: Jesus.

INTERDEPENDENCE OF BROTHER-SERVANT-LEADERS

The cardinal principle for function within the church is the principle of interdependence.

The New Testament style of church leadership flows along with the cardinal principle. Servant leadership, as seen in every part of the Christian Scriptures is, like everything else in the church, mutually dependent, shared, and an exercise in spiritual teamwork.

The principle behind spiritual teamwork was described and illustrated in the Old Testament Book of Ecclesiastes.

> Two are better than one, because they have a good return for their work: If one falls down, his friend can help him up. But pity the man who falls and has no one to help him up! Also, if two lie down together, they will keep warm. But how can one keep warm alone? Though one may be over-powered, two can defend themselves. A cord of three strands is not quickly broken. (Eccl. 4:9–12).

And if the New Testament is clear on anything it is that *the whole church is a team of ministers* (see Rom. 12). The one-man professional style of spiritual leadership and local church care, so comfortable to twentieth-century church-goers, was virtually unknown in the early church.

The concept of a mutual, interdependent style of ministry received a couple of significant applications in the training and ministry of the face-to-face disciples of Jesus and in the leadership strategy of the first-century church. Even though His time was short, Jesus sent out His twelve disciples to announce His coming to the cities of Galilee in teams—two by two (Mark 6:7). Theoretically, He could have reached more people, more towns, if He had sent the Twelve out in twelve directions, one by one. But He knew and meant for His followers to get the message that men work best in teams. He used the same strategy when He sent out the seventy in Luke 10.

When the early church began to apply Jesus' kingdom principles to the life of the New Society as recorded in Acts and the epistles, it, with only a few exceptions, chose its local leaders, sent out its missionaries, and received its ministry according to the same biblical principle.

Teamwork in ministry:

> twelve apostles ministering in Jerusalem
> seven men to distribute food
> Phillip, Peter, and John evangelizing Samaria
> Peter and six brethren bringing the gospel to Cornelius' house
> prophets and teachers of Antioch ministering to the Lord together
> Barnabas, Saul, and John Mark
> Barnabas and Mark
> Paul and Silas
> Paul and Timothy

The unfolding saga of the establishing and continuing life of the local churches of the first century reveals that, when it comes to local church leadership, there are no apparent departures from the teamwork principle.

THE PRINCIPLE OF PLURALITY OF PASTORS

Pastors, elders, overseers, shepherds, bishops—terms interchangeable in New Testament usage—were nearly always chosen in plural and functioned together in the local churches.

There is not one reference to "*the* elder of the church at. . . ." It is possible that there were some expectations to that pattern. If so, they are not mentioned in the New Testament. The normal pattern was for the shepherding of the local church to be the work of a team.

The biblical principle of leadership in the local church is the principle of plurality of pastors (elders).

In its early years the twelve apostles, functioning as a team, were unquestionably leaders of the first church, the explosive Jerusalem congregation. But they gave more and more responsibility to other men, starting with the team of seven appointed to serve the food distribution needs of the large Jerusalem church (Acts 6). By the time Barnabas and Paul returned to the Holy City with famine relief gifts from the Gentile church in Antioch (Acts 11:30), a team of elders had been appointed, who received the contribution.

They weren't called elders, but the group of prophets and teachers at Antioch (Acts 13:1–3) was evidently functioning as a team of spiritual leaders in that local church, when they were told by the Holy Spirit to commission Barnabas and Paul to go out on mission.

The two, accompanied by young John Mark—a team of three—toured Asia Minor, preaching and winning converts in each city. They stayed only a short time in each place (an average of no more than six months). Often abruptly, under fierce persecution and threat of death, they would leave behind a tiny group of "baby" Christians to go on to the next city on the Spirit's agenda to repeat the procedure.

With seeming recklessness, they left these newborn spiritual infants in the hands of the Holy Spirit alone. He would have to take care of them. They would have to take care of each other. There was no other option.

Then after several months or a couple of years, Paul and Barnabas, the church planters, headed home—toward Antioch. And on the way they stopped again in each city (Acts 14:21–23). On this return trip "they (acting as a team) appointed *elders* for them (the new Christians) in each church. . . ." During the time between the initial and return visits, these young churches were leaderless in any official sense. Then the apostles appointed not one, but a team of elders (pastors) to give spiritual leadership in each local congregation.

There are at least four good reasons for looking to a team, instead of a single individual, for local pastoral leadership.

First, because everything in the life of the church is to function on the basis of the principle of interdependence. Even in controlling the affairs of the church, leaders must experience the necessity of dependence on each other. They are to be working together on such an interdependent norm that, in order to minister, they find it necessary to learn submission to each other. In order to sustain the servant-leadership style, leaders must know what it means to honor each other, believe in each other, care for each other, support each other in spiritual growth and ministry, and trust each other to the leadership of the Holy Spirit. Even in leading, planning, guiding, and instructing the church, the element of mutuality—the unique feature of the church—is to be preserved. To local church leaders, leading is to be the ultimate experience of body life. The leadership team of the church is to be a microcosm of the ideal quality of fellowship, life, and caring, possible in the church.

Second, pastoral plurality is both desirable and necessary, because nothing is to be done in the church to obscure the truth of the headship of Jesus Christ. There is to be no confusion over who is head. A dominating one-man leadership is easier to confuse with headship than a plural leadership team in which mutual submission is clearly demonstrated. No single individual, however gifted, is to run the church according to his own pleasure, or to treat the church as his own property. In 3 John 9–10 a domineering man is exposed as trying to control all the affairs of a church. His leadership is condemned.

Third, the church is to be the expression of the personality of Jesus Christ, not the expression of the personality of any man. No single member of the body is to be allowed to leave his personal imprint on all the church's life and work. The church is to be dominated by the Spirit of Christ flowing through many lives. The disunity of the church can be traced, in part, to the practice of elevating strong men, their dynamic personal ministries or their special interpretation of the gospel, to a place in the church above the gospel itself. Many of these men were truly men of God, used powerfully at strategic times in the history of the church. Often, there was no intent on their part to found a new faction and yet. . . . Years (in some cases, generations) after the death of these strong men there still are churches, denominations, movements, schools of thought, whose first commitment is to teach the gospel in the light of that great man's interpretation or experience or style of ministry.

Fourth, pastoral plurality is needed because of the divinely-designed personal limitation of every man of God. The work of God—even just the shepherding of that work—requires far more than the limited resources of any one person. The greatest of multi-gifted, Spirit-filled men, working alone, is purposely hobbled by human limitation—physical, intellectual, emotional, spiritual, and charismatic limitation.

Elders (pastors) serve the body together, as a team. They share a threefold commitment: to love and minister to the Lord who has given them their life and ministry; to love and minister to each other, to be together, to be one; and to love and minister in and to the body, to provide Jesus the head with a healthy body, knit together with healthy relationships, which will be responsive to Him.

BUILDING THE TEAM

The official recorded history of the early church tells how some of the biblical teams were drawn together. These can be studied to discover principles of team building. The story of Jesus inviting the Twelve to be with Him and shaping their lives for ministry is there to be read. The appointment of "the Jerusalem seven." The mutual commitment of the responsible brothers of the Antioch church. The formation of a succession of apostolic teams who carried the Good News to the gentiles. The choosing of elders for the churches of Asia Minor. Letters to Timothy and Titus outline ideal qualities to be sought in men who are chosen for specific office in the church.

In the Acts and the New Testament epistles, it is clear that in every local church the responsibility for servant-leadership was placed with two basic teams. The two are mentioned together in connection with the local church in two passages: (1) the Philippian letter is addressed to "all the saints in Christ Jesus at Philippi, together with the *overseers* and *deacons*," and (2) the outline of spiritual qualifications for the candidates for both types of ministry, in 1 Timothy 3.

The principle of spiritual teamwork is being rediscovered in many places in our time. There are many stories to be told of the calling together of modern ministry teams. Their stories reveal both fundamental similarity and broad diversity in the team-building process.

Told here is our team-building story. I gladly share it, not because I think it is the best or the most effective, nor because there are not others which have come into being more smoothly or that are more biblical, but because it is the story I know best. I believe the telling of it (complete with its reit-

eration of failures and weaknesses) may serve to give someone courage to press for needed change in the leadership
structures of the churches, and perhaps even to avert some
painful mistakes.

I have dreaded board meetings since my first fulltime year
as a pastor. The typical church board meeting is far from the
simplicity, openness, and freedom which characterized the
decision-making bodies of the church in Century 1. The
only ones I have ever know were run according to *Robert's
Rules of Order.* Robert, through his *Rules,* has been given
awesome authority over the functioning of the church of the
living God. Not until recently have I, in more than four decades of exposure to church business procedures, heard anyone ask whether *Robert's Rules* is truly consistent with revealed biblical principles of church life. Nor have I ever
heard anyone question the theological and spiritual basis on
which the word of this man has been given precedence over
the Word of God in the conduct of church business.

The truth is that the adoption of Robert as the authority
on church order has brought destructive elements into the
church! The result of following this man-made system has
been to bind church leaders to a formal structure which
vastly inhibits anything personal. Voting (the "democratic
process") forces brothers to take sides, often without truly
listening to each other. The process leaves little room for
sharing inner, personal feelings—which may be more in
tune with God's voice than all the brilliant arguments mar-
shalled to win votes, and which certainly have more to do
with the weightier matters of soul-fellowship and spiritual
harmony. Furthermore, the cold formality of the process
practically forces the church to concentrate on institutional
matters.[5]

In contrast to the typical motivations involved in this process (i.e., to be "right" and to win votes), the church's
leadership meetings need to be characterized by a new purpose and desire: to build each other up, so we can be the

kind of people God wants in the church. One of the primary goals of "business" meetings, as of all church gatherings, is to build a deep bond of love and support for each other that transcends institutional concerns. It is in the context of fellowship, union in Christ, and spiritual growth, that business concerns may surface and be dealt with on the ground of true affection for one another.

Up until about four years ago the leadership meetings of our local church were typical of the kind of "democratic tragedy" I've been describing. In our renewal process it has seemed to me that church business was one of the last vestiges of tradition to give way to the New Wine. Small groups were renewing deep fellowship. Supportive one-to-one relationships were blossoming. Even the worship services had begun to change. But church board meetings were as tension-ridden and relationally destructive as ever!

As constitutionally designated chairman I chose to take some risks to seek to bring the "personal" into the rigid structure. I felt certain the "group people" on the board would respond.

Step 1 was to add to the board meeting agenda thirty minutes of one-to-one structured personal interaction. I would use one of the Serendipity relational games[6] (choosing carefully to keep them "masculine," since all our board members were men), or the simple assignment: Share with another man the two most significant happenings of your week and the two greatest concerns of your life right now, and pray specifically for each other.

There was some murmuring in the camp, but by twos they would scatter around the meeting room and begin to talk and pray together.

Step 2 was to add a second monthly board meeting for which there would be no agenda. We would meet for lunch on a Saturday "just for fellowship." About half the board members responded. At least two good things happened at these luncheons: (1) half the board was getting to know each other better, more personally, and (2) we sometimes found ourselves discussing church life and coming to "unofficial" decisions in a pressure-free atmosphere which allowed for sharing of personal feelings and prayer, leading toward true consensus. These decisions later were made "official" when the board met in its formal business session.

At the same time, I began to teach both the board and the church the biblical qualifications of spiritual leadership. At election time, 1 Timothy 3 was read and applied to the selection process.

From there we moved to teaching and discussion in which we dared to be confronted with the fundamental differences between our existing style of church leadership and that suggested by the New Testament. A couple of times the Sunday morning study of the patterns of biblical local church oversight would end with this, or a similar question: "There is the New Testament pattern, and here we are with our present *modus operandi*. The two are miles apart. What would we have to do to get from where we are to where the New Testament church is?" Then the congregation, in small groups or the whole, would interact on it.

The following pages, from what we call our "book of policy," which was developed later, comprise a basic summary of the teachings presented at that time. They have been updated to coincide with conceptual growth to date.

JOB DESCRIPTION OF AN ELDER

From the New Testament

1 Peter 5:1–3	Elders *shepherd* (pastor) the church.
Acts 20:28	1 Peter 5:2 says that to shepherd (pastor) is to:
	tend (care for needs),
	guard (protect),
	guide (lead),
	fold (gather) the flock of God that is your responsibility.

212

	1 Peter 5:1–3 says they are to pastor the flock of God (church) voluntarily, according to God, not for personal gain, with eagerness, not "lording it over," and by example.
Acts 15:2–29	Elders *judge* and *decide* —in matters of church and discipline —in matters of conflict between members (see also 1 Cor. 6:1–11).
1 Timothy 4:14	Elders *appoint the church's workers* (see also Acts 13:1–3).
1 Timothy 5:17	Elders *rule, (oversee, lead)* the church (see also 1 Tim. 3:1–2, 4–5; Acts 20:28).
1 Timothy 5:17	Elders *preach* and *teach.*
Acts 11:27–30	Elders *receive and disburse gifts.*
James 5:14–15;	Elders *pray*
Acts 13:1–3;	—for the sick
Acts 14:23	—for the church
	—for needed workers
Acts 13:1–3	Elders *meet together* —to minister to the Lord —to be led together by the Spirit

Practical Application

Elders are the "official" servant-leaders of the local church. They are its pastors. They are called from the body for the spiritual nurture, protection, leadership, and gathering together of the believers. They teach, preach, lead, and model, to develop a loving, working, ministering, believer-priesthood.

It is the function of elders to set the pattern of life for the rest of the church, by the way they themselves live in the Spirit. The life of the body is to be modeled in their life together as a team.

When necessary, they administer discipline, decide doctrinal issues, and work for reconciliation between believers.

213

They lead the church toward response to the world-wide, as well as local, commission of the church.

The authority of elders grows out of actual ministry and relationships of love.

SELECTION PROCESS FOR ELDERS

Biblical Insights

Acts 20:28 — *The Holy Spirit makes a man an elder.*
Therefore, the process of selection in the local church must include ways to recognize the Holy Spirit's choice and must leave room for Him to communicate His will.

Ephesians 4:7–11 — *Jesus Christ, the Head, gives the spiritual gifts the elder needs in order to minister.*
The primary gift an elder must possess is the pastor (shepherd) gift. Other spiritual gifts which may be especially helpful for elders are the gifts of teaching, prophecy, evangelism, etc.

Acts 14:23 — *Apostles, founders of churches, appointed the first elders in each local church.*

1 Timothy 4:14; Titus 1:5 — *Later, already-appointed elders selected new elders.*
Therefore, elders (spiritual leaders) must have a very significant, even dominant, role in the selection process.

Acts 14:23 — *Fasting and prayer preceded the selection of elders.*
The purpose, undoubtedly, was to ascertain the leadership of the Holy Spirit. Therefore, prayer and fasting on the part of the elders and the body ought to be part of the selection process.

214

Teamwork in Ministry

1 Timothy 3:1–7; *Elders are selected from men of a high*
Titus 1:5–9 *level of spiritual maturity.*
This requires time to know them as persons, to observe their gifts, ministry, maturity, and relationships. (Church oversight requires people in whose lives the stature of Christ can be observed in an advanced stage of development—in temperament, family relationships, personal habits, priorities, reputation, and practical spiritual ministry.)

1 Timothy 4:14 *The laying on of hands seals the appointment.*

Hebrews 13:17 *Congregational responsiveness and adaptation to the ministry of those selected is essential* if the ministry of an elder is to be profitable for the church and joyful for the elder.

(Our "book of policy" includes a statement of "Practical Procedure" based on the above biblical insights. These procedures are open to flux. They will be described as our team-building story continues.)

JOB DESCRIPTION OF A DEACON

From the New Testament
The Greek word for deacon is translated:

1. "servant," Matthew 23:11–12; John 12:26
2. "minister," Mark 10:43, KJV
3. "assistant," Philippians 1:1, *Amplified Bible.*

Acts 6:1–3 *Caring for widows,* distribution of food and funds.
Administrating the caring ministries of the body. The deacon is no figurehead. He is one who is charged with specific

215

tasks in the body. And he is chosen for his ability to do a practical job of serving.

1 Timothy 3:10, 13 *Serving.*

Practical Application

Every deacon is to be involved in a specific, practical, necessary area of ministry in the body as requested by the elders or the congregation. Needed ministries:

1. Care of persons and families (i.e., personal service to widows, orphans, divorced, sick, infirm, aged, needy, unemployed, imprisoned, bereaved, lonely, etc.) The number of deacons needed is related to the number of persons and/or families to be served.

2. Helps Team (oversees distribution to those in need, coupled with financial planning and guidance for individuals and families).

3. Treasurer.

4. Trustees (care of church property).

5. All other practical ministries connected with the life of the body, either temporary or permanent.

The office of deacon is not an administrative office. Deacons should advise and counsel the elders in decisions that affect the life and ministry of the local church, but the final decision is by consensus of the elders. The deacon should meet regularly with the other deacons and elders for fellowship, interaction, planning, mutual ministry, and prayer.

SELECTION PROCESS FOR DEACONS

Biblical Insights

Acts 6:2–3   *Deacons are selected by consensus of the local church, to fulfill specific ministry responsibilities in the local church. Therefore, it is proper for the congregation to be involved in selecting and affirming deacons.*

1 Timothy 3:10;   *Deacons are selected only after a time*

	of testing (proving).
Acts 6:1–3	The testing involves ascertaining, through observation, the wisdom, good reputation, and spiritual vitality of the deacon-candidate. Therefore, the people chosen should be those who are known and trusted in the body. If others seem to have deacon potential, they should be given assignments that bring them to the attention of the congregation and allow their lives and ministries to be observed.
Acts 6:6	*Prayer by the leaders of the church (apostles, elders) preceded the final appointment of the deacons.*
	The reason for prayer was to ascertain the leadership of the Holy Spirit. Therefore, prayer must be part of the selection process for deacons.
1 Timothy 3:8–13	*Deacons are selected only from among men and women of a high level of spiritual maturity.*
Acts 6:6	*Church leaders (apostles, elders) seal the deacon's appointment with the "laying on of hands."*

Practical Procedure

Deacons should be selected as follows:

1. If there is a need for a specific kind of ministry in the body that fits within the bounds of the biblical job description of a deacon, and a person is available who has gifts, maturity, and desire that fit the need, that person should be nominated as a deacon.

2. Nominations may be presented by the elders or members of the congregation.

3. The elders consider the nomination(s) against the biblical criteria and church need and recommend to the

217

congregation those they feel should be affirmed.

4. The nomination(s) are presented to the congregation for affirmation.

5. The person is appointed to the specific area of ministry as a deacon with public laying on of hands by the elders.

This entire process is to be bathed in prayer, with fasting. (End of quotation from the "book of policy.")

THE MINISTRY LEADERSHIP TEAM

From this point, major concentration will be on the development of the team of men charged with pastoral ministry in the church, the elders. We began by alternately referring to them as "The Ministry Leadership Team." At present, their alternate designation is "The Pastoral Team."

The guiding biblical principle for church oversight is:

> Pastoral leadership is by a team of men chosen from among the local congregation for their spiritual maturity, giftedness for ministry, and the exemplary quality of their lives.[7]

After the time of concentrated teaching and interaction mentioned earlier, the subject came up repeatedly, whenever a few of us were together, formally or spontaneously. The conviction grew among us that change had to come in the basic leadership structure of the church. This need was felt because of the maturing congregational commitment that the church can be what the New Testament says the church can be only if we are living in tune with the biblical principles—whatever that might involve.

"CHOOSE . . . MEN FROM AMONG YOU"

The two pastors (a youthful assistant named Ron Rogers and myself), not knowing who else to call into the selection process at that point, being the closest thing in the church to biblically appointed spiritual leaders, set about praying for insight as to whom the Holy Spirit might be calling to be a part of the first team of elders. We covenanted to fast one day each week, following the model of the apostles in Acts

14:23. Instead of eating the first two meals on Friday, we spent the lunch hour together praying. This was our pattern for six months.

We determined to pursue this process without a specific number in mind for team size. We believed that the Holy Spirit had already given the congregation the precise number of men for which His plan called. He would lead us to these men.

During the time of our search, the Spirit brought to our minds eight specific men who should comprise the first pastoral team. Ron and I would be members, along with six others. In the process we asked the men themselves to consider whether or not the pastor-elder role might be something they wanted, or that God wanted for them.

The selection process revolved primarily around a search for spiritual maturity, a specific cluster of spiritual gifts, and the leadership of the Holy Spirit (as we, the men, and, finally, the congregation, might be able to ascertain it.)

As we sought to evaluate each man's maturity, our basis for comparison was our own local congregation: Who are the mature (the spiritual elders) of *this* congregation? They might be more or less mature than the elders of another local church, but that is not the point. Those who lead a church need only be spiritual elders to the body of which they are a part.

Spiritual maturity is defined in many places in the Bible. To speak in generalities, the great objective of the spiritual development process is "attaining the full measure of perfection found in Christ" (Eph. 4:13). Spiritual maturation entails healthy growth in integration of all aspects of life around Jesus, the Head (Eph. 4:15). It is the prize to which *all* believers are being called, for which their gifted spiritual servants are to be preparing them, and toward which they spur each other on (vv. 11–16).

First Timothy 3 and Titus 1 speak in specifics about the advanced level of this spiritual integration expected in anyone who is called into local church oversight. Biblical leadership requires a sound evaluation of oneself, an ability to grasp and respond to biblical truth, and a certain level of expertise in the development of healthy, open, personal relationships. Christ is to be observably Lord of the man's temperament and life style. I do not think this means that only perfect men may serve in pastoral ministry. In our search for the Holy Spirit's men to serve our congregation, if we knew that a man was seeking to deal with the spiritual issues involved in his relationships, temperament and life style, and had been making good progress in these matters for some time—even though in some areas of his life there were unresolved problems and obvious imperfections—we counted him as mature. Given the relative immaturity of all of us in the church (including the two pastors who were doing the evaluating), we could not go for perfect men. There were none. So, we went for men who, when compared with the congregation of which they were a part and in which they would serve, were "more advanced" in the areas pointed up in the Timothy and Titus passages than were their spiritual peers. God would have to complete their maturation on the job.

A man's marriage relationship is probably the most significant key to evaluating his readiness to lead the church. There are at least three reasons why, in this aspect of life, a leader must be right.

(1) The marriage relationship pictures for the world, the church, the family, and the elder himself, the nature and function of the relationship between Christ and the church (Eph. 5:21–33). If, as a shepherd of the church, one's marriage is allowed to deteriorate, or to remain in an indifferent or destructive state, then an essential visible model of the redemptive relationship is missing. The nonverbal message inherent in Christian marriage becomes confusing, and our "religion," it may be concluded by those who watch, is mere words.

(2) It is probable that the quality and direction of a person's leadership in the church can be accurately predicted or measured by the quality and results of his leadership at home, with his wife and children (1 Tim. 3:4–5). It is sometimes difficult to evaluate one's leadership in the larger, less intimate body of the church. A strong public presentation of himself can get a man by, even though it may take years to know whether his spiritual leadership has strengthened the church's unity and obedience to Christ, or undermined it. But if you know the truth about the quality of his relationship with his wife and children and other family members, you can know quickly the quality of his leadership in the church. He must be able to lead his family, minister to and serve his family's needs, be positively and redemptively dealing with the problems in and of his family, and be seeking to overcome the weaknesses in his own leadership in that setting, or the church which suffers under the same leadership will not fare any better than the man's family. Here again, perfection is too much to expect, but growth and maturity are indispensable.

(3) The spiritual power released in the Christian community in response to effectual prayer is definitely affected by the attitudes of the community's husbands toward their wives (1 Peter 3:7). A man (especially a servant-leader) is to live with his wife "as an heir with you of the gracious gift of life"—as a fellow-member of Christ's body. All the relational principles that apply to the body, apply to the man's relationship with his wife.

Marriage problems may not render a person unusable for church leadership. But one's attitude toward his relationship with his spouse is a significant barometer of his readiness for spiritual authority.

Authority and ministry (servanthood) are so closely linked in the New Testament church that it's like the show ballad says about love and marriage—"You can't have one without the other." Authority always grows out of, and is a part of, ministry. There is no position in the church where a person has authority but is not involved in ministry. If he has a ministry he will have authority. No one has real authority in the church unless he is a "minister." Furthermore, whatever authority the Christian leader has is to be exercised only in the form of ministry to others (Matt. 20:25–28). If it is my "minister" who seeks to lead me, I am more likely to pay attention.

One of the keys, therefore, to a successful search for the Holy Spirit's people to lead the church is to find those who already have authority, based on personal life and ministry, and to appoint those actual spiritual leaders to serve the church.

We asked the Lord to help us discover those who were already involving themselves in varieties of ministry that were clearly "pastoral."

Our existing local church structure (set up according to the provisions of our denominational book of *Discipline*) called for an election process commencing with the board's appointment of a nominating committee, which would preselect candidates for the prescribed offices (usually two for each office), and prepare a ballot for consideration by the congregation. Whereupon the body would vote, electing its officers.

Ron and I were in the delicate position of having sought the mind of the Spirit in the selection of men for offices for which "church law" did not provide, to man a system of church government totally different (even contradictory) in philosophy from the policy our offical denominational constitution prescribed. So, our agreeing prayers, as election time neared, focused increasingly on the need for the Holy Spirit to pave the way, removing or employing the constitutional obstacles to a whole new form of local church organization. A key point in the process, we believed, would be the membership of the nominating committee.

Here is what happened:

The three chosen by the board as nominating committee were three of our most spiritually alive and mature Christians. In fact, all three were on our list of "wanted men" (for eldership). All three had already expressed strong convictions that the church should move to a more biblical style of leadership.

From this nominating committee came the proposal to replace our existing form of government:

BE IT RESOLVED that in the church elections of April 8, 1973, the local leadership of Our Heritage Wesleyan Church be selected in the following manner:

1. The Nominating Committee bring to the congregation for election two "pools of leadership" corresponding to the two biblical leadership groups.

2. These two groups be designated as (1) the MINISTRY LEADERSHIP TEAM (or local elders) and (2) ASSISTANTS-IN-MINISTRY (or deacons).

3. The MINISTRY LEADERSHIP TEAM be nominated considering three criteria:

(a) spiritual maturity (outlined in 1 Tim. 3:1–7 and Titus 1:5–9),

(b) spiritual gifts (specifically gifts of pastor or shepherd, leadership or administration, and teaching or preaching).

(c) the leadership of the Holy Spirit.

This team should meet together often, perhaps each week, to do three things:

(1) Minister to each other in a body-life fellowship.

(2) Minister to the Lord in prayer, worship, and Bible study,

(3) Minister to the body in any way that leads to spiritual growth.

The emphasis shall be on ministry rather than "business."

4. The ASSISTANTS-IN-MINISTRY be nominated considering the same three basic criteria:

(a) spiritual maturity (Acts 6:3 and 1 Tim. 3:8–13),

(b) spiritual gifts (especially wisdom and leadership),

(c) the leadership of the Holy Spirit.

5. Both of these groups (THE MINISTRY LEADERSHIP TEAM and ASSISTANTS-IN-MINISTRY) meet together, as needed, as The Local Church Board.

6. All other "officers" and committees, as needed, be appointed by the Local Church Board, giving consideration to spiritual gifts and the leadership of the Spirit.

7. Both of these groups be "open-ended." That is, they may be added to or resigned from during the course of the fiscal year.

The congregation approved this proposal by unanimous vote. Later, convinced that the Bible gives the ministry of governing to elders, and that deacon ministry is a nonruling function, item 5 was deleted.

A short time later, candidates selected according to the new criteria were elected elders and deacons. The nominating committee had nominated the very same men (elders) that were on the minds of the two pastors after six months of heart searching and prayer. Others had been discussed in the committee meetings, but for sound reasons had been set aside. The congregation followed suit. After one or two nominations from the floor, the original group was overwhelmingly affirmed.

At that point, a most time-consuming, alternately exhilarating and exasperating process began that eventually gave our church its present "Pastoral Team," composed of five men who, together, are capable of giving growth-producing brother-servant-leadership to this segment of the body of Christ.

COMMENCEMENT

The first nine months of "eldership" were mostly frustrating. The approved proposal had said the team would meet weekly. It did not happen exactly as planned. Only one or two, other than Ron and myself, evidenced any inclination to commit themselves to meet regularly. So, from a team standpoint, the first three-quarters of a year our movements were a little like those of a grasshopper with a couple of legs missing. Even so, the four who met regularly began to know each other better and began to share in common the frustration of the failure of the team to develop.

Also, the hit-or-miss mutual "discipling" that was possible, helped one man to decide that his gifts and desires equipped him to serve the body more effectively and happily as a deacon rather than an elder. The others honored his feelings, and our number was reduced to seven.

In desperation borne of fear that our dreams of shared pastoral leadership were never going to materialize, we managed to get all but one to commit themselves to a one-day "retreat" at a mountain cabin. There was to be no agenda—none of us who had expressed concern had any idea how to organize the meeting so that the right issues would be dealt with in the right way and so that we might come away with a commitment to become what we'd been selected to be. Uncertain, we decided to simply trust the Spirit in the men.

About 6:00 A.M. one Saturday, six of us climbed aboard Larry Richards' station wagon and headed for the Mogollon Rim. We would return about eleven hours later. Upon arrival at the borrowed cabin, we built a fire, made coffee, and sat down around the stove to look at each other. I think someone finally interrupted the frivolous flow of typical male chitchat with, "Well, what do we do now?" All eyes turned to me. (After all, isn't the pastor always in charge? Doesn't he always have a plan?)

"I don't know," I said, "I didn't plan an agenda. What *do* we do now?"

From that Alphonse-Gastone-style nonbeginning, the conversation turned to a sharing of personal feelings, of varying intensity, about our failure to make significant progress toward the building of the pastoral team. Frustration, anger, guilt, apathy, etc., all found expression. By day's end, we had mutually agreed that we would no longer be "pastor and church board," but must become, together, the church's "leadership team."

We drove down the mountain later that day with a shared commitment:

—to spent three hours together each Saturday morning, unless providentially hindered (7:00 to 10:00 A.M.)

—in our meetings to concentrate first on our relationships with each other.

—to let our ministry and decision-making flow "naturally" from the context of a developing commitment to each other.

There was immense diversity on this developing team of six men. (Another had resigned the office a few weeks after the retreat, for personal and spiritual reasons.) By profession, we were a heating and air-conditioning contractor, a corporation vice-president, a Christian education specialist and writer, a free-lance electronics engineer, a pastor, and an assistant pastor. The last two were paid staff of the church. By age, four were in their early forties, one early fifties, and one mid-twenties. By church background (before O.H.), we were Evangelical Free, Episcopalian, two kinds of Baptist, Wesleyan, and Campus Crusade for Christ (not a denomination). By personality and gift-clustering, we were even more diverse. All but the youngest had been involved in a traditional style of leadership in their former churches. Two had been ordained. One was a licensed minister. Four had had formal training for ministry. The other two were readers and students of the Bible.

For almost a year-and-a-half we grew together in an authentic fellowship of love, mutual caring, and brisk confrontation. Team-building. Week after week we grappled with the spiritual issues our personal lives and ministries were raising. With Bibles in hand and hearts open to each other and the voice of the Spirit, we found answers for church problems. We had committed ourselves to "consensus decision-making" and every action we took had the unanimous consent of the entire group. The tension and dread was draining out of church business meetings for me. The "elders' meeting" became the high point of the week for several of us. We were coming to love and trust each other. There was growing freedom to risk and to share with one another our personal struggles. There was power and joy in our times of prayer.

We seemed on the brink of plunging headlong into full-orbed shared pastoral leadership of the local church. The Pastoral Team was on its way to reality!

Then . . . changes came. And serious mistakes were made which resulted in an extremely painful series of complications that, by some evaluations, set team-building back about two years.

The changes: Glen, faced with a difficult family decision, was released from eldership, with expressions of blessing and sorrow from the other team members, and rejoined his family in the Episcopal Church. Ron, needing time away from full-time ministry to sort out important spiritual questions relating to his family and his future, also asked to be relieved of his responsibilities as an elder. Larry's ministry to the church-at-large entered a developmental stage of many months duration in which his travel commitments made it virtually impossible for him to function in other than an "advisory" capacity. His name remained on the list of team members, but his ministry to the other elders and to the church was strictly sporadic and limited.

How to Un-Build a Team

This left three of the original men (plus Larry) to go on with what felt like being short-handed. The Scripture prescribes no arbitrary numerical formula, so this should not have been cause for concern. It was time to wait and see what God would do with the "3-plus," and how He would add to it. But, like Peter in Acts 1, we began to feel the need to find replacements in order to bring the team back near its original number. It seemed to me that three were not enough to carry on the pastoral ministry we'd been envisioning. The others, while not feeling it as strongly as I, concurred. (Almost two years later, one of the men told me he had had serious misgivings but had failed to express them out of deference to my strong feelings. So the action we took was not a true consensus, though we thought it was.)

Earlier, one brother, Howard, had been invited to join us for elders meetings. He seemed to be elder material. He had now met with us for several weeks, and was becoming well-known to us. We could have responded to our sudden attritions by simply bringing Howard to the congregation for affirmation as an elder. But adding one to replace the loss of "two-plus-Larry" (actually, we had by this time lost four of the original group) did not satisfy us in our over anxiousness.

So together we prayed and fasted, and selected four men from among the members of the congregation (including Howard) to join the elder team. We concentrated, as before, on spiritual maturity (though we did not take special pains to get close enough to truly judge this), spiritual gifting for pastoral leadership, and the voice of the Holy Spirit (though unlike the original six months of prayer-with-fasting, we determined that just two or three weeks, leading to the established annual election date, were sufficient to determine what the Spirit was saying.) In addition, we slipped into the process a search for someone to represent a segment of the body which we were trying to tie in more tightly.

The four were willing to serve, and the congregation affirmed their appointment (though with not nearly as much enthusiasm as it had affirmed the original eight. Some members of the congregation did not concur with one or more of our choices.).

Orientation for new team members consisted of the assignment to voluntarily read *Brethren, Hang Loose,* study

Scripture passages on eldership, and an overnight retreat (which not everyone attended).

The following is my perception of what happened. It may have been seen differently by others on the team.

The new members seemed to perceive the function of elders on the old, traditional level: i.e., establishing policy, making decisions, conducting business. (This was through no fault of their own. There was simply not enough specific preparation for the office. Their chief source of instruction was previous experience serving on, or observing, the typical church board.) They did not automatically sense the priority of fellowship and of personal commitment to the other team members, as the absolutely essential context out of which church leadership and personal ministry emerges, under the tutelage of the Spirit. As a result, the focus of argumentation changed. It had been an open exchange aimed at discovering together what the Spirit was saying and what was best for the church, through hard struggling with ourselves, our motives, our needs, and the Scriptures, in intense interaction and prayer. It became "church business" all over again. Being right became more important than being right with each other. Leadership became more important than spiritual unity under Christ's headship.

If the preselection process had been thorough enough, and the new members had been added one at a time, perhaps our simple attempt at orientation would have been sufficient. As it turned out, there was a deep need for much more. The new elders deeply needed initiation into: (a) a sense of the essential and primary place of fellowship and personal commitment to each other, (b) basic and advanced skills of relationship building and maintenance, (c) the unique and personal pattern of argumentation that leads people into close, loving relationships even while debating difficult issues, and (d) the biblical priorities which must guide the meetings and ministry of the church's leadership team. Furthermore, the "old" elders needed to prepare

229

themselves for the adjustments that are inevitably called for when an intimate group is "invaded" by even one—not to say four—new personalities.

There was no way the new members could have understood the depth of love and joy and fellowship the others had known. No way they could have known the awful sense of disappointment the old members now felt. And the old members were so bewildered by the unexpected changes, it was several months before their feelings could be articulated.

At the same time we were trying to figure out what had gone wrong with the team spirit, two heavy church issues were being forced upon the elders. For the first four months they struggled with the issue of spiritual nurture of our children—discussion of which revolved around the rigidly unamendable proposal of one of the new elders that the church return to a strictly traditional style Sunday school program. While that issue was still being debated, intense pressure was brought upon the elders to open the church to a strong charismatic emphasis. Both hit at a time when the elders themselves desperately needed to come to grips with the relational issues between them.

And, to complicate things further, I was away for two months of this period—leaving just two (three with Larry) of the old team to work through these extremely difficult issues with four new members who, for all practical purposes, had had little or no personal orientation to the biblical pattern of church oversight.

At the height of the pressure, which was punctuated with angry exchanges between the elders themselves, the new elder whose Sunday school proposal was being rejected, resigned and left the church. At the same time, Rod, another member of the old team, became so disillusioned by the disastrous breakdown of team relationships that he resigned from eldership, feeling that he could minister more effectively in the church without official designation.

I watched all this from a distance, knowing I could do nothing about it, beyond writing letters, until I returned. My heart was breaking too. But I was beginning to see what had gone wrong, and beginning to learn some very painful lessons that would guide future team-building—if we survived the tidal wave resulting from the mistakes we had already made!

But before it was over, I would make still another colossal blunder.

I came back from my leave determined to do several things aimed at picking up the pieces of our pastoral team, and getting it back on the track: (1) I would personally assume the reins of church life again, not depending on the team for decisions and direction. (2) I would personally take control of leadership of the weekly elders' meeting. (3) All institutional considerations by the elders would be postponed indefinitely until we could refocus on the priorities that must guide church leadership. (4) I would spend more time with the men on an individual basis, for the purpose of refocusing the vision of the church and the vision of the team and to deal with problems I saw between the men.

I did not realize that my drastic unilateral action was actually setting the team-building process back still further. Each of these men was a true believer, indwelt by the Holy Spirit. Even the least mature possessed a deep desire to be a man of God and to minister life to the church. It was a mistake to assume that they had gained nothing from their "summer of discontent." In fact, they had learned a great deal about leadership, even through some very negative lessons. They had made some tough decisions and had dealt wisely and lovingly with challenging pastoral problems. And they had learned about sticking together through rugged, uncomfortable times. My actions to solve the problem said to them (non-verbally), "You have failed." I did not realize that I had given this message until Pat, one of the original group, shared his hurt with me several months later. Because of this

231

strong unspoken message, some of the men backed off for a time from what had been a deepening commitment to minister.

What I should have done was to honestly share with the elders what I saw the problem to be, to suggest a course of action to deal with it, and to ask them to join me in it . . . as a team.

WE LEARN BY MISDOING

Let me pause to lead a brief tour through the rogues gallery of errors, committed in our vast ignorance of the team-building process, which now (by the miracle of 20/20 hindsight) we are able to see more clearly.

In seeking to add to the team of elders, eight major mistakes were made:

1. *Yielding to the pressure of an arbitrary number* forced us to select more men than were truly ready for eldership.

2. *Yielding to the pressure of an arbitrary election date* forced us to take short-cuts in the essential process of "knowing" the candidates.

3. *Failure to reach a true consensus* left us to take action unaware of the "check" of the Spirit.

4. *Failure to take sufficient time to know the new members before finalizing their appointment* caused us to make choices based on shallow evaluations.

5. *Seeking a "representative"* made us willing to overlook significant problem areas and gave credibility to disunity.

6. *Too many new members were added to the team at one time,* setting up a situation in which uninitiated men dominated meetings, thus disrupting team continuity.

7. *Failure to provide sufficient orientation for new team members* left them to rely, for knowledge of how to function, on experience with the old traditional structures from which we were trying to get free.

8. *My personal "take over"* set team building back by

communicating lack of confidence in the men and the team process.

Our positive response to these "lessons" came several months later, when the elders and congregation established a set of flexible guidelines for the appointment of new members to the team. The following is reprinted from our "book of policy," and must be viewed as "in flux" (note the beginning parenthetical qualifier.) The time sequences are completely open-ended, allowing unlimited flexibility to move at whatever pace seems right to the elders.

SELECTION PROCESS FOR NEW ELDERS

(Not to be considered law, but guiding principles.)

When the Holy Spirit seems to be saying to the elders, to anyone in the body, and/or to the person himself, that someone has the gifts, maturity, and ministry that qualify him to be considered for eldership, let the following process be initiated:

1. Nomination. Anyone in the congregation may submit the names of people to be considered for the office of elder. These should be submitted to the elders. The elders will consider each person suggested.

2. Candidacy. The elders, by consensus, decide whether or not a person should be a candidate for the office of elder. In response to the biblical instruction to "know those who labor among you" (1 Thess. 5:12), the elders will take a reasonable amount of time to get to know the candidate. The purpose of this testing period is to familiarize the person with the office of elder and the team process, and to give the elders themselves opportunity to develop their relationships with the person and to evaluate his spiritual maturity and ministry potential.

3. Congregational consideration. Following the testing period, the elders may present the candidate's name to the congregation for their consideration. The members of the congregation will be given a reasonable time (i.e., two

weeks, a month) to express themselves regarding the candidate. They may do this by letter or by personally presenting their thoughts to the elders. If there are objections, whatever time is needed will be taken to confront and work through the problems involved.

4. Affirmation. When the elders, having considered any objections, are ready to do so, they may present the candidate's name to the congregation for affirmation as an elder.

5. Laying on of hands. Upon affirmation by the congregation, the new elder is confirmed by the laying on of hands of the elders in the presence of the congregation.

6. Term of service. Elders will serve as long as they serve well and there is no biblical cause for removing them from office. An elder may remove himself from office, if he feels he should. Temporary leave or sabbatical leave may also be arranged from time to time, as needed.

7. Prayer. This entire process is to be accompanied by prayer, with fasting. (End of quotation from the "book of policy.")

DROPPING BACK TO PUNT

Mistakes notwithstanding, as we began to regroup, we knew God had given us the men who held the office of overseer, and if we would seek to instill in ourselves, and apply to our ministry together, the biblical principles of brother-servant-leadership, we could still become what His plan prescribes for the church's shared ministry team. Diverse and weak as we were, He could and would ultimately make us one in esteem and experience—His team—if we would simply be willing to be together, consistently and at length, and not allow ourselves to be satisfied with less than a biblical style of team relationship and leadership.

Erratic meeting attendance and clinging prejudices slowed our rate of developing mutual esteem to snail's pace. The original commitment to be together, to concentrate on our personal relationships, and to minister from fellowship, was extremely difficult to rebuild. Each man, from his personal perspective, battled disillusionment, which often led to depression, criticism, and expressions of frustration. But together (when we were) and on a one-to-one basis (when we could), we kept the process going. Building relationships. Polishing up the dream. Expressing our frustrations. Explaining each other to each other. Praying. Acting only in consensus. Clinging to hope. Dependent on the Spirit. Returning repeatedly to the biblical principles. Two years of this, and still only scant signs that the team was about to "gel."

We came, during those two years of rebuilding, to share together the leadership of all the church's worship services. We also began to share teaching responsibilities to the point where I was teaching only about half the time.

At one point, our nonattendance and apparent non-relationship brought us to such a place of disjunction that no decisions could be made, and I feared the "team" would go out of existence. I felt almost alone again in the leadership of the church.

I recall sitting in the Worship Celebration one Sunday morning, watching one elder leading the meeting, and listening as another brought a message (teaching), and hearing still another sharing insights and raising questions as a member of the congregation, mingled with the prayers and interactions of other body members. I caught the distinct feeling (it hit me with the impact of a vision) that the leaders of our congregation (both "official" and "unofficial") were all sounding their leadership trumpets for a charge in as many directions as there were voices. I remembered the Pauline warning about the uselessness of trumpets giving "an uncertain sound" (1 Cor. 14:8, KJV). And I realized how really tenuous and dangerous our situation was. We were well-supplied with leaders—good leaders—but still the church was without the leadership it needed, because we had risked everything for a concept—shared ministry and leadership—that was not working because our leaders were not together.

The actual leaders of the church simply must be together, or the potential is for the church to disintegrate under their leadership!

I had struggled with this problem (as I know others in the church had too). I had fielded repeated criticism that the church lacked leadership and direction. I had had my own times of intense frustration, bitterness, and criticism over the slowness of the team to "come together." There seemed no recourse at the time of my "trumpet vision" but to trust that God knew where we were and how to get us through it. I had no more answers. So I sat back to wait.

In addition to waiting, I did two things: (1) I asked each man to search his heart to see if he really wanted to be a pastor-elder. I told each, individually, that he need not feel under obligation to remain on the leadership team if he was not comfortable with the role. (2) I appealed once more for the "former original elder" who had resigned in the heat of conflict two years before, but who had continued to have an effective ministry in the church, to return to the team—for the sake of that needed "certain sound."

Over the ensuing few weeks, the team began to change. Two men, at separate times and for unrelated reasons, chose not to further pursue the ministry of elder. The former original elder was welcomed back. Larry's travel schedule opened up and he was able to promise increased participation in the future. And a twenty-four hour overnight retreat at Lewis's cabin near Payson included twenty-three hours of unprogrammed personal interaction that produced essential breakthroughs to esteem and relationship. Again, as though we had lived it all before, we returned home with the refreshingly hopeful beginnings of a viable team.

Six months later, changes in the direction of my own ministry removed me from the local church leadership scene for several months.

These good men (Pat Porter, Rod Wilke, Larry Richards, and Howard Graham) lived out a depth of commitment to the church and to each other, a level of understanding and competence in ministry beyond anything I had seen in them before, except in potential form. I am not at all sure that they had changed. Perhaps it's just that the scales had fallen from my eyes, and I was seeing them as they were in the Spirit.

I still reflect on the beauty of that original "Ministry Leadership Team" experience. But in terms of spiritual power, effective ministry, and real authority the present team, while more reserved, more hesitant to risk, more careful to move, is ready to "rule well." We have borne the cross of defeat and weakness. We have suffered the blows. We have emerged from the fire. There will be more crosses, more blows, more fire. Growth is demanded. But we will make it. We *are* the Pastoral Team.

DECISION-MAKING

I stated earlier that decision-making by the elders is not a democratic process in which decisions are finalized by majority vote. It is a spiritual exercise known as "consensus decision-making."

We see it in operation in Acts 15. The language of the biblical account indicates that there was very pointed and lengthy debate among the elders of Jersualem on the issue of gentile compliance with the Mosiac law. After all sides had been heard, James, one of the elders, evidently sensing what the whole group felt, made a statement that pulled together the group's real consensus. It proved acceptable to the gathered shepherds. And the action was taken. James had "struck a consensus." And the elders and apostles agreed that what he spoke was what the Holy Spirit wanted them to do at that time (vv. 25, 28).

The underlying spiritual principle upon which consensus-making operates is stated by Jesus in Matthew

237

18:19. It is a statement usually applied to prayer, but its context (vv. 15–20) is actually a discussion on how to handle a tough decision in the church—and the authority given to the church in such a situation. It states that God stands with believers when they agree, when they harmonize, on any matter.

One of the church's essential commitments is that Jesus Christ is Head of the church. Those who desire reality and not just credal words sense the need for practical means to be found through which to "tune in" on the desires of the Head for His church. It seems to me that consensus decision-making on the part of the leaders provides at least one key answer to that necessity. Engaged in by faith in the desire and ability of Christ to lead the church, consensus becomes an exciting adventure in spiritual communication, spiritual unity, and faith.

Stated most simply, the consensus-making process involves; (1) thorough discussion of the issue to assure that all persons who have feelings and/or opinions on it are carefully listened to, their true feelings shared, their sharing valued; (2) prayer and waiting on God; and (3) arrival at a decision all can go with together.

A consensus is not when everyone says, "That's wonderful!" It is when no one says, "We should not do it."

A consensus is lacking when one member of the decision-making body, after prayer about the issue, talking about it, looking at it from all sides, and hearing others' points of view, says, "I cannot agree that this is what God wants us to do."

When the members of the group agree that this is what God wants us to do at this time, the group has reached consensus.

If it is some pet project of mine, and the elders cannot reach consensus on it, I have no other recourse but to take it as the direction of the Head for now. It may be the end of the matter. Or, it may be brought back for more discussion.

Some churches use consensus decision-making even when the whole congregation is involved in the decision. We seem to be coming to this more and more, but to date still combine it with an occasional ballot.

Leadership teams are the best equipped to function by consensus. Even a spiritually immature "representative" governing body could be benefited by the process. However a leadership group may have been selected, consensus-making could force it to face important interpersonal issues.

Here the biblical essentials for brother-servant-leadership become significant. The best consensus-making can be done by (1) leaders chosen for their spiritual maturity, appropriate spiritual gifting for the office, and chosen under the direction of the Holy Spirit; (2) leaders whose first priority as leaders is to be "together"—in close personal fellowship with each other; (3) leaders who envision themselves as a team of ministers under the leadership of the Holy Spirit. As described in Acts 13:1–3, consensus decision-making in such a context of spiritual unity and unity of purpose is a natural.

There has not been a vote taken among our local leaders (the old church board, followed by the new pastoral team) for five years—even through some intense and stormy debate.

WHO LEADS THE TEAM?

One question raised by the concept of pastoral plurality, team leadership, is Who leads the team? Is there not, in Scripture, the concept of "the one man with the 'mantle,'" a "chief shepherd," or "ruling elder," or "principal pastor"? The one person through whom the Holy Spirit most often speaks to set the church's direction, around whom the members rally in unity, who is acknowledged as leader even by the other leaders, and at whose feet the "buck" (responsibility) inevitably stops?

Was not Moses such a charismatic leader, alone at the helm of Israel in its escape from slavery? And Joshua, at the head of Israel's invasion columns? And the judges, raised up to deliver God's people from their perennial oppressors? And isn't it obvious that James was the Jersualem church's "presiding elder," who spoke for the whole church in the controversy over the law and the gentile churches? And there was Paul, heading teams of missionaries, and continuing to speak authoritatively to the churches even after he had left them. And was not Timothy sent to serve alone as shepherd-leader of the Ephesian church?

In the Old Testament—that chronology of living pictures, shadows and types—the "lonely charismatic leader" is the norm. But, in the New Covenant, the "lonely charismatic leader" is Jesus Christ! He *alone* is the "Chief Shepherd"[8] (1 Peter 5:4), the "great Shepherd" (Heb. 13:20), the "one Master" (Matt. 23:8), the "one Teacher" (Matt. 23:10), the "head over everything" (Eph. 1:22), the "head of the body" (Col. 1:18), the "high priest" (Heb. 3:1), the "Wonderful Counselor" upon whose shoulders "the government will rest" (Isa. 9:6). The rest of us "are all brothers" (Matt. 23:8), who achieve greatness (if we do) only on the basis of a servanthood that chooses abasement over self-exaltation and gives its soul and life for other people . . . like Jesus did (Matt. 20:25–28; 23:11–12). When the Leader sends some to special responsibilities in the church, there may be lonely times and lonely vigils and lonely stands in lonely outposts of the spiritual warfront, but these are not the norm—at least they are not intended to be permanent. The norm in the New Covenant is teaming for brother-servant-leadership—mutuality in support, ministry, and responsibility.

In Matthew 23, Jesus severely castigates the religious leaders of His day for their practiced self-exaltation: religious nit-picking in the name of "leadership"; legalistic foolishness perpetuated simply for the sake of controlling the lives of people; motivational hypocrisy; religious pronouncements and manipulations done in the name of "piety" that were only a cover-up for the leader's own inner spiritual decay and failure to respond to God; coveting for themselves places of honor at religious gatherings and welcoming respectful titles and greetings that told puffy egoes they were "somebody" in the eyes of men. As already noted, John, the elder (3 John), warns against the ministry of the church leader who "loves to be *first*."

Christ affirms one church for its hatred for "the practices of the *Nicolaitans*," and warns another to repent because it has tolerated among its members in good standing those "who hold to the teaching of the *Nicolaitans*" (Rev. 2:6, 15). Scoffield and others believe that "Nicolaitans" is an epithetical byword coined by wedding two Greek words— *nikao*, to conquer, and *laos*, the people (of God). It is highly probable that the "Nicolaitans" are those who advocate practices and teachings in the church that place God's people "under" in a way never intended by the Head. This probably indicates that the seeds of the hierarchical system of church leadership that developed only a few decades later, and which led to the clergy/laity caste system, which today continues to conquer the laity, were already sprouting in the infant church, having been sown there by an enemy.

There is only one legitimate route to "chiefhood" in the church of Jesus Christ: the route of genuine self-giving servanthood, which only has in mind benefits to others. The true servant is one of the brothers by identification and true position, who has no desire to lord it over the others. He is found in the position of a slave, underneath, supporting the rest, so that they may be free. The effect of his servanthood is that the others find strength and courage to be all God has created them to be.

But what does that say to the suggestion that one of the local team of brother-servant-leaders will inevitably rise to the place of charismatic leader or presiding elder?

I do not see such a concept taught under the New Covenant. Instead, the overriding emphasis is on shared leadership, plurality, and complete mutuality among the members of the team of shepherds, bishops, elders, overseers, guardians, pastors, leaders (all those terms designate the same basic service—care for the spiritual leadership needs of local church).

Jesus never indicated that one of the Twelve would be their leader after His ascension.

Timothy and Titus are sometimes cited as examples of one man sent into a locality to serve as chief elder or principal pastor. Both men were traveling companions of Paul, whom he sent on special assignment from time to time. Timothy, for instance, was sent to Ephesus, to conduct an *apostolic* function there—the strengthening of the church through teaching, evangelism, and modeling, and the appointment of elders. Like any other apostle, Timothy spoke and acted with singular authority, based on his own gifts and personal ministry. It was seen as a temporary situation. "Do your best to come to me quickly" writes Paul (2 Tim. 4:9), whose apostolic support team was suffering from attrition and commissionings. When Timothy went to Ephesus, he was temporarily in charge. But his assignment was to turn oversight of the church over to a team of local men, then to move on as quickly as possible.

Titus, like Timothy, was frequently sent to struggling New Testament churches to bring the strengthening, affirming ministry of an *apostle*. Crete was one such assignment. He, too, was sent to appoint elders in the Cretian local churches (Titus 1:5), to deal with relational issues, and then to rejoin the apostolic team (3:12). He possessed the gifts and authority (and the backing of the apostolic team) to do the job. It was lonely, yes. Heavy with personal responsibility. But it was only a stepping stone to leaving an interdependent team of pastors in every locality on the island where there were Christians.

Peter and James are sometimes thought to have been successive presiding elders of the local church at Jerusalem. This conclusion is drawn from the fact that several incidents are told, between Acts 1 and 12, in which Peter plays the role of spokesman, channel, and trail-blazer, and finally is the focal point of an enemy attack on the church. Then, after a brief special mention in Acts 12:17, James' leadership seems to be notably respected. In 15:13, it is he who catches the consensus of the apostles and elders engaged in intense debate, and makes the proposal which all agree is in harmony with the Holy Spirit's desire for the church. In 21:18, it is especially noted that he was there, with the elders, to hear Paul's report of what God was doing among the Gentiles.

This may indicate a sort of "head elder" role. But that has to be read between the lines. There is another possibility.

In a team of pastor-elders, functioning together as brother-servant-leaders for each other and the local church, the gifting and working of God in the life of a particular man may give him greater impact and/or visibility in the life of the church. He may fill a body function that makes him more often the center of attention. He may be looked to for counsel or leadership by the other elders. He may be especially gifted to catch the direction of discussion and strike a consensus, therefore it is he who most often chairs the decision-making sessions. But, it is strictly the result of the Spirit's gifting and the Lord's design for the man's personal servanthood. Both he and the others may be perfectly comfortable with such an "effect" (1 Cor. 12:4–6).

But the New Testament does not teach that it is necessary or more desirable, for the effect of God's working, to place a single person in the "spokesman" or "bell sheep" role among the others equipped by gift and call to serve the flock as shepherds. In fact, it may be more in keeping with His design, to enable five men to function so totally as one, and to be so beautifully complementary to each other, and with

243

such perfect diversity and equality of intensity, that neither they nor the church can see any clear distinction in terms of who is leading the leaders. They are "together." At one time, one seems to be leading. At another time, his brother is the spokesman. At still another time, the guidance, teaching, and nurturing seem to be flowing from the team, acting as one man. This phenomenon seems possible from New Testament descriptions of the life of some churches. It has the glorious potential of providing the church with a style of leadership that least obscures the headship of Christ.

The Elder/Younger Principle of Discipling

The appointment of a congregation's spiritual elders to the office of elder is actually only one phase in the operation of a broad principle within the church. The gift of pastor is not given to pastors alone. A congregation may have many men and women who engage in shepherding (nurturing, protecting, guiding, enfolding) ministry to and for other members of the body. Even people with the kinds of spiritual impediment which may prohibit them from pastoral appointment, or who may never be led of the Spirit to accept the office of overseer, may have significant pastoral ministries.

In every Christian group, some will be more experienced in the application of spiritual principles to life, more knowledgeable in certain areas of biblical truth than the others. There is a sense in which, if in any aspect of the Christian life one is more mature than another, the more mature ministers to the less mature, to bring his "younger" to where he is in spiritual growth. In which case, the one has functioned in an "elder" role. Next day, the same two may switch roles. The act of discipling is simply the process of the elder sharing his life in Christ (with all it involves of knowledge and search, power and failure, competence and need) with the younger, and the younger receiving what his elder shares as coming from the Lord, and sharing what the Lord is giving him with his elder. All the biblical pictures of discipling are those in which one or two men and/or women are observed sharing their lives in Christ with another or a group of others.

In some cases this interchange becomes an extended intimate relationship between elder and younger. This is extremely desirable for both. (As a younger, I want that, and welcome it—even search for it.) Nevertheless, if the church's style is one of sharing and openness, whenever they get together, believers will be discipling each other in the natural flow of their interaction. The goal of all spiritual intercourse is to bring the younger to eldership. When the church then, led of the Spirit, chooses its elders (its pastoral team), it merely affirms those the Spirit has selected from a continually filling "pool" of spiritual elders.[9]

Notes

[1]*The Analytical Greek Lexicon* (Grand Rapids: Zondervan Publishing Co., 1970), p. 344.

[2]Ibid., p. 243

[3]Matthew 20:28, NASB marginal reading is "to give His *soul* a ransom for many."

[4]The Greek word is καθηγητής , which means *leader, to lead, conduct, or guide,* rather than "teacher" or "master" as some translators render it.

[5]Adapted from Larry Richards, lectures given at the Dynamic Church Seminars.

[6]Available from Serendipity House, Scottsdale, Pa.

[7]From the Appendix of this book, p. 331.

[8]*Lexicon*, p. 333.

[9]Additional bibliography:

Bob Smith, *When All Else Fails Read the Directions*(Waco: Word Books, 1974).

Watchman Nee, *The Normal Christian Church Life* (Washington: International Students Press, 1969).

Paul Landrey, "Teamwork in Mission", an unpublished paper (10 pages) drawing together the biblical basis for spiritual teamwork, Basic Principles of an Effective Team, Basic Concepts of Team Leadership, and Basic Principles of Team Formation. Landrey is a missionary with Overseas Crusades.

W. Graham Pulkingham, "God's Authority—A Gift to His Family," a set of four lecture tapes, available from The Fisherman, Inc., Box 18648, Houston, Tex. 77023.

11
Fire in the Assembly

At O.H., the participants really were a "family of God" to one another. The worship service was spontaneously directed—anyone could stand up and share a testimony, request a song to be sung, ask for emotional or financial assistance, or simply shout praises to God. The communication was open and highly honest. A diversity of personalities and spiritual gifts worked in harmony together regardless of differences of opinion. Confrontation and disagreement were freely and openly shared without fear of upsetting the family relationships already established. An environment of freedom allowed people to be themselves—the same person at church and at home. Three hours of singing, laughing (families do have a sense of humor), handclapping, and excellent biblical teaching are the unique trademarks of the Our Heritage family.

—Stephen Porter[1]
Northern Baptist Seminary

The meetings of the church are intended to be more than a sitting-and-listening-without-getting-involved affair. (That is, if the biblical historical account is to be taken as authoritative.) Fine, even spectacular performances were presented by the temple priests in Jerusalem, but under the New Covenant even the finest weekly musical/oratorical/liturgical performance would not do for a royal priesthood, which counts all believers in its number.

The record of a few early Christian meetings is preserved

for us in the New Testament. They are never called "worship services," even though the early Christians often worshiped together. Jesus prophetically designated them as times when His followers would "come together in my name" (Matt. 18:20). Luke speaks of their "meet[ing] together" (Acts 2:46), and that they "came together to break bread" (Acts 20:7). Paul refers to "your meetings . . . when you come together as a church" (1 Cor. 11:17–18, 33; 14:23, 26). The author of the Letter to the Hebrews speaks of "the assembling of yourselves together" (Heb. 10:25, KJV). When the original Christians assembled, it was not merely "to worship." It was to be "the church-together"—whatever that might involve. The focus of the meeting might deal with anything and everything involved with association "in Jesus' name," and "remembrance" of His person, work, life, and teaching.

ECCLESIA

The nature of the church is to be together. Christianity is, by nature, not primarily individual but collective. It calls people to assemble.[2]

The Greek word translated "church" is *ecclesia*. *Ek* means "out of." *Klesis* is "a calling." Its original usage was to refer to the assembling of a specific group for a particular purpose. The word literally designates "the called-out ones assembled." God has called out a people from the world system for Himself. Together or not, they are His "called-out ones." But by the use of the word "church" (*ecclesia*) to describe them, God indicates His intention that these called-out ones assemble together. If each one God calls out were to maintain his independence, there would, in fact, be no church![3] It is important for the church to be together.

WHY CHRISTIANS GATHER

The reasons for the Christian meetings are all based on the truth of the corporateness of our relationship with God.

First, God's plan is that there be no independent Christians. Watchman Nee, in *Assembling Together,* notes three important biblical revelations concerning the church which strongly convey this divine intention.

(1) Everyone who is born of the Spirit becomes a child of God, and with many other divine offspring, a member of the family (or household) of God (Eph. 2:19). I am not God's only-begotten child. God is my Father, and every born-again believer is my brother or sister. Only in living relationship with this forever family can the fullness of relationship with the Father be experienced.

(2) Believers together comprise God's house (habitation, dwelling, temple) (Eph. 2:19–22). The old desert tabernacle was replaced by the succession of destructible temples on Mt. Zion in Jerusalem. Under the New Covenant, a new indestructible earthly temple has been built for the habitation of God. God's new house is a living house built with many "living stones" (1 Peter 2:5), upon the "chief cornerstone, Christ Jesus" (Eph. 2:20). The sanctuary of the Lord is no man-made edifice, it is His people. No "place" is holy. Only His people can be holy. No lifeless thing or structure, however functional, will reveal the living God to the world. This He can accomplish only through a people who, together, are the living, breathing house of God. Everyone who has founded his/her life on Jesus is one of His living stones. By the Spirit they are "joined (fitted) together" (Eph. 2:21) to form His holy temple.

> If a house is to be constructed, stones must be built on stones and stones must be joined to stones. . . . We dare not say that living stones standing alone become dead stones, but it is certainly true that a stone, though living, will lose its usefulness and miss out on spiritual riches if it is not joined to other stones to become God's habitation. We can contain God's richness only when we are joined together with other living stones; then God can dwell in our midst. That is why there must be a conviction in our hearts that we must be the church.[4]

(3) Together, believers become the body of Christ (Eph. 1:22–23; 1 Cor. 12:12). It is impossible for those who are one with Christ to be independent from each other. First Corinthians 12 teaches lucidly that neither ear nor hand nor feet can declare its independence from the rest of the body. The members are useful only if they are in the body. A hand or an eye must be attached to the body or it is not only useless, it quickly dies. Oneness is not an option to body members. The biblical teaching about the church as the body reveals that the Lord has not given to any one person the whole fullness of the life and experience with God. The life we share is a strictly interdependent life. Isolation robs us of fullness, for as Ephesians 1:23 declares, "The church . . . his body, (is) the fullness of him. . . ." Unless we live in the church, in vital union with each other, knowing God in His fullness and experiencing the full richness of His life are impossible!

Hence, Christians gather because of the inescapable corporateness of their relationship with God.

Second, Christians meet because they are drawn together by the Holy Spirit. The original verb tense in Matthew 18:20 indicates that someone acts upon the "two or three" to bring them together. In Acts 2, the first response the Holy Spirit produced in the three thousand converts who had just received Him as a gift, was to begin meeting together for the apostles' teaching, interaction, breaking bread, and prayer (Acts 2:38–42). The Holy Spirit's pattern is to draw people together.

Third, Christians gather because they bear in common the name of Jesus (Matt. 18:20). "In Jesus' name" is the phrase which describes the Christian believer's authority. It is the passkey to relationship with God and kinship with each other. Of all earth's peoples, we are the only ones who have given allegiance to Jesus and are personally identified with His name. Our authority for gathering, the attraction by which the Spirit magnetically draws us to each other, the reason we have for assembling, is Jesus—His name, His person.

There is, in fact, no other legitimate "gathering place" for us. In the Old Tesament, the Lord would receive His people's sacrifices and worship only at the place in which He had placed His name. That place was the holiest place in the temple on Mt. Zion. (See Deut. 12:5-14). Under the New Covenant, the place of His name is still the only "official" venue for meeting. No extravagance of architecture, no perfection of performance, no human personality with magnetic charisma, no statement of theology, no effective use of mass media, or any other earthly thing that may be used to attract churchgoers is any substitute for the simple call to come together in Jesus' name.

Fourth, meeting is important for Christians because the Lord is present in the gathering (Matt. 18:20). While it is true that Jesus is near in the loneliest, most solitary moments of a person's life (Matt. 28:20), it is nonetheless true that the most powerful and overwhelming presence of the Lord is experienced in the meeting of believers together.[5] We as body members visibly gathered, in effect, cause the living Jesus to physically materialize before our eyes! This is the only time we see the physical presence of the Lord. We often do not recognize Him because we hesitate to believe He is incarnate in the aggregation of faulty friends which is the church. But around us when we gather, contained in a collection of earthenware jars,[6] is the physical/spiritual presence of the Lord. Those who are not longing for something better than the body, who look and listen with the eyes and ears of faith, see and hear the Lord whenever the body is together.

There are no strings attached to the promise: whenever we meet, He is with us. It is not just worship services or prayer meetings Jesus attends. Whenever a few of His friends gather—whether for worship, prayer, praise, teaching, communion, sharing, business, work, problem-solving, or play—or just to be together—Jesus is there! It's a spiritual assembly.

Fifth, Christians are drawn together because the reality of the body of Christ becomes clearest when we are assembled.[7] I know the body is real seven days a week, and does not go out of existence between weekends. It is probable that the body's most important work is done on weekdays as believers function in the world as salt and light. But when it's scattered, I do not see it so clearly. When, on the other hand, we come together, it is easy to see the body and it is difficult to deny its reality. Our corporateness is unmistakable when we are gathered. Our indivisibility may even then elude our comprehension, but the reality of our "bodyness" is closer and clearer when we can actually see the members together.

Sixth, Christians gather to stimulate spiritual growth. This reason for assembling also is to govern what we do when we are together. According to 1 Corinthians 14, a guiding principle for the believers' meeting is the principle of edification.

oikodomay (1 Cor. 14), the act of building . . .

(spiritual) advancement, edification.[8]

The church has a responsibility to speak to unbelievers. To touch them. Communicate the gospel to them. Win their allegiance to Jesus Christ. It needs to be able to speak their language. Answer their questions. Challenge their errors. But the regular gatherings of the church are not for that purpose. Unbelievers are not normally excluded. They are welcomed. Invited to join themselves to Christ. But . . . the regular meetings of the church are for the maturing of believers.

Unless the meeting is a special meeting designated specifically for evangelism, the planning of the church's gatherings should not be aimed at making them attractive to the unsaved. The spiritually growing church gathers its members to meetings geared to the spiritual man, the Christian. They should be geared to the expectation that believers who share in the assembly want to grow. We can expect followers of Jesus to desire spiritual things. So, church gatherings should never be designed to satisfy the whims of the carnal or worldly or careless Christian, or the person who does not know Jesus in the first place. Instead, what happens when we're together should lead the believer forward toward spiritual adulthood.

If he does not now have them, we should expect the believer to develop desires for edifying fellowship, close interaction with and ministry to fellow members, real prayer, genuine worship, and growth-producing teaching which moves beyond milk to meat[9]—beyond human likes and dislikes to ministry that touches real spiritual needs.

It is not an abdication of the evangelistic call for the church to concentrate in its gatherings on helping Christians grow up. Mature believers, no longer at the mercy of "every wind of teaching,"[10] who are part of the supportive fellowship of love, who are getting to know the Son of God, naturally reflect the glory of the living Christ. They are witnesses. It's their way of life.

Seventh, Christians meet to keep filled with the Holy Spirit. "Be filled with the Spirit" (Eph. 5:18) offers the challenge. The original verb's tense allows the interpretation: "Be *being* filled. . . ." No single crisis here. It is the indispensability of a continually intensifying relationship.

What is involved in keeping filled with the spirit? The challenge is actually one phrase within a rather long Pauline sentence which explains it:

> Do not get drunk with wine, for that is dissipation, but be filled with the Spirit, speaking to one another in psalms and hymns and spiritual songs, singing and making melody with your heart to the Lord; always giving thanks for all things in the name of our Lord Jesus Christ to God, even the Father; and be subject to one another in the fear of Christ (Eph. 5:18–21 NASB).

To keep the Spirit-filling fresh is to live life in a context of interaction with others who love the Lord. It is being together, sharing mutual gifts and encouragement and worship, sitting at each other's feet to receive from each other as from the Lord. All are essential elements in the process of perpetuating the Spirit-filled life.

The Spirit-filled fledgling church was renewed in its Spirit-fullness in the midst of a meeting of its members to share together the harsh reality of their life in a hostile city (Acts 4:31). I do not believe this was to be a one-time happening. Whenever believers gather, they should experience renewal of their capacity to receive and appropriate the fullness of the Holy Spirit for their daily reality.

RING OF FIRE

Perhaps the most radical biblical statement about the work of the Holy Spirit was made by John the Baptist in his prophecy concerning what Jesus Christ had come to do:

> The ax is already at the root of the trees, and every tree that does not produce good fruit will be cut down and thrown into the fire. I baptize you with water for repentance. But after me will come one who is more powerful than I, whose sandals I am not fit to carry. He will baptize you with the Holy Spirit and with fire. His winnowing fork is in his hand, and he will clear his threshing floor, gathering the wheat into his barn and burning up the chaff with unquenchable fire (Matt. 3:10–12).

The power of Jesus is the potency to cleanse, change, and deliver His followers from the chaff (sin, impurity) of their lives, by "soaking" them in the Holy Spirit, who fills their lives, bathing everything with a cleansing renewing fire. The fire of the Spirit ultimately leaves nothing behind but clean, unadulterated "wheat"—the pure, precious harvest of life. In the work Jesus came to do in us, the Holy Spirit and cleansing fire go together.

Christians of this generation have nearly talked themselves hoarse about how the Spirit comes—but have said little about the fire. How does the fire come to the church? What is Jesus-the-Baptizer's method or medium for distributing the cleansing fire of His Spirit?

A revealing phenomenon accompanied the original outpouring of the Holy Spirit. Ten dozen disciples met together. A little before nine in the morning, the room was violently invaded with a tornadic roar. And . . .

> there appeared to them *tongues as of fire distributing themselves, and they rested on each one of them.* And they were all filled with the Holy Spirit (Acts 2:3–4 NASB, italics added).

When the Holy Spirit fills the lives and beings of believers, at the same moment He distributes the promised fire among them. The fire of the Holy Spirit by which Jesus will thoroughly transform and purify His followers is literally "distributed." Each one of His friends is specifically given a share of the fire.

This is awesomely important. Were we able to see this truth, we would approach and respond to each other with the deepest appreciation and the highest esteem. The fire by which I am to be cleansed, the fire by which the church is to become all that the Lord intends, is brought to the church in the crude clay containers of the members of the body. It is not the prerogative of "special, spiritual" people or "leadership types" in the church to bring to it the perfecting fire. The fire distributes itself and rests on each one of us! A share of the fire by which the Lord intends to deliver me from the eternally useless chaff in my life, He brings into my life in the person of the brother next to me, and in all the other members of the body with which I have to do.

Hence, surrounding each of us who are in the family of God is a veritable ring of fire, through which the Lord of harvest will ultimately eliminate our impurities. The interaction of our lives, the developing intimacy of our fellowship, the investment of significant amounts of quality time with each other, then, are vital parts of the process of our purification. Exposure to each other, working through our irritations and discomfort with each other, and termination of the aloofness and solitariness that stands between us, are experiences of exposure to the fire of the Holy Spirit, distributed in the church. Reconciliation with, accommodation to, acceptance of, and deep involvement with each other, are necessary to the sanctifying work of the Holy Spirit in our lives.

When the church gathers, then the Pentecostal fire takes on special significance. Each coming together of any part of the body of Christ is a gathering together of the distributed flame. Together as Christians the opportunity for exposure to the Spirit's fire is maximized.

The fact that each of us shares a piece of the fire dictates the kinds of meetings Christians are to have. The apostle Paul gets into the specifics of the style of meeting that makes best use of the fire, in 1 Corinthians 14. The meeting style of the early church is described like this:

What then shall we say, brothers?

When you come together, everyone has a hymn

(something to sing)

or a word of instruction, a revelation, a tongue or an interpretation

(something to share).

All of these must be done for the strengthening of the church (v. 26).

THE FIRE AND PROPHECY

A most strategic aspect of these "wide open" assemblies was something called "prophecy." Its priority in the church is underscored by the fact that it is the only spiritual gift which is included in all four of the Pauline gift lists. The major thrust of 1 Corinthians 14 is to show how prophecy is the most desirable and one of the most valuable of all God's gifts to the church.

The word "prophecy" is basically untranslated, having been brought directly over from Greek to English with no change that would explain its meaning. Consequently, it is vastly misunderstood, even in the church.

The most basic Greek usage of the word (outside the church) was to designate "one who speaks for another." In the world of the first century it had become common to use the word to refer to "one who speaks for a deity," or "one who interprets the will of God."[11]

The angel, in Revelation 19:10, told John that "*the testimony of Jesus* is the spirit of prophecy." Joel indicated (in the prophetic message Peter quoted to explain the Holy Spirit's doings on the day of Pentecost) that "prophesying" (i.e., speaking for God) would be a widespread practice wherever the Holy Spirit was being poured out—

Your sons and daughters will prophesy.

He said it twice (Acts 2:17 and 18).

There are people with full-blown, set-apart, prophetic, or speaking-for-God ministries. They are called "prophets" and "prophetesses," or, to translate, "speakers for God." And there are special "prophetic messages" which are sometimes given in the church, by which the thoughts of the congregation or individuals are galvanized and focussed around a special "word from the Lord." The charismatic renewal has brought a revival of this type of prophecy. A sense of miracle may attend such words. But New Testament prophesying also includes the simplicity of a testimony or insight shared in a meeting of the body, in a meeting of two or three believers, or in the world. Such prophesying (speaking for God) by ordinary believers was a part of most meetings of the original Christians.

In the style of meeting our congregation shares (described at the beginning of this chapter), prophesying (speaking for God, interpreting what God is doing) is something we experience nearly every time we get together. Not everything said in these meetings is prophesying. Some is problem sharing which often leads to prophesying. Nonetheless a good part of what happens falls within the broad definition

257

of the biblical word. Some of it falls within the special definitions. It is not all spooky and it often doesn't seem miraculous (though I believe it is), but it *is* prophesying—the Holy
Spirit speaking through His people.

The cleansing aspect of what happens is described in 1
Corinthians 14:25 . . .

> If the whole church should assemble and . . . if all
> prophesy (speak for God), and an unbeliever or an
> uninitiated believer (a believer who is lacking something
> in the development of his spiritual understanding and
> experience) enters, he is convicted by all, he is called
> into account by all, the secrets of his heart are disclosed
> (to him); and so he will fall on his face and worship
> God, declaring that God is certainly among you. (Para-
> phrased and expanded to include word meanings.)

That's Jesus, in the midst of His church, threshing the
wheat and burning the chaff! The distributed fire surrounds
us in the meeting. The gathered intensity of the Spirit's
flame leaps from soul to soul. The cleansing process goes
on. Through each other the Holy Spirit speaks. We are con-
victed of sin through each other. We find ourselves called to
answer for the residue of bitterness and selfishness that
clings to our life-in-the-Spirit. Inside, the covering is being
torn off the stark reality of our secret unbeliefs, fears, hos-
tilities, prejudices, conceits, lusts, hurts, guilts, resentments,
resistances to God, and failures at love.

In the Corinthian-style church meeting (I speak from personal experience), prophetic and exhortative voices may
speak and exciting new light breaks in some neglected area
of life. But, in the same meeting, God's message may come
in the form of very uncomfortable, self-abasing feelings that
reveal the unholiness of our responses to fellow believers
who are speaking. Repeatedly, I have been forced to deal
with such inner evidences of lack of love. Sometimes, our
whole church has been given the painful choice between
acceptance of the difficult-to-accept person who rises to

share, and resentment of him leading to rejection. It's always a time when heart secrets are laid bare, the voice of God speaks, and no one dares to say with self-exalting pride, "I heard God speak today." In those times, whoever says it, says it with a humble recognition that God has spoken to his personal lack or sin.

And in the fire, we see the face of God. We know He's there. And that He is intent on changing us.

That is how it is when true believers get together and speak with one another for God. And that is why meeting has to be more than a performance, a speech, a "sitting-and-listening-without-getting-involved" affair. Because each true believer has the Spirit's fire . . . for each other's sanctification.

A basic requisite to the body's life, therefore, is: In the church everyone is to come together to contribute something: and everyone may share in the meeting. It is essential to the unity, growth, and power of the church. And it is essential to the experience in the church of the full impact of the "shared Jesus" and His distributed cleansing fire. It's God's plan for when believers are together.

METAMORPHOSIS IN THE MEETING

The evolution that brought our church to its present meeting style was an alternately agonizing and satisfying process stretching over four or five years. The dream of an open, participative gathering sprouted and grew from the ground of a growing understanding of the biblical doctrine of the spiritual giftedness of the every-believer priesthood. The vision was sharpened by the descriptions of the original Christians' meetings as told by the New Testament, and of the unique Sunday evening meetings at Penninsula Bible Church, Palo Alto, California, as told by Ray Stedman in his book *Body Life*.[12]

From the outset, it seemed that that real, spontaneous meeting-style was the way the church ought to be whenever it gathered. It seemed to contain the potential for introducing reality into a hitherto sugar-coated assembly. And Jesus had promised the day when worshiping God would be an experience of spirit and reality (John 4:23).

Small groups were springing up and thriving in many places in the local church. People involved in them were tasting spirit and reality. But when the Sunday services came, there was little of either—other than a new sparkle in the eyes of a handful of renewed people and a new openness on the part of the pastor to share his personal struggles. Some of us longed to loosen up this rigid wineskin and let the Spirit-wind blow through the meeting place. From the pulpit came extensive teaching of biblical body-life principles, our need for each other, the need for reality in our expression of worship and fellowship, the New Testament church's meeting patterns, etc.

We decided to start by turning the Sunday evening service into a Stedman-style body-life meeting. So, we met in the Sunday school building. Sat in a circle, or on the floor. Allowed the whole meeting to "erupt" spontaneously from the hearts of the believer priests. Sang the songs the priests wanted to sing. Learned to sing the Scriptures. Shared the happenings of our lives. Joys. Insights. Hurts. Burdens. Experiences in sharing Jesus in our world. Prayed for each other's requests and then checked up during the weeks following to see how God answered. Prayed for the sick, and saw some healed. We let the teaching come spontaneously in response to questions members of the group were asking. It was a genuine experience of truth and spirit. And it was intensely relevent to the lives of the participants.

But the conviction grew that while what we were experiencing together Sunday nights was real and powerful, the main body of our church still gathered in impersonal formality that increasingly seemed like a great barrier to much that we now knew a believers' meeting could accomplish.

In desperation to see the barrier begin to crumble, I broke into one Sunday's "order of worship" with the following insurrectionary move: I asked everyone to stand up, find someone nearby who was not a member of his/her family, and talk to each other for a few moments. "Give each other your name," I instructed, "and tell each other where you lived between the ages of seven and twelve, and how you heated your house in those days. And keep talking until I tell you to stop!"

It was heavenly bedlam. After the initial looks of shock, they did as instructed. Everyone talked to someone at church that day. To my ears the din of human voices in conversation was sweeter than organ music.

Afterwards, I explained why I had done it. And "Friendship Time" was added to the weekly order printed in the bulletin.

After a lengthy period of time to deal with the aftershocks of this addition (some people loved it, others were extremely threatened by it), I began to ask for questions from the congregation following my sermons. The questions were slow in coming, so I "planted" a few: that is, before the meeting I would ask two or three people to be ready with a question for me, to help break the ice.

Next, we added a pause before prayer to ask if anyone was hurting and would like to have us pray for them specifically. A few would stand and share.

Later, a section was added to the order of worship, in which spontaneous sharing was encouraged. This would open the meeting to even more reality and involvement with each other, in a sharing of current life experiences, testimonies, praise items, spiritual insights, exhortations, and personal concerns. At the beginning, and occasionally through our period of learning to meet together this way, a few people would be preselected to stand and share what I knew God had been doing in their lives that week. The emphasis was on sharing from life as it is happening now.

For eighteen months after the body-life section was added to the meeting, our commitment to teach the congregation to function in this more personal, spontaneous way would be tested again and again. The sharing would alternate from Sunday to Sunday between reluctant, dull, irritating, and wonderful. Major complaints about it were that "I don't come to church to listen to *those* people talk—I come to listen to *you*, pastor"; "Why does *she* always share those irritating things every Sunday?"; and "The service is getting too long." (Indeed it was getting longer and longer—1¼ hours, then 1½, then 1¾, then more. It's a matter of simple arithmetic. If more than one person is going to speak, more time is required.)

Many complaints were used as springboards for teaching. Those who were irritated were taught that their irritation was evidence that their love needed to grow. Those who didn't want to listen to anyone other than the pastor speaking in church were taught about the believer-priesthood and the spiritual gifts. Those who felt the service was too long were taught both of the above and reminded (not too effectively, I fear) of the length of typical sports events, concerts, and movies, and that the New Testament places no sixty-minute time limit on Christian meetings.

And sometimes the sharing *was* irritating, unprofessional, and too long. And often those with something really edifying to share were reluctant to speak, thus giving the floor that Sunday exclusively to the socially or emotionally needy, who would share to meet their social and emotional needs. (Even that can be edifying, but it is also often quite uncomfortable and doesn't seem edifying at the time.) Our response to this problem was to exhort and teach on the necessity of everyone bringing something with him/her to the meeting, of willingness to participate and not just to watch, and of the "edification-criteria" for what takes place.

Criticism and testing notwithstanding, at about the

eighteen-month mark we become aware that we had broken through to a refreshing level of freedom. It became unnecessary to plant people to share or ask questions. Whenever there was opportunity given, someone was expecting it and ready. And the quality of the sharing was more often recognized as spiritually beneficial to the body, and was maturing.

Gradually, with leadership of the meetings being shared by the elders and others, the whole gathering has been opened to its priesthood. Leaders see to it that important elements are not overlooked, i.e. mutual ministry, acknowledgment of the praiseworthiness of God, growth-producing teaching, prayer, news of body and personal needs, etc. They introduce needed elements, and give guidance, exhortation,and correction as needed.

It is more like a family gathering than a presentation to an audience. It is extremely informal, largely spontaneous, and sometimes disturbingly real. It lasts about two-and-one-half hours.

With all its spontaneity and freedom, there is order. Normally, the meeting consists of these elements:

—singing, praise, and worship,

—biblical teaching followed by questions, further insights, interaction, or debate,

—sharing of personal needs, prayer requests, victories, common concerns, exhortations, etc.,

—prayer for specific persons and problems (occasionally with the laying on of hands),

—the Lord's Supper, at least monthly.

Sometimes the meeting ends with the congregation in a circle, holding hands, singing Malotte's "The Lord's Prayer," *a capella*. In addition, there is freedom to set everything aside to deal with a personal need, or to let the teaching come (in a nonsermonic fashion) from the sharing of the congregation itself. When congregational business concerns require attention by the whole group, these are made a part of this same Sunday morning time together.

After the meeting, there is often a Love Feast (pot-luck dinner), followed by games, sports, swimming, special classes, or lengthy conversations. For several months this was an every-Sunday pattern.

The Sunday meeting (called "Celebration") is now our only congregational meeting of the week. The functions of the Sunday evening gathering having been brought into the larger Sunday morning session rendered the evening meeting unnecessary. So it was cancelled, to make more time available for our families to be families.

Time lapses: (1) Eighteen months to come to significant freedom in sharing and spontaneous participation; (2) About four years to move through the steps outlined above leading from pulpit-centered formality to believer-priest-centered participation.

Over any period of months, many of the gifts of the spirit listed in Romans 12:6–8; 1 Corinthians 12:8–10 and 28; and Ephesians 4:11 are being exercised in these meetings—occasionally in the traditional "charismatic" manner, but usually in a more natural way, amid the reality of a group of people speaking to one another out of their lives and their relationship with the living God.[13]

FANNING THE FIRE

This kind of free-wheeling public interchange opens the door to one very vexing problem: If everyone is encouraged and permitted to speak for God in the church, the gathered saints are often going to be exposed to the ministry of the spiritually immature, the weak, the selfish, the overbearing, the mistaken, the confused, the wrong in attitude and doctrine, the divisive, and the unspiritual. And, alas! even the spiritual are sometimes overtaken by error, faulty logic, or mistaken interpretation of the Word and of what God is doing in their lives. And yet, it is to such a faulty conglomeration of stumbling saints that the Spirit of God has given His gifts, His voice, and His fire.

264

For this reason, the Bible includes careful instructions, which are intended to guard both the freedom of the Spirit to speak through whomever He will and the order and soundness of the church. (See 1 Cor. 14 and 1 John 2:18–27, for instance.)

Perhaps the clearest statement offering a step-by-step response to whatever is said in the name of the Lord is 1 Thessalonians 5:19–22:

> Do not put out the Spirit's fire; do not treat prophecies with contempt. Test everything. Hold on to the good. Avoid every kind of evil.

(In several versions, that section is a single sentence.)

Two ways are disclosed in which the Holy Spirit's fire can be extinguished: (1) having contempt for prophesying (ordinary believers speaking for God), and (2) failure to use one's judgment with regard to what is said.

As we have seen, the meetings of the biblical church include broad participation and speaking for God by ordinary believers. It is one important way the sanctifying fire of the Spirit does its life-changing work in us. To have contempt for prophesying is to make light of that process, to belittle or despise the sharing or teaching or praying of fellow saints, to avoid exposure to it by refusing to gather where believers are interacting, to treat such mutual speaking for God as optional or secondary, to disregard what is said, or to despise the person saying it. All these actions and reactions are powerful steps toward "quenching the fire of the Spirit."

Such negative reaction toward interaction in the body of Christ is not merely a personal matter having to do with aesthetics, emotions, or personal preferences. The danger is of specifically hindering the work of the Spirit to change us, by trying to stifle His uncomfortable prophetic utterances.

They may irritate, produce discomfort, challenge values, or give rise to angry, carnal feelings. They may be wrong and need correction. They may not have neat and polished ways of saying what they have to say. They may talk through their noses about things better kept to themselves. But the fire of God's Spirit is on them, and the Spirit is speaking through them. And through interaction with them, we are being cleansed and transformed. So . . . "Do not put out the Spirit's fire; do not treat prophecies with contempt."

There is an oft-overlooked second factor in the kind of response we are to have to what people say in the name of the Lord: *Test everything.* (The same instruction is given in 1 Cor. 14:29.)

The Holy Spirit's fire can be put out in the church if believers gullibly "soak in" everything anyone says or teaches in a purportedly Christian context, without being discriminating and making conscious personal decisions to receive or to reject all or part of what is being said. The biblical imperative is not "Be suspicious of everyone and everything they say," nor "Be so afraid of being led astray that you dare listen only to a narrow variety of Christian people who fit some predetermined theological or ideological pigeonhole." Such spiritual paranoia inhibits the work of the Spirit more than it protects the saints from error, and is itself a growth-inhibiting form of error. At the same time, we are instructed to test everything, to judge carefully, to scrutinize everything that anyone is saying in the Lord's name.

It is the responsibility of every Christian to bring his mind to church. We are to be thinking while the brothers and sisters interact, the teachers teach, the preachers preach, the prophets prophesy, and the exhorters exhort. Also, we are to be applying our powers of judgment while listening to Christian radio, television, or tape; while reading Christian literature; while singing or listening to Christian music; and while studying the Bible and/or praying with Christian friends.

God has given His people at least two things to equip them to examine and choose a response to everything said in His name.

First, He has given us the written Word of God, the Bible. In a context of warning about deceivers and imposters in the church, Paul tells Timothy,

> All scripture is God-breathed and is useful for teaching, rebuking, correcting and training in righteousness, so that the man of God may be thoroughly equipped for every good work (2 Tim. 3:16–17).

No one is such an authority in the church that what he says need not be checked against the Scriptures. When a "speaker for God" says something that doesn't square with what I, as a Christian listener, think the Bible teaches, I should not "buy" the idea until I have had time to go to the Word to do my own research on the matter. The Scriptures have the final word. It is not disrespectful, unbelieving, nor unspiritual to do this. It is imperative.

The second part of God's equipping of us to judge what is said, is "the anointing of the Spirit" (1 John 2:18–27). Sound judgment is not merely a matter of being knowledgeable of the Bible. True Christians are indwelt by the Holy Spirit, and are in personal relationship with the living person who not only knows, but is the Truth. This relationship is personal and functions on personal communication between the two parties, the believer and God. The indwelling Spirit "will guide you into all truth," promised Jesus (John 16:13).

Listening Christians should be being taught continually to dare to think and feel, and to trust their inner gut-level feelings about things said in a Christian context. If one is uneasy about what is being taught, he should not receive the teaching without asking the questions he feels or taking the ideas to the Word for verification. Leaders would do well to exhort believers repeatedly to have confidence in their ability and authority to judge whatever anyone is saying. "Anointing" is a transfer of authority. Because he/she has the Holy Spirit, the ordinary believer has the authority as well as the serious responsibility to judge everything that is said in the Lord's name. This judging is not at all unloving—it is positively commanded.

Recently Joyce was talking with Audrey and me, telling us how, when a certain brother shared in the meeting, she felt terribly uneasy and simply would not listen to what he was saying. "Was that the wrong thing to do?" she asked. "Absolutely not!" we replied, "That man's word comes out of a life filled with deception and bitterness. Your uneasiness was the result of the Holy Spirit within you, making you sensitive to the spirit of error." Without knowing the Holy Spirit was speaking, she had made the right choice. We simply had to assure her that she had the authority to judge, and to help her to recognize the Spirit's "voice" for what it is.

All believer-priests, elders, pastors, prophets, teachers, evangelists, and other speakers for God, being human, are continually prone to error. None is able to interpret God perfectly. Therefore, the words of all must be carefully tested in the light of God's written Word and the Spirit's shared authority.

In every case of exposure to someone speaking, singing, or praying in the name of the Lord, the Christian listener's response is to have two important elements:

(1) He is to esteem his fellow Christian, and to guard his freedom to speak.

(2) He is to judge carefully what his fellow Christian says, and guard his own freedom to make such judgments.

Such Spirit-anointed judgment is bound to turn up mistakes amid the truth. A good teaching may be laced with ignorance, inexperience, or prejudice. And God often chooses to say genuinely edifying, soul-searching things through immature believers who don't fully understand what they are saying. Human prejudices (of both speakers and listeners) often color the presentation of a vitally needed word from the Lord. When one's testing turns up error, inconsistency, human discoloration, wrong attitude, or a wholly mistaken idea, the Pauline instruction is to make a

268

conscious spiritual decision, (1) to receive and assimilate what is good and true, and (2) simply to have nothing to do with the evil and untrue.

There are times when the error should be confronted publicly and immediately (i.e., Paul upbraiding Peter for his misleading and damaging nonverbal message to the gentile believers, in Gal. 2). There are gentle and loving ways to do this. I remember the time a sister rose to share her healing experience, and then proceeded to generalize it into a theology of healing which gave the impression that the only reason people are not healed when they pray is personal lack of faith. The next Sunday, in direct response, a respected spiritual brother simply shared his experience of exercising faith over a long period of time (his family with him) for the healing of his eyes, in which no "miraculous" healing took place, surgery was eventually required, and his trust in God was actually strengthened through the experience. At other times, the public correction must be even more direct and pointed.

The double motive in all Christian correction and rebuke: (1) to save the mistaken fellow disciple from his error, and (2) to guard the body against spiritual disease.

When public correction would be confusing to the listeners, it is best to deal with the matter privately (i.e., to correct some important gaps in Apollos' message, Acts 18:24–28, Aquilla and Priscilla chose to invite him to their home after the meeting "and explained to him the way of God more adequately.")

Normally, when gathered Christians are simply sharing their lives with each other, talking about their struggles to live out Jesus' life, even interpreting some of these things, those who are knowledgeable need to listen to the *spirit* of the person sharing. In a context of teaching about how to handle differences of conscience and spiritual understanding, Paul reminds the church that superior knowledge is not to have the final word . . .

269

Knowledge puffs up,
but love builds up (1 Cor. 8:1).

This does not mean I leave my brother in ignorance and misleading others. But my response to him—correction, rebuke, or my general attitude toward him—is to come through as self-limiting love.

It is not necessary to contradict every word the brother says which may not be totally correct. When the church is being hurt, public or private correction is demanded. But sometimes the Spirit will do His correcting through the Word, the brother's ongoing experience in God, and the positive ministry and modeling of other members of the body. The best setting for effective correction is a loving personal relationship in which growth is being stimulated through one-to-one interactions between friends.

DEFICIENCIES AND POTENTIAL

I see both great potential and major deficiencies in our meetings. A study of early Christian documents, some of which describe the church's meetings of the first and second centuries, discloses that a much greater place was given to the Christian meal, the Lord's Supper, which was usually celebrated as part of a Love Feast which also became an occasion for providing food for the poor.[14] Our usual pattern is to celebrate a very personal and informal version of the Lord's Supper in our meeting on Sunday per month. For a while, as I said, a weekly Love Feast followed each Sunday meeting. Then, because some felt it was more burdensome than helpful on a weekly basis, it was made an occasional happening—perhaps monthly.

We lack (I speak for myself, though I am quite certain I confess also the weakness of others) the depth of appreciation for the power of the Communion meal (Lord's Supper) that the early Christians seemed to possess. Keys to understanding seem to be missing that could make this the dynamic event it was to them. It may be simply, on our part, the sin of ingratitude for the sacrifice of Christ. Or it may be our life-long experience with the mundaneness, coldness, and unrealness of ritualism that has attached itself to the church's traditional approach to Holy Communion. There is fear that weekly repetition of the meal, given our weak emotional grasp of its symbolism, may just bury its true power deeper beneath the wet blanket of our tradition-laden mindset. It does not seem that a live understanding would grow simply through dutiful repetition.

We must, I think, search diligently until we understand, appreciate, and can experience what the Lord envisioned the night He took bread and broke it. . . . New twists on the old custom are helpful, but are not enough.

Our open-meeting style has brought us into some experiences of genuine spiritual shaking and renewal (see Acts 4:31). So, perhaps, my hungering for more that can clearly be recognized as "the power of the Spirit among us," is, again, the sin of ingratitude for and blindness to what He is already doing in our midst. But I sometimes feel that we are bound by fear and an undue sense of propriety.

We have watched, mostly from a safe distance (though some of us have gone "inside"), the self-centered emotionalism of some of the so-called pentecostal/charismatic tradition—the exaggeration and intoxication of one's own human emotions.[15] (As a child and youth, I watched such emotionalism from inside the Wesleyan/Holiness movement of which I was and am a part.) And we want something more genuine. But, could our fear of excess and counterfeit actually be keeping us from being receptive of the powerful presence of the living Spirit, and the shaking dynamic of certain spiritual gifts?

We want no empty show, no empty catch-phrases, no empty gifts, no more psychological manipulation of truth or tongue. But the *Spirit*—however He would shake and renew us and stir us to boldness in speaking God's Word, in living in one-souledness, in radical self-giving, in powerful testifying to the resurrection of Jesus, in serving one another[16]—let the *Spirit fill* the gathered church!

Jesus came also into every peaceful meeting, however small, He who alone was both leader and fellow-fighter among His followers. Often in meetings of this nature, the radiant cross and the thronging mass of people watching the execution of Jesus were all but visible. The voices raised at the crucifixion of Jesus and the shouts of His friends and enemies rang out from Golgotha.

What was seen and heard in such Spirit-filled gatherings often led to unintelligible speech and to actions that were hard to understand. Nevertheless, what dominated their meetings was the fiery judgment of the last battle, which gave flaming birth to light and warmth and brought the fresh air of the future world; for here the Christ was truly present in person, in the power of God's Word pregnant with the Spirit, and in the powerful virtue of goodness, pureness and strength.

In prayers, psalms and hymns, and in commentaries on the Bible which the prophets and teachers made during the meetings, the Word came into its own. The moral impact of Biblical truth exacted purity and truthfulness in actual life, practical love in actual work. There was nothing of the exaggeration and intoxication of one's own human emotions in the exultant enthusiasm which broke in freely from the Holy Spirit. On the contrary, the genuine, surging power of the Holy Spirit revealed the authority of the Christ, which came down straight from the other world like a stroke of divine lightning. Sometimes, on hearing for the first time the proclamation from those who had been taught by the apostles, whole crowds would embrace the faith under this impact of God.[17]

Notes

[1]Stephen Porter, summer intern, sharing his perceptions of the weekly meetings at Our Heritage Church, for a seminary publication.

[2]Watchman Nee, *Assembling Together* (New York: Christian Fellowship Publishers, Inc., 1973), p. 35.

[3]Ibid., p. 36.

[4]Ibid., pp. 5–6.

[5]Ibid., p. 38.

[6]2 Corinthians 4:7.

[7]Nee, *Assembling,* p. 36–38.

[8]*The Analytical Greek Lexicon,* Zondervan, p. 284.

[9]1 Corinthians 3:2; Hebrews 5:12–14.

[10]Ephesians 4:14.

[11]*Analytical Lexicon,* p. 354.

[12]Published by Regal Books Division, Gospel Light Publication, Glendale, Calif., 1972.

[13]Malachi 3:16.

[14]Acts 20:7; 1 Corinthians 11:17–34.
Justin Martyr, *First Apology,* 65–67, about A.D. 138; Tertullian, *Apology,* 39, after A.D. 200. Source: Eberhard Arnold, *The Early Christians After the Death of the Apostles* (Rifton, New York: Plough Publishing House, 1970), pp. 220–225.

[15]Ibid., p. 27.

[16]Acts 4:31–35.

[17]Arnold, *The Early Christians, pp. 26–27.*

12

"The Annual 'Speaking-in-Tongues Crisis' Has Been Cancelled"

I . . . refuse to be distinguished from other men by any but the common principles of Christianity . . . I renounce and detest all other marks of distinction. But from real Christians . . . I earnestly desire not to be distinguished at all . . . Dost thou love and fear God? It is enough! I give thee the right hand of fellowship.

—John Wesley

"Pastor, I received 'the baptism' last night!"

The residue of old prejudices implanted in me by the church since early childhood, caused by stomach muscles to tighten noticeably at those words. And the old prejudices were not alone. They had been confirmed and strengthened in later life as I watched the turmoil that boiled up in many churches when some of the faithful were drawn into the charismatic movement.

"Oh, oh!" I groaned inside, "It's happening in *my* church."

I had often talked about what my response would be. I had said I was open, if the Holy Spirit wished to work in this manner among us. I had boasted that God could do whatever He wanted to do with Our Heritage Church.

But when members of our church began to report that they had been to charismatic meetings and had "come into the baptism of the Holy Spirit" and were speaking in tongues, I was inwardly afraid.

But I could not deny that, in some of their lives, there was definitely a new awareness of the reality of Jesus and a new commitment to His Lordship. And when I went back to the Bible to search out what my response should be, I could not deny that speaking and praying in tongues is a biblical gift given by the Holy Spirit.

One instruction is certainly crystal clear: "Do not forbid speaking in tongues" (1 Cor. 14:39). I determined that, whatever response the church and I should make, we would not disobey that imperative.

But respond we must, for many in the church were being touched by the score or so of enthusiastic charismatics among us. Two or three of our weekly home study/sharing groups began discussing "the baptism," "spiritual gifts," and "tongues." The tapes of well-known charismatic teachers were introduced into the group meetings. And a few of these earnest Christians, zealous for the good things brought into their own lives by their new experience, began to press the contention that unless every Christian experienced something similar to what they had experienced and received the "attesting sign" (a new language), there would always be something essential missing from their Christian lives. In addition, those who were now "moving out in the gifts of the Spirit" began to gather in new and separate meetings to encourage each other in the new experiences and to pray and praise the Lord.

A wide spectrum of spontaneous responses erupted in the rest of the congregation: i.e., searching the Scriptures, earnest seeking to "receive," confusion, jealousy, self-condemnation, frustration, fear, resentment. A number of the negative responses were based on prejudice, unfounded fears, and biblical ignorance, to be sure. But some were normal reactions to verbal and nonverbal messages that sometimes came across as spiritual pride, egotism, separatism, and contempt for the "lesser" spiritual relationships of fellow believers—a holier-than-thou-ness that quickly built walls between brothers and sisters. More than one person felt a deep sense of rejection. A few people experienced tremendous emotional pressure to "enter in," in order to be socially and spiritually accepted by their "Spirit-filled" friends. Many of us, positively, found God speaking to us concerning our genuine need for a more real and intimate walk with Him.

There was struggle and pain in the body of Christ, and not a little confusion.

God was doing something significant in the life of the church and its people. I wanted neither to miss it nor to mess it up. But the confusion, conflict, and divisive aspects of what was happening demanded positive response. Since this was in the days before the development of our team approach to pastoral ministry (ch. 10), if anyone was to speak to the issues involved, it would have to be me.

The outgrowth of my concern was a seven-Sunday series on the ministry of the Holy Spirit. I intended to let the Bible say exactly what it says about the Holy Spirit, spiritual gifts, and spiritual baptism. My approach was to discuss the whole scope of the Spirit's ministry in the lives of people. I attempted to show that the Spirit is indeed involved in baptizing and equipping (gift-giving), but that His work is not primarily confined to "great experiences." The Holy Spirit's ministry includes such basic and important activities in our lives as . . .

illuminating (John 16:13–16)
 i.e., convicting (John 16:8–11), teaching (John 14:26), leading (Rom. 8:14)
regenerating (Titus 3:5)
 i.e., new birth (John 3:5–8), new creation (2 Cor. 5:17), resurrection (Rom. 8:11)
sealing (Eph. 1:13–14)
 i.e., stamping us with God's mark of ownership
baptizing (Luke 3:16; Acts 1:5; 1 Cor. 12:13)

> i.e., positioning us in Christ (Rom. 6:3–5), introducing us into the stream of life in the Spirit (Rom. 8; 1 Cor. 12:13)

indwelling (1 Cor. 3:16; 6:19)

> i.e., "Christ in you" (Col. 1:27)

cleansing (Acts 15:8–9; Luke 3:17)

> i.e., sanctifying, purifying

equipping (Eph. 4:11–12)

> i.e., the gifts of the Holy Spirit (1 Cor. 12; 13; 14)

filling (Eph. 5:18)

> i.e., diffusing Himself through our beings (Acts 2:4, *Amplified Bible*), empowering (Acts 4:31–33).

The study sought to show that baptism with the Spirit is not just an added blessing for a few willing Christians, but it is the whole stream of the Holy Spirit's powerful working, into which true believers are placed when they receive Jesus Christ as Savior and Lord. The term covers the entirety of the transforming work of the living Christ carried on in our lives by the Holy Spirit. One may speak of "spiritual baptism" or "baptism in the Spirit" to describe a significant and crisis *moment* in the whole-life experience with the Holy Spirit. Life-changing experiences, in which the Spirit's reality breaks in on us with new awareness and power, in which we touch new levels of surrender to God's will, or in which we are newly equipped by His added gifts to serve God more effectively and enjoy Him more fully, are often part of the great baptizing work of Jesus Christ. But there is also an overarching continuity in all the Spirit does, a singleness of purpose in every phase of His process. The New Testament theologians and prophets employ the term "baptism" (Greek: to be placed or introduced into) to describe several aspects of the new and living relationship with God opened to us in Christ: (1) introduction into the Holy Spirit (Acts 1:4–5); (2) entrance into spiritual union with Christ Jesus, including His death, burial, and resurrection (Rom. 6:3–7); (3) placement by the Spirit within the body of Christ, the church (1 Cor. 12:13); (4) assuming the family likeness of (being "clothed with") Jesus Christ (Gal. 3:26–29); and (5) the outward symbol of spiritual baptism, water baptism (Acts 10:44–47). The unity and wholeness of Christ's spiritual working in us is emphasized by Paul when he says, in Ephesians 4:5, that one of the things on which unity of spirit is based is the "*one* baptism" in which all Christians share.

The spiritual gifts named in Scripture, including tongues (new unlearned languages), are as needed in the church today as they were in the first century, I said. The church must be open to *all* the gifts of the Holy Spirit. But, in order for there to be unity in the body, we must grasp and appreciate the New Testament's clear teaching concerning the wide diversity of spiritual gifts and experiences (1 Cor. 12:4–30; Rom. 12:6–8). None of the gifts, including the new languages for prayer and worship, is universal among Spirit-filled Christians (1 Cor. 12:29–30). It is ultimately the will of the Spirit Himself which determines the exact personal distribution and corporate configuration of His spiritual equipments (1 Cor. 12:11).

Before I could complete the series, fifteen people who had experienced "the baptism" left and became part of another congregation. A spokesman told me they were leaving because I was teaching false doctrine. How, he intimated, could it be otherwise, when I was "closed to the Holy Spirit."

From my perspective, I had honestly been struggling to preserve the unity of the Spirit. But my prejudice and fear had been stronger than I had realized and had detrimentally influenced my approach to the matter. I had failed to communicate love, acceptance, and confidence. The group felt scolded, attacked, and rejected.

Now, I was on that end of the stick. I felt scolded, attacked, and rejected. I suppose I could have suffered it all for Jesus, and felt quite pleased with my martyrdom, if it had not been for a letter I received from one of the "defectors" the following week. It was addresed to me, with a note: "The enclosed is from one of the E.P.N.L.G. (Exclusive Private Narrow Little Group). I didn't think you 'tagged' Christians." I recognized the abbreviation as a quote from one of my sermons in the series. The letter was a heart-cry in free verse, the gist of which was contained in the first two lines:

Just tell me you love me

No sermons or scoldings . . .

I was stung by this revelation of my own self-righteousness and unloving attitudes which, in spite of my best efforts, had undermined my communication of the truth.

I apologized publicly for my lack of love and understanding. I appealed to them to stay: "We can learn together to function in oneness and harmony around Jesus." It was too late. They had made their decision.

Not everyone with a "prayer language" left at that time. Thank God! Some stayed. In the years that have followed, they have had a strategic role in helping us to open up to a new dimension of fellowship.

This break was one of the most difficult for me to accept. I loved these people. Several had been converted to Christ under my ministry.

I cried a lot in those days.

"Why can't the body be one?" I bawled. "If what has happened in these people's lives is of the Spirit, why does it have to divide the fellowship of true believers? It must be possible for Christians to live together with this! God doesn't intend for them to leave. I don't want them to leave. Then, why are they leaving?"

The bad news is that our experience to this point has been repeated in scores of churches around the world, as a side-effect of the modern charismatic renewal.

The good news is that it doesn't have to end like that. There is "unity-in-diversity" for the people of God . . . if they ache for it badly enough. Our subsequent experience as a group which includes both tongues-prayers (those who stayed, those who returned after the exodus, and others who have joined us) and non-tongues-prayers has convinced us that we *can* pray (and live) in symphony.

Because we chose to fight for unity between these two schools of theology and Christian experience, we have been maligned from both directions at once! Those whose theological views exclude tongues after the completion of the New Testament, have warned us that we have opened the church to a dreadful heresy. Those whose views judge us slow to allow the church to "move out in the gifts," have labeled us as inhibitors of the Holy Spirit. We have resolutely insisted that both so-called charismatics and noncharismatics are brothers and that their separation from each other over such an issue constitutes a gross sin against the body of the Lord. We have demanded reality and scripturality in the use of the so-called sign gifts (i.e., tongues, healing, etc.). We have sought to give freedom for anyone to share what he has in Christ with the body. It has been costly (in terms of attritions in both directions) to try to live by these convictions.

Those who have chosen not to separate, though they have found it a decision often fraught with discomfort, have entered as a church family into a process of reconciliation that has been a rare growth experience. By choosing to stick it out together, we have been acting out the conviction that, if Jesus is our mutual Lord, if there is one body, and if one Spirit lives in all who belong to God, then, it must be possible to work out practical spiritual unity regardless of the diversity He has created in us. If we can stay together long enough to choose unity over disunity with enough spiritual fervor to carry us over the rough relational struggles, it will lead, through the pain, to true spiritual maturity.

Our goal has been development of a congregation of people who have actually broken through the ideological and attitudinal barriers to genuine enjoyment of and delight in each other's personal and spiritual uniqueness. Who experience Christian unity, not alone on the theoretical level, but on the practical and personal level.

In our experience, at least four key elements which are essential to oneness of spirit have characterized our life together in the face of charismatic differences:

1. *Refusal to accept the legitimacy of division between true followers of the Lord.* All who confess Jesus as Lord are called to live together in harmony. Committed to that premise, we can work through our differences, whatever they are. In fact, the process of working through will help us to grow up in Christ.

2. *Determination to allow the Bible to say exactly what it says about the Holy Spirit and His gifts.* As soon as I became aware of my prejudices and sought to approach it without reading my preconceptions into it, I discovered the Bible saying many things that shattered some of those preconceptions and radically rearranged my previously concretized pneumatology and ecclesiology. Some of my fellow members who have and use a "prayer language," have been reading and studying the gift passages without resorting to the teachings of an "authority" for the interpretation. As a consequence of trying to listen to the Word itself, some are discovering not only the solid biblical legitimacy of their own gift, but also the authenticity of the Holy Spirit's filling, working, and gifting in others who have not been given a new language. It is not that everyone here is now in full agreement on all points of the issue, but I think we are discovering that even in nonuniformity we can be one in Spirit and in mutual esteem.

3. *Expectation that God may speak to the church through whomever He will.* Even the person who is interpreting his experience with God from a place of immaturity, misinformation, confused theology, ignorance of Scripture, misunderstanding of his own emotions, or mixed motives,

may be bringing to the church in his person and/or his faulty words, God's message. Those who, by the Spirit and the Word, judge carefully whatever is said in the name of the Lord (1 Thess. 5:19–22) can hear the sometimes hidden message and even interpret it for the edification of the church. Thus, we can dare to be accepting of every person, whatever his experience or gift.

This does not for a moment mean that every word anyone speaks is to be received as God's message. But the person is to be valued. Whatever God is saying is to be "extracted" and heard, the rest ignored or rejected.

4. *Determination to accept and affirm each other, apart from any necessity for full agreement on matters of doctrine and experience.* This includes affirmation of each other's gifts.

We have tried to say both verbally and nonverbally, publicly and privately: "*All* spiritual gifts are needed and welcomed in our church." At the same time, we have sought to affirm the full range of person-gifts (the choice uniqueness of each person), the less spectacular gifts of the Spirit (i.e., helps, mercy, giving, exhortation, etc.), the unlisted gifts (i.e., Spirit-led writing, music, art, etc.), and the spiritually useful skills and talents (which may include any human ability offered to God). Our servant-leaders have determined that, if possible, every person, whether or not his gift has been discovered, should know that he/she is indispensible to the life of the body.

It requires setting aside selfish interests and taking specific risks to give ourselves to the task of preserving the unity of the Spirit. But it can be done where spiritual kin are willing to choose to commit themselves to each other, to take the risks, and to count on God to make the struggle for oneness work for their good.

One Sunday, about two years ago, we became aware that the charismatic issue had been largely diffused. Unity was winning. One of the brothers—who speaks in tongues—

stood to make a statement to the congregation. He was completely poker-faced as he declared, "I would like to announce that the 'annual speaking-in-tongues crisis' has been cancelled for this year!"

The wonderful thunder of uninhibited laughter that shook the place spoke eloquently the joyous news that the fever had broken and full healing was coming.

"MY BROKEN BODY"

Focussing on the potential of division over spiritual gifts is not intended to give the impression that the "problem of tongues" is the only or the greatest problem alienating true believers from each other today. It is merely that this problem is typical of the issues that cause spiritual Christians to divide up the church over anything that makes them uncomfortable, calls for sacrificing self-interest, demands growing up, or challenges them to genuinely love and accept one another and do the hard work of keeping the unity of true believers intact.

I have watched fellow members of Christ's body walk away because they disagreed with some doctrinal position; because they didn't like someone in the church; because "the people weren't friendly"; because the church was getting "too personal"; because the church was too formal; because the church was too informal; because the church refused to fire or censure the youth director who used an inappropriate word in the Sunday worship service; because the church wasn't evangelistic enough; because the services were too long; because the leaders were allowing too much freedom in the meetings; because the leaders were inhibiting freedom; etc.

And I cried when every one of them left.

I suppose I should be thankful that people just walk out on me when they disagree. In the days of the reformers, those with whom they disagreed were sometimes burned at the stake!

How contrary to the admonisments of the Bible!

If the New Testament is clear on anything it is in its insistence that any kind of division between believers is to be utterly shunned. *Disunion is totally unacceptable in the body of Christ.*

"THERE SHOULD BE NO DIVISION IN THE BODY" (1 Cor. 12:25).

Many of the dividing lines that believers today accept as valid between them are actually specifically condemned in Scripture.

No Division Over Leaders

In 1 Corinthians 1:10–13 Paul particularly censures the practice in the Corinthian Church of separating from fellow believers on the basis of allegiance to certain effective spiritual leaders and teachers.

Certainly Paul, Apollos, and Cephas have been unusually influential in the spiritual development of various people. Does that justify the existence of a Paulist segment of the church to lift up the supremacy of Paul's work over the others? Paul is aghast at the idea.

"You have divided Christ!" he exclaims in verse 13.

Hero worship and personal preference for leaders is certainly natural. But in the church they are part of the self-life Jesus has called on us to deny. First Corinthians 3:3–6 identifies as carnal, not spiritual, separatism based on an overbalanced loyalty to men who have been significantly used of God.

It is natural that there be a tie of appreciation and love between the convert and the man or group who brought him to Christ. But it is not spiritual for him to cling in any kind of exclusive or divisive way to those instrumental in his salvation. And as the babe in Christ matures, it is expected that he will start to develop a more God-centered view of the church and its ministry (1 Cor. 3:7–9).

No Division Because of a Supposed Superior Commitment to Christ

First Corinthians 1:11–12 again specifically denounces separation from other true believers on the proposition of allegiance to Christ alone.

It is carnal to declare "I am of Paul," or "I am of Apollos," or "I am of Cephas." But this passage also insists that it is no less carnal and divisive to declare "I am of Christ," when in saying it one is setting himself or his group apart from other true Christians.

Every true believer testifies correctly, "I belong to Christ." The error comes when there is a spirit of division, exclusivism, or superiority. There cannot legitimately be a nonsectarian sect of believers (contradiction of contradictions!) who separate themselves from other believers on the basis of self-proclaimed allegiance to Christ alone. Allegiance to Christ automatically involves allegiance to all who belong to Him.

Spiritual growth is important. The Spirit-filled life is certainly not only desirable but is commanded by Scripture. But no experience of filling, no deeper or higher level of spiritual growth or maturity, no expansion of one's capacity as a channel for Christ's life and power, no amount of "advanced knowledge" of the Word and will of God or the person of Christ or the work of the Spirit, no vision, no new light, no depth of doctrinal understanding, no confessed nearness to or allegiance to Christ, is ever justification for division in the church—whether that division be actual or attitudinal.

No Division Over Opinions

Galatians 5:20 lists divisions and discord in the body based on differences of opinion among "the works of the flesh." One of the works of the flesh disclosed there is "party spirit" (Phillips), "factions" (NASB), "sects with peculiar opinions" (*Amplified Bible*). The Greek word is *hairesis*. The KJV translates it "heresies," but the lexical meaning of the word does not communicate the same thing that heresies has come to mean to most of us. The English word "heresy" has the connotation of theological error. But in the Greek word, theological error is not the issue. It comes from the root *haireo*, which means to take, to grasp, to seize, to get into one's power, to conquer, to take in. The word *hairesis* carries these ideas: the act of taking, capture, or choice, a chosen opinion, a sect, a body of men separating themselves from others and following their own tenets, dissensions arising from diversity of opinions and aims.[1]

Other words and phrases are used in the New Testament to warn against doctrinal error itself and to deal with it in strong terms. But what are being tagged here as completely contradictory to and in opposition to the fruit of the Holy Spirit in the lives of believers are divisions (factions, parties) based on differences of opinions.

What is said here to be the work of the flesh is not the differences of opinions themselves, nor the holding of erroneous opinions, but the separating of ourselves from others who are indwelt by the same Spirit—preferring and choosing to gather exclusively with those who have "captured" us or whom we have "captured" with this or that special opinion.

All such exclusivism and giving in to personal preferences in the body of Christ grows out of self-interest and is motivated by the flesh, not by the Spirit.

There are key doctrines surrounding the person of Christ[2] that are a part of the kind of faith necessary to enter into relationship with God through His Son, and to be given the right to be called God's child.[3] The Bible, God's recorded Word, reveals these truths. And departure from or refusal to accept those key truths automatically makes impossible the unity of the Spirit, because they are so essential that to deny them is to deny the Lord. Without this basic trust in the Lord, the Spirit does not indwell. And without the indwelling Spirit, there is no hope of unity of the Spirit.

Doctrinal error of that destructive sort demands—in fact produces—separation and division. Unity of the Spirit does not exist where the Lord is denied.

Denial of vital doctrine is not the primary issue raised by the word *hairesis* in Galatians 5:20, though that may be included. The definition goes farther than that in dividing between flesh and Spirit. The vital point for the living church is: different opinions or interpretations or personal preferences are not to be considered grounds for dividing into factions, parties, or sects.

Paul wrote the fourteenth chapter of Romans to show how to handle differences of opinion in the church. The underlying supposition is that there *will* be differing opinions among Christians:

> Accept him whose faith is weak, without passing judgment on disputable matters (Rom. 14:1). We who are strong ought to bear with the failings of the weak and not to please ourselves. Each of us should please his neighbor for his good, to build him up. For even Christ did not please himself. . . . May the God who gives endurance and encouragement give you a spirit of unity among yourselves as you follow Christ Jesus, so that with one heart and mouth you may glorify the God and Father of our Lord Jesus Christ. Accept one another, then, just as Christ accepted you, in order to bring praise to God (Rom. 15:1–7).

Allow and live with differences of opinion, Paul is saying, And at the same time "be of one heart and mouth" with one another.

We are in "one accord," not when we agree on every interpretation of every Bible passage, but when we (1) recognize our oneness in Christ, (2) accept each other as we are, (3) commit ourselves to the spiritual well-being of our brothers, not ourselves.

We, in our strictly limited humanness, desperately need to be challenged by the experiences and perspectives of our brothers. Such challenges can, if we are open to what the

Spirit may say through our "different" brothers, actually lead toward fullness—fullness of perspective on God's infinite truth, fullness of experience of God's infinite life, and fullness of humility for involvement in Christ's infinite servanthood.

> Perhaps we need to pray for a fresh outpouring, not of the Spirit but of humility to reexamine our brother's position in the light of where he has been and where we have been and what we are looking for together—recognizing (can there really be any doubt?) that God does not treat any two people alike at any stage of their spiritual development.[4]

No Division Over Race

The New Testament radically declares that there is not to be racial segregation and division in the church. First Corinthians 12:13; Galatians 3:28; Ephesians 2:11–18, and Colossians 3:11 all state the irreversible principle behind this truth.

The church at Antioch, described in Acts 13:1, exemplified it. There, in spiritual leadership and bound together in a deep fellowship along with Paul, Barnabas, and Manean (who was a member of the royal family), were two men who were probably black—"Simeon who is called Niger (black)" and "Lucius of Cyrene" (a city in northern Africa).

The full richness of the New Testament quality of fellowship is out of reach to the congregation that does not accept without question or rationalization the practical dimensions of the *whosoever* gospel. When the church gathers or reaches out to touch its community, whatever it does must be an operational expression of the truth that

> There is neither Jew nor Greek, slave nor free, male nor female, for you are all one in Christ Jesus (Gal. 3:28).[5]

No Division Over Social Differences

The same passages also make it clear that social distinctions ("neither slave nor free man") are never to be allowed to separate believers from each other. James 2:1–9 calls preferential treatment of people on the basis of social or economic status distinctions "sin."

Personal preferences, leaders, personal loyalties, disagreements, race prejudice, diversity of spiritual experience, misunderstanding, persecution, trouble in the church, criticism, being snubbed, differences over interpretation of Scripture, personality conflicts. . . . None of these things, by any stretch of acceptable exegesis, is sufficient reason to separate from one's brothers and sisters in Christ! And we clearly fly in the face of the Word of God when we do it.

THE ONLY BIBLICAL GROUNDS FOR DIVISION

There are only three legitimate biblical reasons for division in relation to the church. All the other reasons with which we bombard one another are disavowed and condemned.

1. Life and Death

The first scripturally acceptable wall between people is the unavoidable split between spiritual life and spiritual death.

There is no way those who have not received Jesus Christ can experience spiritual oneness with those in whom He lives. Automatically there is a barrier. On one side is life, on the other death (John 5:24). One is in the light, the other darkness (Acts 26:18). One is a citizen of Christ's kingdom, the other is a captive of the ruler of this world (Phil. 3:20, NASB; Eph. 2:2). One has peace with God, the other is still at war with His Creator (Rom. 5:1; 8:7). One possesses the life of God, the other does not (1 John 5:12). One is united with the Son, the other is separated from Him (Rom. 6:5). One is a child of God, the other a child of wrath (Rom. 8:14–16; Col. 3:6).

If you are not a Christian and I am, there is a wall between us that cannot be broken down, unless you too choose to follow Jesus.

Even in this, however, it is not God's intent that we make separating ourselves from non-Christians the personal passion to which we dedicate our lives (1 Cor. 5:9–13). In the church's earthly expression the weeds and the wheat often grow together and are not separated until the judgment (Matt. 13:24–30).

God Himself caused this kind of division when He "rescued us from the domain of darkness and brought us into the kingdom of the Son he loves" (Col. 1:13).

2. Discipline

The second division allowed in Scripture is a temporary separation. It is described in 1 Corinthians 5.

The sinning Christian who will not stop his gross sinning when he is confronted with it,[6] is to be deprived of all normal contacts and fellowship with his spiritual kinfolk. He is to be literally turned over to Satan! Put out of the church. Not allowed to participate in its meetings. The rest of the believers are not to associate with the disciplined one.

This is not meant to give license to the "Christian" practice of snubbing and separating from each other because of personal preferences or differences of opinion. We are speaking of disciplinary action, taken by the entire local body of believers, who have judged an individual persistently guilty of extremely serious, personally and corporately destructive sin.[7] It is clearly to be the last resort, accompanied by sorrow that leads to repentence on the part of the whole fellowship (1 Cor. 5:2), who have loved and cared for the brother until the time of his separation.

It is clear from what Paul says in 2 Corinthians 2:5–11 that the intent is not that this separation of the body from a rebellious individual be a permanent division. Six months have gone by since Paul's instructions to remove the offender from the fellowship.[8] He's talking about the same individual—the object of the church's chastening—when he says:

290

> The punishment inflicted on him by the majority is sufficient for him . . . Forgive and comfort him, so that he will not be overwhelmed by excessive sorrow. I urge you, therefore, to reaffirm your love for him . . . in order that Satan might not outwit us (2 Cor. 2:6–11).

At every point in this disciplinary process, the emphasis is on saving the offender, and on restoring him to forgiveness and full fellowship in the church. For the church it is intended as a time of renewal and intensification of the members' care and concern for each other (2 Cor. 7:11).

The body in any community must be living out a high degree of oneness if the New Testament brand of discipline is to have its desired effect—the development of a true spirit of repentance leading to full restoration.

3. Geography

The third division the New Testament allows is a geographical division. This is the only permanent division permitted between people who are indwelt by the Spirit of Christ.

If I move from Phoenix to Tucson, I separate from the church I left behind. Immediately, I become a part of the Christian community in my new place of residence. It is physically impossible to be part of a community in which I no longer reside.

> Locality is the divinely-appointed ground for the division of the Church, because it is the only inevitable division. Geographical distinctions are natural, not arbitrary, and it is simply because the physical limitations of the children of God make geographical divisions inevitable, that God has ordained that His Church be divided into churches on the ground of locality. *Any division of the children of God other than geographical implies not merely a division of sphere, but a division of nature. Local division is the only division which does not touch the life of the church.*[9]

The New Testament affirms no other divisions between

291

those who have life in the Son.

THE CHURCH'S FORGOTTEN DOCTRINE

Sensitivity to the real spiritual oneness of Christian believers has been largely stifled and ignored through centuries of persistent, rational justification of our evermore proliferating divisions. The followers of Jesus Christ have fought and divided over nearly every doctrine except the doctrine that all men born of the Spirit are one body in Christ, and over every conceivable practice except the practice of "preserving the unity of the Spirit in the bond of peace."

The true spiritual church, the body of Christ, into which every believer has been baptized by the Holy Spirit (1 Cor. 12:13), cannot be divided. In its spiritual reality it is not divided. But the earthly, physical expression of it is tragically splintered. Even the observing pagan can argue convincingly that there is not "one church," but hundreds!

Those "observing pagans" were on the mind of Jesus as He prayed His "high priestly prayer" of John 17.

> My prayer is not for them (the disciples) alone. I pray also for those who will believe in me through their message, *that all of them may be one . . . so that the world may believe that you have sent me* (vv. 20–21, italics added).

This is what Francis Schaeffer calls "the final apologetic." The unconvinced world waits to be convinced by our oneness that the gospel is true.

Inside every true believer in Jesus Christ there is a spiritually inborn cry to be one with fellow members of the body of Christ; regardless of differences. We, as the Scripture says, share the same life, the same Holy Spirit; together, we share the flow of that life between us as those who are one. There is no need for someone to invent spiritual unity between Christians. It is an eternal reality. It needs now to be recognized . . . and preserved.

The Bible doesn't allow for irreconcilable differences between brothers. Christians are not permitted to consider their oneness obsolete.

Beautifully and sovereignly, the Holy Spirit is including in the great spiritual awakening, that presently appears to be sweeping the world, a revival of this vital neglected truth.

TOUCHES OF SYMPHONY

The original Greek word for "agree," as in "if two of you on earth *agree* about anything you ask for" (Matt. 18:19), is actually the ancient root of the English "symphony." To agree in Christ, then, is not for everyone to be saying exactly the same thing, nor to be thinking exactly alike, any more than a symphony is every instrument sounding the same note or playing the same melody. The beauty of the symphony is its masterful blending and flowing together of a multitude of sounds in harmony, under the baton of its conductor.

That is the church living out the unity of the Spirit.

In all the discord that surrounds us in the world—and in the church—when lives come together in harmony, it is great music heard among the saints and all over the cosmos.

None can tell the story of the finished symphony. That may have to wait until the Conductor's authority is universally acknowledged in the splendor of His millenial reign. But we can describe a few touches of symphony, as possible examples of the richer, fuller song that we will one day play together.

Personal touches . . . .

I had a hard time remembering that this warm, open lover of the Lord Jesus across the room from me was a Catholic "brother" of the Society of Mary, who would soon complete his training for the priesthood. My conservative evangelical upbringing had provided me with some internal conditioned responses. One of them was a quiet alarm which automatically warned me that people who were a part of certain religious groups were unlikely to be true followers of Jesus.

But I couldn't deny that there was a real warmth of the Holy Spirit between us. And I loved this bearded young man with the medium long hair, because I knew he was my brother in the Lord.

He suggested we pray for each other before He left. At the close of a simple shared prayer Brother Gary took my hand. The oneness we felt at that moment made it natural for us to embrace. As we held each other for a moment he said, "The peace of Christ be with you." And I responded, "And with you, *brother*."

At that moment we could not have agreed on some points of theology and practice which are very important to each of us. But Jesus is Lord of his life and of mine. The Spirit of God is in his life and in mine. We were not sharing merely mind to mind. We were sharing, and thus preserving, the unity of the *Spirit* in the bond of peace. We were not concentrating on differences. If circumstances were to permit us to go on in continuing fellowship, we would be able later to discuss even those differences. A deeper personal relationship in Christ can make such discussion not only possible but very productive.

What we were concentrating on was our mutual share in . . .

> one body and one Spirit . . . one hope . . . one Lord, one faith, one baptism, one God and Father of all, who is over all and through all and in all (Eph. 4:4–6).

And it was good.

Some liked Bob's teaching and some did not. But he had the capacity to minister life to many people. As I sat in his adult Sunday school class, I occasionally swallowed hard to put down the twinge of theological tension that climbed up from deep down inside me, when he explained what he felt about the believer's security. Bob and the class knew that we did not exactly agree on the subject. And without putting each other down we even occasionally discussed both sides of the issue during the class.

But Bob understood grace. And whenever he talked about God's love and God's forgiveness and God's acceptance, I saw God more clearly through his eyes. My life in Christ was enriched. And the members of the class grew as Christians, became more confident and consistent. The spiritual gift of teaching was clearly operating.

Besides this, the mystical warmth and oneness in the Holy Spirit was there. Our relationship continued long enough and went deep enough that we could discuss the points on which we differed, even sometimes to the point of tension. But there was also the love of Christ, the indwelling presence of the Holy Spirit, the mutual commitment to Jesus as Lord. *And* the determination to live out oneness in Christ; the two-sided refusal to let differences of opinion separate us. And we share a deep sense of appreciation for the value of each other's ministry.

So, in the setting of week in and week out local church life, we chose to try to preserve the unity of the Spirit. We chose to "hang together."

Local touches . . . .

The universal church can be defined as, simply, all believers on Jesus Christ everywhere. The local church, then, is that part of the universal body of Christ living and meeting in a certain locality. In the New Testament, the term "church" (in the local sense) is used of all the Christians in a particular city (i.e., the church at Ephesus), and, secondly, those who gather together regularly in a certain meeting place (i.e., the church at Philemon's house).

No further definition is needed. Nothing more is required. Having received Jesus Christ by faith (John 1:12), having confessed Him as Lord (Rom. 10:9), each person is baptized immediately by the Holy Spirit into the body of Christ (1 Cor. 12:13). From then on, he is in the universal church. And, from the spiritual standpoint, he is also, without any further qualification, a member of the local church in whatever community he resides.

One has an option with regard to reception or rejection of Christ, but no option with regard to membership in the church. If one chooses Christ, one gets His church too. There is no such thing as belonging to Christ, but not belonging to His body.

One does not "join" the true and living church (as we moderns understand joining). One merely recognizes his union with other believers and lives it out in accordance with the teachings of Scipture (or fails to do so). But when Christ is received the question of church membership is settled. One is automatically placed by the Holy Spirit into Christ's body, the church.

We concluded that this means that all who gather with our congregation are members of our local expression of the church, whether they have ever officially joined or not. We further concluded that it is unbiblical for us to require people to join (with its attendant demand for a certain level of spiritual maturity, doctrinal agreement, promises to abide by certain arbitrary "rules," majority vote by the rest of the congregation, etc.). Our only option as brothers and sisters, we came to believe, is to accept those who already have been accepted by the Lord Himself, or to reject them in the face of the fact that Christ lives in them, and that refusing to accept them is tantamount to refusing to admit Christ into our fellowship.

The Scriptures seemed to condemn the membership policy handed to us by denominational fathers. For example:

> Accept him whose faith is weak . . . for God has accepted him (Rom. 14:1, 3).

> Accept one another, then, just as Christ accepted you, in order to bring praise to God (Rom. 15:7).

We saw ourselves as actually caught in the position of arbitrarily and unnecessarily dividing the body of Christ by placing unbiblical "additional requirements" in the way of unity with true believers.

An entry in our so-called book of policy tells the rest of the story:

> By unanimous action of the Church Board
> . . . The membership of Our Heritage Church was expanded to include "all true believers in Jesus Christ who regularly attend the meetings of the church." The Scriptural basis for this policy is Acts 2:47; 10:44–47; 11:17–18; Romans 10:9; 14:1; 15:7; Ephesians 4:4–6; I Corinthians 12:3, 13, ff. . . . This means that, without ceremony or further special action, if one is a member of the Body of Christ by having received Jesus Christ as Savior and if he attends this church regularly, he is received as a full member of this congregation.

To some churchmen, such an undemanding approach may seem simplistic and even dangerous. We have found, on the contrary, that when the practical thrust of church life is to bring all members from spiritual weakness and infancy to spiritual strength and maturity, and when the church's leaders and policy makers are chosen only from a developing reservoir of mature people, most of the dangers to be dreaded for such an open-door policy are defused.

With confidence in the faithfulness of the Holy Spirit, we may dare to allow the church to be one.

Ecumenical touches . . . .

Bob Galley, pastor of Tri-City Community Church (Christian and Missionary Alliance), and I were together in a group discussing mutual church needs and struggles. Bob was telling how their congregation was chafing under the limitations they felt because they were without a church building—public school rental was cramping their freedom to do some of the things they wanted to do. The discussion also revealed that many of their families lived closer to our meeting place than to the school.

"Why don't you come and use our building?" I blurted out in a flash of inspiration. "There aren't any problems we can't work out to make it possible."

He couldn't sleep that night thinking of the possibilities. Next day, we met to talk more about it.

There are some significant differences between the two groups. But both are soundly evangelical. Both give allegiance to Jesus as Lord.

From that beginning, the leaders and then the congregations of both churches were brought into the discussions, which stretched over several weeks. Many began to sense the positive potential of "joint use." Advantages we could see included:

—better stewardship than having such a large amount of money invested in two separate, partially-used facilities.

—possible close cooperation between the two churches in certain aspects of ministry.

—community testimony to the unity of the body of Christ.

—opportunity to pioneer a needed new concept for the evangelical world. Skyrocketing building costs demand new approaches to providing church facilities.

There were some problems to be worked out: (1) scheduling of Sunday meetings and other events, (2) joint care of buildings and grounds, (3) sharing the costs, (4) liaison, in the event of problems, and to encourage cooperation and fellowship.

The first year was to be a trial year. Future possibilities under discussion included joint ownership, permanent leasing arrangements, merging of certain ministries (i.e., youth ministry).

A new sign was prepared designating the property as a

COMMUNITY WORSHIP/FELLOWSHIP CENTER

and listing information on both congregations side by side.

After several months in which the arrangement seemed to be "going off without a hitch," pressures from their district leaders forced T.C.C. to abandon the idea of permanent joint use. They launched a building fund drive. Before long they will be gone. But for a short while it has held promise of fulfillment of a dream—to be able to say to the world,

"We are one in Christ!" and to demonstrate it in a really tangible way.

Lord willing, we shall try again.

LET THE SYMPHONY BEGIN

I am not talking about trying to be one with anyone who denies the Son of God. I am only interested in recognizing and working to preserve the basic spiritual oneness that belongs to all whose lives have been invaded by the living Spirit of Christ.

We are one!

This is a call for us to act like it.

The questions raised by this call cannot be easily answered. There are problems involving strained relationships between Christians, divisions between Spirit-filled men and women, doctrinal differences between evangelicals, that defy easy solution. I am not wise enough to tell specifically how each of these can be bridged, or at least lived with. I am struggling with these things in some of my own relationships.

But I have enough confidence in the prayers of Jesus Christ, the vision of the Spirit-inspired apostle Paul, the reliability of the Word of God, to declare: there *is* a "unity of the Spirit," a "one accord" kind of church experience, a "no division in the Body" possibility, a peace, a oneness available in the church. An actual experience of oneness in which love and peace bind believers together in one body, the joints (relationships) of which are in good health—even though we differ in knowledge, understanding, wisdom, experience, personality, and interpretation.

My personal conviction progressively deepens that denominationalism is unbiblical and that God has called us to something better. Could the answer be as simple as leaving the denominational structure in response to that conviction? But how could dividing from my spiritual brothers and sisters in the denomination be a step toward unity? That sounds like a contradiction. Especially when I find independence to be equally as inconsistent with the biblical revelation which teaches the *inter*dependence of members and assemblies within the living church.

The solution is not a great megalopoliptic organic merger of evangelical denominations and independent churches. In fact, we are confronted with the impossibility of trying to put the ecclesiastical humpty dumpty back together again. Each generation of the King's men has added its own human, structural, and doctrinal bulges to the pieces it held. Any new superchurch which could, conceivably, be constructed by organizationally merging all of the denominations would only create a grotesque and human "lumpy humpty"—still not much like the unwrinkled church the Spirit says Christ intends to present to Himself "in all her glory" (Eph. 5:27).

The problem is that we have for centuries neglected and ignored a vital biblical doctrine that is closely related to the lordship of Christ. The solution is a rediscovery of this doctrine and a real commitment to it on the part of true believers.

It is the doctrine of "The Unity of the Spirit."

Christ Himself is the common foundation under us all and the common bond between us through the indwelling Spirit. And no other idea is presented in Scripture but that together in Christ any two or more of us, if we value it enough to pay the price tag on it, may enjoy an exciting, fulfilling kind of fellowship with brothers and sisters in Jesus—a sharing of our lives which touches the world, the angels, and the believing community, with the rich symphonic hymn: "We are one heart and one soul!"

There is hope for the broken body of Jesus.

Hope that in Christ men like me can overcome proud aloofness, commitment to secondary things, insensitivity to broken fellowship, and forgetfulness of the unity of the Spirit.

My spirit says there must be hope.

The Bible holds it out as part of the gospel's promise. Perfection of our oneness will have to wait until the kingdom age, but however unfinished, let the symphony begin *now!*

Notes

[1] Definitions of *hairesis* gleaned from *Liddell and Scott's Greek-English Lexicon* (London: Oxford, 1944); and *Thayer's Greek-English Lexicon of the New Testament* (Grand Rapids: Zondervan, 1972).

[2] John 3:16; Acts 16:31; Romans 10:9; 1 John 4:1–4, etc.

[3] John 1:12. Also, Watchman Nee suggests that the seven "ones" of Ephesians 4:4–6 constitute the basis for the unity of the Spirit. *The Normal Christian Church Life* (Washington, D.C.: International Students Press, 1969), pp. 61–63.

[4] Editorial, "Can We Get Together?" *The Presbyterian Journal,* May 1, 1974.

[5] Amplified Bible.

[6] Matthew 18:15–17 gives instructions for confronting him in his sin.

[7] First Corinthians 5:11 lists the kinds of activities that, if a man persists in doing, he may be temporarily removed from the fellowship.

[8] *Halley's Bible Handbook* (Grand Rapids: Zondervan), p. 496, sets the date of the writing of 1 Corinthians at Spring, A.D. 57 and the date for 2 Corinthians in the Fall of the same year.

[9] Watchman Nee, *The Normal Christian Church Life,* pp. 63–64.

13
The New Society

"I'll take this one."

Ten-year-old Carolyn held the rough, brown spherical shape in her small hands and gazed at it like it was the most wondrous of gems. She had worked and saved her allowances and earnings all summer for this moment. And now, at last, she held the hidden treasure.

No one knew exactly what was inside the geode[1], until, upon its purchase, it was cut, revealing whatever crystalline formations nature had left. But Carolyn saw it with the eyes of a believer. She had never seen its inner beauty, but she knew it was there. And she would give all she had saved to experience it.

In a moment, its splendor would be hers.

The kingdom of God is such a treasure. It is hidden in ordinary looking packaging which masks the richness of its splendor. The person who decides to follow Jesus holds it in his grasp, and knows something of its awesome value. Others may see a dull, brown shape of doubtful worth. But if he wants to, the child of God can see the secret splendor with believer's eyes. And, if he chooses, and chooses again, he can pay the price demanded and go inside the sphere. There he can touch and taste and hear and smell and see the reality of the new world that is coming!

THE KINGDOM DREAM

From the earliest moments of collapse of the human community under the weight of the consequences of willful sin, hope for a new society has been implanted in the hearts of men (Gen. 3:15). Until, from the pen of a later prophet, Isaiah, comes the prerevelation:

> For to us a child is born, to us a son is given, And the government will be on his shoulders. And he will be called Wonderful Counsellor, Mighty God, Eternal Father, Prince of Peace.
> Of the increase of His government and peace there will be no end.
> He will reign on David's throne and over his kingdom, establishing and upholding it with justice and righteousness from that time on and forever.
> The zeal of the LORD almighty will accomplish this (Isa. 9:6–7).

The people of God, hearing this promise, expected the birth of a special child, who, from the time of His appearance on man's scene, would be God's appointed governor, through whom the kingdom of heaven would be established among men. It was Christ's destiny from eternity to head the development of a new human society.

Six months before Jesus' public ministry began, the desert baptist, John, began to prophesy and baptize in preparation for the formation of the kingdom. As personal envoy of the king, his message was:

> Repent, for the kingdom of heaven is near (Matt. 3:2).

The governor was on the scene. "Project: the kingdom" was about to be inaugurated.

When Jesus dawned and John's light began to pale, the kingdom-dream was what He too preached. His first message seemed an echo of John's (actually, it had always been His own):

> Repent, for the kingdom of heaven is near (Matt. 4:17).

Jesus' dream is bigger than the church. In fact, when He spoke of the "God movement" and called people to join Him in it, He seldom used the word "church."[2] Instead He chose an appellation which encompasses all the meaning in church and vastly more. He spoke continually of "the kingdom of God" or, as in Matthew's record, "the kingdom of heaven."

It was always on His mind and lips. Even after resurrection, to the moment of ascension, the kingdom was still His most talked about subject (Acts 1:1–9).

The Kingdom is Now

The "nowness" of the kingdom must be understood. Its earthly emergence, according to Isaiah, John, and Jesus, began with Messiah's life among men, and was to continue from then on forever. Those who were near Jesus were told that some of them would "see the kingdom of God come with power" before they died (Mark 9:1).

Perfection of the new nation will not be seen on this side of the Second Appearing of our Lord, when every knee bows before Him and every human and heavenly tongue confesses His lordship.[3] But nearly 2000 years ago Jesus' earthly ministry introduced into the world the authentic "advance contingent" of the coming kingdom—a visible society intended as a living prophetic glimpse of the spendor of the society to come.

The nowness of the kingdom becomes readily apparent as you follow the biblical story of His life. In Matthew 6:19–34, He tells His followers not to consume their energies in anxiety over the daily necessities of life, but instead to give themselves to an intense search for the kingdom of God. The direct implication is that when, as those who have received Jesus Christ, we seek the kingdom, *we can and will find it* for our present lives and times.

The teachings of the Sermon on the Mount (Matt. 5; 6; 7), the Sermon on the Plain (Luke 6:17–49), and all but the clearly eschatalogical kingdom teachings, have about them the unmistakable ring of contemporaneity. The student of the Word is forced to read-in a great deal of purely rationalistic interpretation in order to miss the obvious: Jesus expected His listeners to respond to His teachings in the present tense of their lives.

LAW, GRACE AND THE NEW SOCIETY

Disciples of the Lord are never called upon to *build* the kingdom. Isaiah states that that is what the governor-prince is to do. The stark truth is, the moment man (even the spiritual person) sets about through human manipulation and organization to build God's kingdom, it becomes another of man's kingdoms, not God's. It's a mistake Christians repeatedly make. It's the reason there is so much "wood, hay and stubble"[4] stacked neatly about, with signs all over it saying, "This is the church" or "This is the kingdom of God"—when much that bears such designation is neither church nor kingdom!

Our part in realizing the "new society dream" is to forthrightly *seek* (Matt. 6:33), *see* (John 3:3), and *enter* (Matt. 5:20; John 3:5) the experience of the kingdom life style.

The constitution and by-laws of the new society are the teachings of Jesus, in the four gospels. Paul and the other epistlers expand on, interpret, apply, and report additional revelation. But the basic principles are thoroughly disclosed by Jesus.

True Christians have made misleading and destructive errors in their perception of the teachings of Jesus. Three are most serious:

(1) That Jesus' kingdom teachings fall into the category of "law" (Old Covenant), were primarily given for the Jews, and therefore, do not necessarily fit with the New Testament concepts of grace, freedom, and life in the Spirit, as taught in the epistles. (2) That the kingdom teaching describes life in the millenial kingdom, and therefore its serious applica-

tion for us is strictly future. (3) that Jesus' teachings are laws which must be obeyed in order to find acceptance with God. The effect of these misinterpretations is to make most of what Jesus says irrelevent and impractical, or an impossible burden, for today's disciples.

It is a tragic mistake. It effectively short-circuits the development of the kingdom dream. And fits nicely into the enemy's destructive schemes by getting believers to practically "write off" or be crushed beneath a major portion of New Testament revelation.

Paul truthfully declares, in Romans 7:6,

> Now, by dying to what once bound us, we have been released from the law so that we serve in the new way of the Spirit, and not in the old way of the written code.

The law from which we have been released does not include the teachings of Jesus. It is the Mosaic law, and it is all Old Testament. The Nazarene nowhere calls what He teaches "law," except when He introduces His "new law"—that His disciples love one another as He loves them (John 13:34). Kingdom teachings are all part of the New Covenant, not the old. And they are pure grace.

The system of law, the program of seeking to please God by obeying commandments, did, indeed, die with Christ at the cross. And there we died to it with Him. No longer are we called upon to meet an external standard of righteousness in order to find pleasure in God's sight. We are free from that impossible millstone. Having entered into living relationship with God by faith in Jesus, *I please God without the law!* (Rom. 3:28)

It is at this precise point in spiritual experience where the teachings of Jesus—the fundamentals of the kingdom— move into focus, not as laws by which rebellious sinners make themselves pleasing to God, but as principles by which forgiven saints enter into a living experience of kingdom society. The issue that turns upon our responsiveness to kingdom principles is not relationship with God and salvation, but entrance into the kingdom life style. Multitudes of believers confess to having been "saved" on the basis of faith in Jesus, but comparatively few have touched the abundance of life promised in the new nation. Ignorance, neglect, or rejection of its precepts have kept many from the cornucopian style of life and relationship taught by Jesus in the Gospels.

CHRIST'S NOT-OF-THIS-WORLD KINGDOM

Jesus' earliest recorded teaching of kingdom principles begins with the simple statement that He taught these precepts to His own disciples (Matt. 5:1). Unless He specifically states it, He does not expect His teachings to be adopted by worldly governments and worldly communities in order to make the world a better place to live. If the world improves itself in spots upon application of some of these concepts, let it be! But let it be understood that the world system is entirely under the power of "the evil one" (1 John 5:19), and it has no intention of becoming the kingdom of Christ. When, as Revelation 11:15 prophesies, the kingdoms of this world become the kingdom of God and of His Christ, it will only be after a violent fight to the death to try to keep it from happening. The new society Jesus is building starts and continues from the point where the Christ is openly acknowledged as Lord. This immediately and radically sets the new society apart from the world.

The blueprint for the kingdom, including all its governmental and relational principles, is given to the redeemed, who are seeking to experience the fullness of Christ under the reign of God on earth, the present-tense living community of Christ.

A RADICAL ALTERNATIVE

Whenever we meet the kingdom in the teaching of Christ, or in its recognizable living expression (i.e., wherever two or three are struggling to live out its principles) we meet a life

307

style that is radically contradictory and diametrically opposite to the world's way of life. We see it in everything Jesus said. But He left no doubt about the transcendent character of His government when compared to world regimes when, in answer to Pilate's cross-examination (John 18:36), He said,

My kingdom is not of this world!

That is the principle. In the same breath He applied it to His specific situation: In the typical worldly kingdom, if the king was in trouble, his followers, if they were worth their salt, would grab weapons and storm the preatorium to gain his release. But *this* king has not trained his loyal troops for that kind of warfare (John 18:36).

The kingdom of Jesus Christ is not a political organization. Its goals are completely different from any human political regime. All His kingdom's goals are spiritual. None of its objectives involve the gain of material wealth, political power, or worldly advantage of any kind. No need to fortify the empire against the kingdom of Christ. It is not in competition for institutional power.

Since that is true, its means of reaching its goals, its methods of expansion, and its approach to preservation, are completely different from the methodology of any system or movement to be seen anywhere in the culture. The strongholds the kingdom will tear down are the intellectual and volitional strongholds of entrenched human resistance to the knowledge and rule of God. We are aiming, not to bring people "under our power," but rather to bring every man's thinking into captivity to Christ.

We fight, but not against governmental leaders, military machinery, human movements, or human foes of any kind. Men are not our real enemies.

> For our struggle is not against flesh and blood, but against the rulers, against the authorities, against the powers of this dark world and against the spiritual forces of evil in the heavenly realms (Eph. 6:12).

Our weapons are not the kind that maim and destroy

soldiers. The instruments of our warfare are:
> truth
> righteousness
> good news of peace
> faith in God
> salvation from sin and hell
> the indwelling Holy Spirit
> the Word of God
> prayer in the Spirit (Eph. 6:14–18).

With this spiritual weapons system we defeat spiritual enemies, protect ourselves against evil's attacks, and advance our Leader's cause.

The new society comes under sharp attack because it rises in radical antithesis to the whole body of thinking and life-patterns of the world-system in which we are called to live the mortal portion of our lives. Therefore, the pressures on Christ's followers to conform to the world are tremendous and endless. Often the church has relaxed its guard and opened itself and its spiritual communitites to absorb and embrace the *modus operandi* and life style of the world. The history of the Christian church has included centuries of repetition of this disastrous process, until the mind of the world influences more areas of our personal and ecclesiastical life than the mind of Christ. We Christians are so used to it, that most of us never think to question the awesome gap between what Jesus taught and the practices and values of the church.

Paul expresses deep concern at this point, when he urges the church,

> Don't let the world around you squeeze you into its own mold, but led God remold your minds from within . . . (Rom. 12:2, Phillips).

The world is likely to think those who live by the principles of the kingdom grossly out of step, even insane. And there is enough of the world in the church, as most of us know it, to cause an extremely confusing phenomenon:

Those who seek to follow Jesus' kingdom teachings will likely find themselves confronted by earnest fellow Christians, whom they may deeply respect, who will try to persuade them, in effect, that the principles of Jesus for interpersonal relationships, priorities, and evaluation of the worth and effectiveness of the things we have to do, are not practical for the times in which we live. Jesus' times were simpler times. In the complex age, they will say, there are additional factors to be considered. Our world will not respond to the fine points of Jesus' principles. He presents the "ideal." But when you come down to the nitty-gritty of living in the present world, a few discreet compromises may be best.

I recently heard a dear evangelical pastor confess in all honesty, "If we really preached the gospel, we'd empty our churches!"

Many of the things to which the church is now committed would be eliminated, and some that it has neglected would be added, if it dared to evaluate the elements of its way of life in the light of the question: Is this of the culture, or is this of the kingdom?

THE KINGDOM: A SOCIETY

Jesus' dreams for kingship go far beyond the prospect of *individuals* living their personal lives according to His teachings, though that certainly is part of it. His dream (a very human word for God's eternal plan) is of a new redeemed society in which His precepts are the living principles which govern all relationships, all the society is and is doing, with each other and in the world. In His vision, it is not primarily I alone who am "the light of the world," shining in my dark, lonely corner. But we together are "the city set on a hill" which cannot be hid. His plan is not primarily that I alone, as an independent follower of Jesus, am to be the living, visible antithesis to worldly philosophies, politics, institutions, and

310

values. It is that together we become a living model of the kingdom community.

God loves, calls, saves, relates to, and "has a wonderful plan for" individuals who trust Him. But the key to the kingdom is not "rugged individualism." It is community, a new society.

In *Eternity,* Robert Webber wrote:

> Individualism—a so-called virtue which has overemphasized a personal rather than corporate faith. It makes biblical interpretation relative to individual experience, misunderstands the body of Christ in community, fosters Christian jet-set heroes, and encourages success-oriented, power-hungry, recognition-hunting pastors, evangelists, educators, writers, and organizational institutional executives . . . . The church is to be the one institution on earth not ruled by the gods of this world. It does not accommodate itself to cultural norms. It functions differently than other institutions because it is rooted in a confession which stands in radical antithesis to the worldly ideologies which rule the institutions of society. Therefore the church as church is a radical witness to the world, a community of different people, a light set on a hill, a salt which has not lost its strength.[5]

Jesus wants His followers to share His dream, not merely of what individuals can become following Him; He desires for us to catch His vision of a new heaven-touched community of redeemed people seeking to live with each other first, and then in the world surrounding them, according to the principles He shared with us in the Gospels.

SEEING THE KINGDOM

We receive spiritual eyesight when we are born again.

> Unless a man is born again, he cannot see the kingdom of God (John 3:3).

Before Christ I was incapable of seeing anything but what was consistent with the rebel organization of this world. I thought, believed, judged, and acted according to the mindset and outlook of the surrounding culture, which I had been taught by precept and example since childhood. But when I received Christ, His mind began to work its way into mine. Now, by the Spirit, I am capable of seeing what I could not. The way is now open for me to *see* the kingdom.

In Matthew 13:15–16, in a dialogue about the kingdom, Jesus tells that the choice to see or not to see is ours. Then He says to His close friends, who are just beginning to catch sight of the new society:

Blessed are your eyes because they see, and your
ears because they hear.

There are many culturally imposed and/or self-chosen barriers filled with spiritual mustard gas which keep us from seeing and entering: i.e., reluctance to recognize Jesus as Lord of the practical matters of our personal lives and our life-together . . . concern for preservation of the comfortable and usual . . . unwillingness to bear others, to give ourselves to/for others . . . determination to protect ourselves from risk . . . resistance against the radical thinking of Jesus which seeks to tear down and overwhelm all the overt and hidden citadels of world-thinking that have controlled our minds all our lives . . . refusal to look and to see something better beyond the status quo of the present level of fellowship, caring, and mutual ministry known in our churches . . . willingness to allow the security of the standing order to blind us to the yet-unfulfilled promises and calls inherent in the teaching of Jesus . . . tendency to stifle the vision of the new community by cowering before the difficult-to-answer question: How do we get there from here?

The "how we get there" has been worked out for us by our King, and waits to be discovered in His gospel preaching and our life with Him.

ENTERING THE KINGDOM

Jesus presses the truth in John 3:5:

Unless a man is born of water and of the Spirit,
he cannot enter the kingdom of God.

At new birth, we receive the capacity to *see* the kingdom, and we also are given the ability to *enter* into the experience of the kingdom.

Before our spiritual genesis we did not have the power to become the society of God. Even if we could have seen it, we could not have experienced it. We could only look at the Sermon on the Mount, etc., and feel condemned, hopeless, lost. For, apart from the wind of the Spirit (John 3:8), the new society principles form a standard so high no mere human being can possible hope to reach it.

Jesus is not holding out an impossible way of life to us, and then saying we must enter into it using only our own ruined resources. He is saying, Look, here's the new style of life you can live together with your spiritual kin right here in this devil-dominated world—now that the Holy Spirit has come into your lives and has begun to live His life in you.

> The kingdom of God is . . . a matter of . . . righteousness, peace and joy in the Holy Spirit (Rom. 14:17. See also Phil. 2:12–13; 1 Thess. 5:24).

There will be relational and spiritual lapses, growing pains, discomforts, struggles, failures, times of wondering if one fits into the kingdom community at all. But once Christ's new life is released in us, we are capable, by His power, to begin to live in the kingdom style.

The kingdom of God, Christ's new society within the old society, is a *spiritual* community. Even though it is expressed physically in the tangible life style of its citizens, the kingdom is not physical.

> Flesh gives birth to flesh . . . Flesh and blood cannot inherit the kingdom of God . . . But the Spirit gives birth to spirit. You should not be surprised at my saying, "You must be born again" (John 3:6–7; 1 Cor. 15:50).

When any of us comes to Christ, we bring with us from our life in the rebel world, strong philosophical and cultural "fortresses" which life-long exposure to world thinking have naturally constructed in our minds as a defense against surrender to the lordship of God. These barriers to kingdom thinking are the intellectual strongholds of human reasonings, wisdoms, and imaginings. All our inner citadels of independence, self-sufficiency, self-willfulness and worldly knowledge are slated for destruction by the Holy Spirit, who will not see His process in us as complete until every thought we have is a captive of Christ (2 Cor. 10:3–6). Our minds *must* be renewed!

It is a hard truth those who would choose to follow Jesus into His new society must face: the kingdom of God does not in any way function according to the thinking of this world system. The pervading reason for the difference is, as already stated, that the fundamental principle of life in the new community is open, continuous, practical acknowledgement that

Jesus is Lord!
He is king![6]

THE KINGDOM ELITE

The best example of the difference between the world's mind and the mind of Christ is seen in the kind of attitudes Jesus says produce the kind of people who are "great in the kingdom," and who are "blessed."

In the so-called Beautitudes (Matt. 5:3–10), His first unveiling of life in the new soceity, Jesus describes the kind of people and qualities that are absolutely essential to the kind of kingdom He is founding. We understand this to mean that the new community of God is impossible without the life elements He notes here.

"The Kingdom Elite":

> Blessed are the poor in spirit,
> for theirs is the kingdom of heaven.
> Blessed are those who mourn,
> for they will be comforted.
> Blessed are the meek,

for they will inherit the earth.
Blessed are those who hunger and thirst for righteousness,
    for they will be filled.
Blessed are the merciful,
    for they will be shown mercy.
Blessed are the pure in heart,
    for they will see God.
Blessed are the peacemakers,
    for they will be called sons of God.
Blessed are those who are persecuted because of righteous-
ness,
    for theirs is the kingdom of heaven.

Those who intend to discover and live in the full experience of the new society will see these values and this thinking as indispensable.

Conversely, the church having assimilated much of the world's mind, the world's values, tends to treat the kingdom of Christ as though it were, after all, a kingdom of this world. The practical reality of the way the church often lives and moves constitutes a nonverbal rewriting of the Beatitudes. If Christ's kingdom were of this world, He would have laid out, as basic essentials, qualities with which modern Christianity would be more comfortable. He would have gathered His disciples around and said:

Blessed (to be envied) are those who are completely adequate and strong, who never display weaknesses or personal spiritual need
. . . for theirs is the kingdom of heaven.
Blessed are the positive, light-hearted, and those who never cry
. . . for they will be comforted.
Blessed are the aggressive, demanding, and cocky, those who know and claim their rights and advantages
. . . for they shall inherit the earth.
Blessed are those who desire the glory of power, goods, success, and acclaim
. . . for they will be satisfied.

315

Blessed are the organizers, motivators, and man-
ipulators of people, who have their corporate growth
objectives clearly in mind, who see people as a means
to reach their objectives, and will not be distracted from
their "higher work" by personal involvements with
misfits or cripples
. . . for they shall receive mercy.
Blessed are those who are careful in their commitment
to God, not to become too "other worldly"
. . . for they shall see God.
Blessed are the fighters and scrappers, who knowing
they are right, tear all who disagree with them to
shreds, and noisily separate from those who are
"wrong"
. . . for they shall be called the sons of God.
Blessed are those of whom all men speak well, with
whom the world is comfortable
. . . the kingdom belongs to them.

The fact that the church in many places functions according to one or more of these rewritten beatitudes, and often
chooses its heroes and leaders on such criteria, does not
change the truth: such is not the thinking of the King.

His word to His followers is that the kingdom, true comfort, the earth, genuine satisfaction, the mercy we need, the
knowable presence of God, the sense of His fathering,
heaven, and superabounding blessedness and joy[7] in the
new society belong, by contrast, to:

The vulnerable (v. 3). The new society is a community
dependent on God, a family of admitted cripples, seeking to
heal each other in Jesus' name. The blessed and truly great
are those who freely and openly acknowledge the gap between the spiritual possibilities and spiritual realities of their
lives, and that they are themselves utterly without the resources needed to deal with the gaps.

The broken (v. 4). The new society is a repenting community, a people broken over their own sins and the sick-

ness of the world. The blessed and truly great are those who allow their hearts to be broken by what breaks the heart of God.[8]

The gentle (v. 5). The new society is a yielded community, a people who own nothing but God. The blessed and truly great are those who claim nothing[9] and demand nothing, who, ceasing rebellion, place themselves under the reins of the Master,[10] are completely moldable in His hands, and continually seek total relinquishment of themselves to God, leading to gentleness of style.

The intense (v. 6). The new society is an intense community, a people seeking godlikeness as though their lives depended on it. The blessed and truly great are those who want God's righteousness and seek God's mind, like a starving man wants food or a man dying of thirst seeks water.[11]

The compassionate (v. 7). The new society is a healing community, an island of concern for persons. The blessed and truly great are those who care enough to choose to get inside the lives of others, to experience what they are experiencing, feel what they are feeling, know what they know,[12] in order to bring true, not imagined, help and healing.

The single-minded (v. 8). The new society is a cleansed community of people who are being perpetually cleansed. The blessed and truly great are those who have surrendered their hearts completely to Jesus that He alone may reign in them, whose hearts are undefiled by their own evil and their own virtues.[13]

The propitiators (v. 9). The new society is a community of reconciliation, seeking to bring alienated persons together into a community of love. The blessed and truly great are those who find the joy of life in a definite, positive, active, initiating involvement in the troubles and conflicts of people.[14]

The despised (v. 10). The new society is a community of the crucified,[15] who are ready to follow Jesus to the loss of all things. The blessed and truly great are those whose life style, a response to the mind of Christ, is so radically contradictory to the world's priorities and ways, so radiant a prophetic condemnation of cultural thinking and values, that it brings them into rejection and'trouble.

The kingdom of God is built of such qualities of life and of such people. They are the new society's nobility.

> As long as we have a self-righteous conceited notion that we can carry out our Lord's teaching, God will allow us to go on until we break our ignorance over some obstacle, then we are willing to come to Him as paupers and receive from Him. "Blessed are the paupers in Spirit," that is the first principle in the kingdom of God. The bedrock in Jesus Christ's kingdom is poverty, not possession; not decisions for Christ, but a sense of absolute futility—"I cannot begin to do it!" (Oswald Chambers).[16]

THE SECRET MOVEMENT OF THE KINGDOM

The kingdom of God accomplishes its objectives in a "secret" movement that is a radical alternative to the style of the world's movments. The principle is enunciated in Luke 17:20–21.

> Having been asked . . . when the kingdom of God would come, Jesus replied, "The kingdom of God does not come visibly, nor will people say 'Here it is,' or 'There it is,' because the kingdom of God is within you."

The kingdom is not a *thing,* a composite of any number of things, nor a collection of things. Of no humanly put together structure or institution can it be said, "This is the kingdom." It is, for this reason, difficult to see, and impossible to destroy. Its enemies may demolish everything they see and the kingdom will be untouched. They may burn its meeting places, confiscate its funds and properties, imprison or execute its leaders, infiltrate its ranks, disrupt its fellowship, cancel its meetings, prohibit its activities, herd its people into concentration camps, martyr its witnesses, ridicule it before all men, smirch its name, discredit its Book, legislate against its freedom or its existence (all these its enemies have already tried), and still it moves on— undefeatable, inexorable, invisible, living, obedient to its King.

The movement of Christ is a quiet movement of God's indwelling Spirit in the hearts and lives of a people vitally linked in spirit with everlasting divinity.

Jesus illustrates the movement of the kingdom with two parables, in Matthew 13:31–33. Kingdom expansion and growth follow the "invisible" pattern. The movement of God is not pictured as a successful corporation splitting its stock, a tornado changing the face of the countryside, or an explosion forcing on its surroundings the will of its detonator. Instead the kingdom is like a mustard seed, the tiniest, most unimpressive of seeds, quietly, naturally growing, in the course of time, into a very large bush that offers protection and a resting place for sojourning birds.

Furthermore, the kingdom moves toward its objectives like yeast in bread dough. The homemaker mixes in a tiny piece of leaven. Then seemingly forgetting the dough and the hidden catalyst, she busies herself with other things. Indwelt by a sensitive change-agent that works best when conditions are right, the dough rises—quietly, naturally, persistently, mysteriously. Yeast doing what yeast is uniquely designed by its Creator to do. The tiny fungus has reproduced itself many-fold, and has given off a fragrant ingredient which dramatically affects its environment.

One quality in yeast makes this miracle happen: LIFE!

The church's business, as the community of the King, is not to make the world notice it. But to produce a new and living nation of people, who, yielding personal allegiance to the King, and indwelt by His life, provide the living Christ with a living vehicle for revealing himself in the world.

In the story of the expansion of primitive Christianity, there are obviously supernormal events. The baptism of

3000 converts in a single day. Dramatic public defenses of the gospel which were often forced upon disciples who would rather have remained anonymous. Public martyrdoms. There is public witnessing and preaching, and persistent missionary activity. There are charismatic figures like Stephen, Philip, Peter, and Paul. But the normal Christian witness involves a process which seems more natural. In 2 Corinthians Paul uses three images to characterize this way of gospel communication. (The presupposition is that the people addressed are not Christians in name only, but that each has had a genuine personal encounter with Jesus Christ, and, therefore, is spiritually alive.)

1. *The fragrance of Christ* (2 Cor. 2:14–17). No need to peddle or huckster the gospel, using the world's methods of pitchmanship to win converts. All living believers, wherever they go, in whatever circumstances they are encountered, bring into the place where they are the fragrance of Jesus. This wordless "fragrance" comes through as a powerful sense of life to those who are being saved, and of death to those who are lost. (It's the yeast, giving off its change-producing ingredient.)

2. *The letter of Christ* (2 Cor. 3:1–18). From inside, where the Spirit has written Christ's message on our human hearts, emerges a renewed life pattern which is observable to the naked eye. The world reads the gospel from the day-to-day pages of the lives of kingdom citizens. We live in confidence in what the Spirit has written. In fact, our confidence is so great, we dare to live before the world with our faces uncovered (v. 18)—purposely allowing others to see and know us as we really are. Confident that, as time passes, this self-disclosure, including openness about our present discrepancies and weaknesses (which we are *not* to hide to "protect" our witness), will allow those who are reading us to see that the Holy Spirit is changing us to be more and more like the Lord! If change is not occurring, a mere spoken witness can lead to disillusionment.

3. *The ministry of reconciliation* (2 Cor. 5:16–6:2). God has reconciled us to Himself through Jesus Christ. He has also reconciled us to each other in His community. Reconciliation (oneness, peace) is attractive. There is a sense in which it sells itself. It needs only to be exposed. As Christ's followers consciously choose to involve themselves as "peacemakers" in the troubled lives of the people around them, the fragrance is sensed, the letter is read, the reconciliation is modeled, in person and in community, and when the verbalized invitation is given, there is solid reason to listen: "Good news! No need to live in estrangement from God and each other. Look what He's done for you in Jesus. His heart is already wide open to you. Come on in! Be reconciled to God."

One quality in the community makes the miracle of kingdom expansion happen: LIFE.

The Kingdom: a Call to Be Changed

Repentance is fundamental to life in the new society (Mark 1:15). To repent (Greek: *metanoia*) is to be transformed in the basic structures of one's life. Put simply, Jesus' call to enter the kingdom is a call to be changed.

Repentance (choosing to be changed) begins when one turns from independence and self-willful rebellion against God, puts his trust in Jesus Christ, and starts to live with God in relationship rather than alienation. But that's mere beginning. No one is fully changed at that point. He is a new creature in spirit, to be sure. But in mind and life patterns, he is not yet fully renewed. Until a person is related to God, and the Spirit of God lives in him, he does not even see what needs to be changed. And it may take significant time in interaction with Christ's mind for the believer to grasp how extremely vast is the chasm between the alignment of most of his life, and the new mindset toward which he is now being led by the Spirit.

According to Jesus in Matthew 7:21, living in the kingdom

requires obedience to God's will. If we miss the richness of the kingdom in any area of life, it will be because we choose to disregard His instructions regarding it. To call Jesus "Lord" is insufficient. The experience of the kingdom is for those who go beyond hearing, knowing, and talking, to *doing* the will of God. In order for this kingdom-constructive pattern to replace the old destructive pattern of the world in every aspect of life, for freedom in Christ's truth to replace the bondage caused by saturation with our godless culture, there must be a continuous bringing of our real lives to the Word of Christ (John 8:31–32), measuring ourselves by it, and adjusting to it.

We will be called upon to be positively responsive to God's serendipitous though often disturbing and puzzling interaction with us, on a day-to-day basis.

Change is inevitable for the people of God. We shall ultimately and completely be like His Son. (See Rom. 8:18–25, 28–29; 2 Cor. 3:18; 5:17; 1 John 3:2.) In the process of reshaping us, God is using as instruments of change (1) the Holy Spirit, living inside our bodies and in Christ's corporate body, (2) the Word of God speaking to our minds and spirits, (3) every circumstance and incident of our lives, and (4) interaction with the members of Christ's body.

We may react to His process with rebellion ("I will not be changed!"), resentment ("Why do I have to suffer all these things?"), independence ("I have a better idea!"). . . . Or with surrender ("Go ahead, God, change me"), trust ("You know what is best for me"), obedience ("Yes, Lord").

Jesus demanded of all who want to experience His new kingdom style of life, "Repent!" Paul issues the imperative, "Be transformed!" (Rom. 12:2). It is as though change were not automatic, but conditioned on our response.

If earth ever sees the kind of community that lives together in the Sermon on the Mount, it will see it emerging among those who repent, who choose to be changed. Discoverers of the kingdom's hidden treasure are those poor in spirit ones, those hungry and thirsty ones who leave the security and comfort of the world's neat systems of value, thought, and living, and place themselves willingly, like a lump of soft clay, in the strong hands of the Potter King. In His hands everything undergoes change. Everything is re-shaped, realigned . . . renewed.

THE KINGDOM IS LIKE . . .

In a world of well-packaged and slick
Products,
The ideas of the kingdom of heaven
Often seem a bit homemade and lumpy.

> But Jesus never presented the ideas
> Of the kingdom of heaven
> As a finished product.
> He pictured God's kingdom as raw material
> Put into our hands.
>> The kingdom is a seed,
>> The kingdom is yeast,
>> The kingdom of heaven is people, not saints.
>>> People growing,
>>> Rising,
>>> Working toward an ideal.
>>>> People not yet perfected,
>>>> But alive and moving.

And any packaging of the kingdom of heaven
Which gets too slick
Seems to lack that lumpy homemade quality
Of seeds and yeast.[17]

Notes

[1]Geode: a hollow, stone-like formation, two to six inches in diameter, often lined with crystals.

[2]Jesus used the word "church" only twice in the recorded biblical narrative: Matthew 16:18 and 18:15–17.

[3]Philippians 2:10–11.

[4]1 Corinthians 3:12.

[5]Robert Webber, "Conservative Radicalism," *Eternity,* June, 1974.

[6]These two lines form an ancient Christian greeting, with one person saying the first line, the other answering with the second.

[7]The word "blessed" (Greek: *makarios*), Matthew 5:3–10, also means "joy."

[8]Lloyd John Ogilvie, *A Life Full of Surprises* (Nashville: Abingdon Press, 1969), p. 15.

[9]J.B. Phillips' translation of Matthew 5:5, "Happy are those who claim nothing. . . ."

[10]Ogilvie, *Surprises,* p. 24.

[11]William Barclay, *The Gospel of Matthew,* Vol. 1 (Philadelphia: The Westminster Press, 1975), pp. 99–100.

[12]Ibid., p. 103.

[13]Dietrich Bonhoeffer, *The Cost of Discipleship* (New York: The Macmillian Co., 1963), p. 125.

[14]Ogilvie, *Surprises,* p. 49.

[15]Bonhoeffer, *Discipleship,* p. 127.

[16]Oswald Chambers, *My Utmost for His Highest* (Fort Washington, Pa.: Christian Literature Crusade), p. 351.

[17]Gordon and Gladis DePree, *The Gift* (Grand Rapids: Zondervan Publishing House, 1976), p. 15.

Epilogue:
A Church Without Walls

Several months after the completion of this manuscript, a new phase of our renewal process began. This briefly descriptive epilogue was slipped in just before the book went to press.

A CHURCH WITHOUT WALLS

On New Year's Eve, our church walked out of its buildings, and plans never to return!

The following Sunday the church met in several locations instead of one—in homes instead of a church building—in the late afternoon instead of morning.

This is the substance of an informational paper, sent to the church's constituency shortly before the move was made.

For Our Heritage Church, Scottsdale

The Next Step: A Church Without Walls

On an eleven-year pilgrimage into change, the congregation of Our Heritage Church has been led into (1) small groups, (2) simplification of programs and ministry, (3) relational style of church life, (4) participatory style of meeting, (5) shared pastoral leadership by a team of local elders, (6) refocussing of giving priorities to comply with New Testament teachings that

Christian giving is basically for people needs, and (7) deinstitutionalization—moving toward functioning not as a "church" but as a family. All these have involved considerable change in church structure.

"The next step" grows naturally out of this long process of refocussing and renaissance. In order to provide a more flexible "wineskin," or structure (Mark 2:22), which will more effectively stimulate real growth into Christ and responsiveness to His headship, we are committed to the following actions:

1. *On Sunday, January 7, 1979, we shall begin meeting weekly in several "house churches."*

From that date on, by deliberate choice, we shall no longer meet at 4640 N. Granite Reef Rd. These buildings are being voluntarily turned over to our denomination.

Characteristics of the house churches:

a. *Geographical location.* Body members will be urged to join the nearest house church, but there will be freedom for each person/family to choose. (Acts 2:44-47; 5:42; 12:12; 16:40; 28:23, 30-31; Rom. 16:5, 23; 1 Cor. 16:19; Col. 4:15; and Philemon 2.)

b. *Team leadership.* Each house church will be shepherded by a carefully selected team of pastors and teachers (elders and others who are gifted by the Spirit for teaching and pastoral care). Team members of all the house churches will meet weekly for mutual discipling and to share and pray concerning the needs of each house church and the larger body (Acts 13:1-3; 14:22; 1 Tim. 3:1-6; 1 Peter 5:1-4; Heb 13:17).

c. *Sunday afternoon and/or evening meeting time.* A timeframe allowing development of greater freedom of thinking, attitudes, and meeting style.

d. *Participative meeting style.* Similar to our present Sunday meetings. Planned to include singing, worship, sharing and teaching of the Word (1 Cor. 14:26; Acts 4:23-35; Eph. 5:18-21).

e. *The shape of a family.* The body will be encouraged by its setting to *see* itself as a family, and will be stimulated by its structure to *live* as a family (Mark 10:29-30).

f. *Closer personal relationships.* Both localness and size will contribute to greater concentration on developing significant relationships with people. The church, unencumbered by the murkiness of institutional expectations, has a chance to *be* what it by nature is, a network of relationships (John 13:34-35; 15:12-13; 1 Cor. 12:12-27).

g. *Completely duplicatable structure.* This simple, dynamic church-form can be developed in any neighborhood, without financial or professional limitation. Body members will be built up and sent out as the Spirit leads and supplies pastoral leaders, to form new house churches (Matt. 28:19-20; Acts 1:8; 13:1-3).

2. *There will be monthly gatherings of the larger body, in which all the house churches will come back together.* The general pattern is expected to be: (a) meeting in the house churches for three Sundays, and (b) on the fourth Sunday, all house churches cancel their meetings in order to gather for the later celebration and "family reunion." Occasionally, these larger meetings will take the form of a retreat.

Purpose: (1) to maintain identification and relationship with the larger body, to guard against becoming ingrown and cultic.

(2) benefit for the whole body from the gifts (teaching and other gifts) in the other house churches.

(3) stimulation of a common sense of mission.

Content of these monthly meetings:

    worship and celebration

    concentrated biblical teaching

327

fellowship and relationship-building.

Place of meeting: rented or borrowed places such as retreat centers, hotel meeting rooms, schools, public recreational facilities, restaurants. There are many such places available in the Phoenix area.

Added opportunity: Other already existing house churches will join us for these monthly gatherings.

3. *Small groups will continue.* The weekday small groups which have been part of the life of our church for more than a decade, which have carried on their indispensable ministry of "spontaneous discipleship," will continue as is. New groups will be formed, as needed.

The goals of these actions include:

1. Spiritual maturity: a) that all may have the mind of Christ, b) that all may bear the family likeness of God's Son, c) that all may know what is spiritual and what is not (Rom. 12:1-2; Eph. 4:11-16).

2. Priesthood development: that each believer may become an able minister with his/her gifts (1 Peter 2:5, 9; Rom. 12).

3. That the network of relationships that the church by nature is, may be strengthened and freed to become more real and practical (1 Cor. 12:12-27; 13:1-13; 1 Peter 1:22).

4. That the church may grow with "the growth that is from God"—in numbers of people and in love (Col. 2:18-19; Eph. 4:16)—in a manner and context which is a biblical response to the Lord's commission to "Go . . . make disciples . . . baptizing . . . teaching them to *observe all that I have commanded . . . .*" (Matt. 28:19-20).

5. That the church may cease to be, in any important sense, an institution, and may be what it is—a body, a family, a shared life (Acts 2:42-47; John 18:36).

COME ON ALONG!
LET'S TAKE THE NEXT STEP . . . TOGETHER.

We had talked about it for years. Never sure when or if ever we would make the move. Together, our five elders had already led the church through significant structural changes. Last fall, four of the five spent a week together in the woods (with the leaders of seven other churches) where they broke through to a new level of unity and a new clarity of vision for the church. Upon their return all five met together, with their wives, to share the impact of that week, and to discuss its implications. The consensus decision to give our church building to our denomination and to move out into house churches seemed literally, to erupt from the fire of renewed vision and deepened trust in each other. Almost immediately the ten of us knew—*Now is the time! This is the voice of the Spirit for us and our congregation.*

For the following month, pastoral team members (elders) led the congregation through a review of four basic biblical themes concerning church life: 1) the church as a ministering priesthood, 2) the church under the headship of Christ, 3) the church as a true community, and 4) the church as a worshiping people. On the fifth Sunday, "the vision" for "A Church Without Walls" was shared.

District officials were informed of our plans. The church property was turned over to them (actually, they already held the deeds). They could sell it, start a new church in it—whatever they felt was best. But we needed it no longer. We asked to be allowed to continue in relationship with the mother denomination. Perhaps, we suggested, they could view us as a "laboratory." The gentle-but-firm official response, which came several weeks later, was that we had moved too far from the *denominational norm,* and a continuing relationship would thus be "improper."

Evangelical house churches exist in all parts of the world.

In the Wesleyan revival, the *norm* was to establish "societies" (churches) divided into "classes" (small groups) without regard to either buildings or professional clergy. House churches have existed throughout ecclesiastical history. Special buildings for Christian meetings were not commonplace until late in the third century. The New Testament records the location of many house churches, known only by the name of the people in whose house they met.

Could the house church be an overlooked alternative into which today's evangelicals should take a closer look?

Someone compared the atmosphere of the last day in our church buildings with the day Israel walked out of Egypt. *Exodus.* Spontaneously, the emotional tone of the gathering flowed from boisterous exuberance to sober worship to expressions of dependence on God to exhortations and needed warnings, sprinkled with touches of nostalgia. The first Sunday in the house churches the excitement continued, but now was tinged with new nervousness, and the inevitable struggle that goes with adjustment and growth.

It is too soon to report great changes or to predict the full potential of being, more visibly, a spiritual family. There are still communication breakdowns, fears, and vast imperfections to be dealt with. The potential for growth is unlimited, both in terms of numbers and in love.

A young man who is active in pastoral ministry in one of the house churches spoke recently, with intense concern: "Our relationships with each other have got to be right or this thing will fall apart!" He's right. The structure that now ties us together is the structure of personal relationship—to each other, to the group, and to God. If we fail at love, there will be nothing left. But, then, is there really anything of value left anywhere in the church, when love isn't there (1 Cor. 13:1-3)?

Appendix:
Ten Basic Principles of
Church Life

A most significant aspect of the process of change in which Our Heritage Church has been involved has been the emergence into sharp focus of some basic principles of church life observed in the New Testament. These ten principles became for us guiding stars, or structural girders, for working with God in His building process . . . on the foundation of Jesus Christ, the apostles and prophets (Eph. 2:19–22).

Principle 1: The church is dependent on the Holy Spirit for the ability to do and to be all God has called it to.

Principle 2: The church is people alive in Christ.

Principle 3: Jesus Christ is present Head of the church.

Principle 4: The ministry of the church is by its royal priesthood which includes all believers.

Principle 5: Pastoral leadership is by a team of men chosen from among the local congregation for their spiritual maturity, giftedness for ministry, and the exemplary quality of their lives.

Principle 6: The regular meetings of the church are for the maturing of believers.

Principle 7: Church fellowship and discipline are facilitated by the development of loving relationships.

Principle 8: Evangelism takes place, as a matter of course, when the church is healthy.

Principle 9: The spiritual nurture of children is primarily the responsibility of their parents.

Principle 10: The local church is part of the greater body of Christ which includes all true believers.